POSTMODERN CONDITIONS

Postmodern Conditions

edited by Andrew Milner,
Philip Thomson
and Chris Worth

 BERG
New York / Oxford / Munich
Distributed exclusively in the US and Canada by
St. Martin's Press, New York

This edition published by
Berg Publishers Limited
Editorial offices:
150 Cowley Road, Oxford OX4 1JJ, UK
165 Taber Avenue, Providence R.I. 02906, USA
Westermühlstrasse 26, 8000 München 5, FRG

© Berg Publishers 1990

All rights reserved.
No part of this publication may be
reproduced in any form or by any means without
the permission of
Berg Publishers Limited.

British Library Cataloguing in Publication Data
Postmodern conditions.
  1. Culture. Postmodernism
  I. Milner, Andrew II. Thomson, Philip III. Worth, Chris
306
  ISBN 0-85496-591-2

Library of Congress Cataloging-in-Publication Data
Postmodern conditions / edited by Andrew Milner,
Philip Thomson, and
  Chris Worth.
      p.   cm.
   ISBN 0-85496-591-2 : $34.50 (U.S. : est.)
  1. Postmodernism. I. Milner,
Andrew. II. Thomson, Philip J.
(Philip John), 1941– . III. Worth, Chris.
B831.2.P66   1989
190'.904-dc20

Typeset in Bembo by Opus, Oxford
Printed in Great Britain by Billing and Sons Limited, Worcester

Contents

Acknowledgements	vii
Introduction	ix
Existentialism, Alienation, Postmodernism: Cultural Movements as Vehicles of Change in the Patterns of Everyday Life *Agnes Heller*	1
Wrapping up Postmodernism: The Subject of Consumption versus the Subject of Cognition *David Bennett*	15
Marat/Sade, or the Birth of Postmodernism from the Spirit of the Avant-Garde *David Roberts*	39
Feminism, Realism and the Avant-Garde *Rita Felski*	61
The Pyrrhic Victory of Art in its War of Liberation: Remarks on the Postmodernist Intermezzo *Ferenc Fehér*	79
The Cultural Contradictions of Postmodernity *Boris Frankel*	95
Postmodernism or Post-Colonialism Today *Simon During*	113
The Issue of Bataille *Julian Pefanis*	133
Marx and the 'Postmodern' Image of Society *John Rundell*	157

Blu-Tack and Temples: Artistic Practice in the Eighties, a Postmodernist View
   Memory Holloway   187

Notes on Contributors   199

Select Bibliography   201

Index   205

Acknowledgements

We would like to thank all the members of the Centre for General and Comparative Literature who have helped in various stages of the production of this book. Special thanks are due to Sue Stevenson for her assistance in preparing the typescript of the essays and to Gail Ward for general administrative and secretarial help.

David Bennett's 'Wrapping Up Postmodernism: the Subject of Consumption versus the Subject of Cognition' was first published in *Textual Practice*, 1:3 (1987), David Roberts's '*Marat/Sade* or the Birth of Postmodernism from the Spirit of the Avant-Garde' in *New German Critique*, 38 (1986), Ferenc Fehér's 'The Pyrrhic Victory of Art in its War of Liberation: Remarks on the Postmodernist Intermezzo' in *Theory, Culture and Society*, 3:2 (1986), Simon During's 'Postmodernism as Post-Colonialism Today' in *Textual Practice*, 1:1 (1987).

Introduction

Andrew Milner, Philip Thomson, Chris Worth

'Postmodernism' in art and 'postmodernity' in society have provided perhaps the single most important theoretical challenge to contemporary modes not only of cultural criticism, but also of social theory and radical politics. Historically, each of these discourses has been constituted to a remarkable extent around an archetypically 'modernist' opposition between the modern on the one hand, and the pre-modern on the other. Within English studies, that opposition takes its characteristically negative form in the Leavisite defence of the values of the pre-industrial organic community against the dissociated sensibilities of industrialization. But however evaluated and however constructed, the opposition between modernist and pre-(or non-)modernist cultural forms has been central to twentieth-century debate in the humanities. A parallel set of oppositions, between feudalism and capitalism, between un-reason and enlightenment, between traditional and rational/legal modes of legitimation, and between organic and mechanical solidarities, informs the modernist moment in anthropology, sociology and also in the more theorized forms of history writing. Each of the grand narratives of emancipation, whether of the nation, of the proleteriat, or of womankind, constituted respectively by late nineteenth- and early twentieth-century nationalisms, socialisms and feminisms, remains predicated on a similar opposition between the prehistory of oppression and the moment of emancipation, both imminent and immanent within modernity. At the point at which these three discourses intersect, in Western Marxist cultural criticism, the dispute between Lukácsian anti-modernism, Benjamin's enthusiastic modernism, and Adorno's tortured dialectic of enlightenment, has constituted one of the most theoretically fertile moments in the intellectual history of our century.[1] It is precisely this modernist dichotomy, of modernity versus pre-modernity, so central to the intellectual culture of the West in the years between, say, the 1850s and the 1950s, which the debate on postmodernity threatens finally to deconstruct.

Within the discourse that is contemporary cultural theory three key texts can be identified as speaking with particular effect to the postmodern condition: Peter Bürger's *Theorie der Avantgarde*, first published in 1974, Jean-François Lyotard's *La Condition postmoderne*, first published in 1979, and Fredric Jameson's essay, 'Postmodernism, or the Cultural Logic of Late Capitalism', published in 1984, the year in which the other two texts appeared in English translation.[2] Each characterizes the postmodern (or the post avant-garde in Bürger's case) as a socio-historical period which post-dates modernity proper. For Bürger, late nineteenth-century high modernism is merely bourgeois art become conscious of itself as autonomous social institution; the avant-gardism of Dada and Surrealism, by contrast, represents an attempt to subvert the institution of art and to overcome the emergent separation between art and life; and the failure of that rebellion, which 'has not occurred, and presumably cannot occur, in bourgeois society',[3] itself generates that peculiarly postmodern condition in which the institution of art persists, but in which valid aesthetic norms do not. For Lyotard, the postmodern can be defined precisely in terms of an 'incredulity towards metanarratives',[4] not only those of aesthetics, but also, and equally importantly, those of science and politics; this incredulity, which has arisen since the Second World War, is in part a consequence of the internal logic of the narratives of modernity which themselves proceed from scepticism to pluralization; but it is also a correlate of those contemporary 'post-industrial' social forms in which knowledge has become 'the principal force of production'.[5] What for Bürger represents an impasse is of course for Lyotard an opportunity. For Jameson, postmodernism is both: it is the 'cultural dominant' of multinational 'late capitalism', an aesthetic populism in which pastiche eclipses parody, as the past is assimilated to the present in 'a field of stylistic heterogeneity without a norm';[6] but it has also its own 'moment of truth' in its internationalism, and in the potential for a political aesthetics of 'global cognitive mapping'[7] which that internationalism suggests.

To periodize the postmodern in this way, as do Bürger, Lyotard (in *La Condition postmoderne* at least) and Jameson, permits a conceptualization in which, to quote Jochen Schulte-Sasse,

Modernity . . . would mean a form of society or social organization characterized by industrialization, so-called high capitalism, etc. . . . The *cultural* precipitates of this socio-historical period should be called modernism. . . . In an analogous manner, the term postmodernity should designate a mode of material reproduction of society that has succeeded the period of modernity; whereas postmodernism should refer solely to the mode of cultural reproduction of that socio-historical period.[8]

Such an understanding informs most, although by no means all, of the papers collected together in this volume. They were originally presented as a series of research seminars organized during 1986–7 by the Centre for General and Comparative Literature at Monash University in Melbourne. At the time all were unpublished, although some have subsequently been published elsewhere. Their underlying thematic unity, and the way in which they canvass a range of quite different disciplinary, theoretical and political responses to the debate over postmodernism, seem to us to justify their collective publication in this format.

For two of the contributors in particular, Agnes Heller and Ferenc Fehér, both former students of Lukács, postmodernism has to be understood in periodizing terms. For Heller, the 'boundless pluralism' of postmodernism, although anticipated in social theory since 1968, is crucially a phenomenon of the 1980s and of the development of post-industrial society. For Fehér, too, postmodernism is a recent cultural phenomenon, not much more than ten years old, although its deeper origins can be located in the museification of European culture over the entire period since the Second World War. David Roberts and Rita Felski both make use of Bürger's attempt to periodize postmodernity in terms of the historical trajectory of the avant-garde rebellion. For Memory Holloway the relevant periodization is that provided by Jameson. So too it is for Simon During, whose paper rejects Jameson's reading of postmodernism, and especially of postmodernist internationalism, but nonetheless adopts a fundamentally similar understanding of postmodernity. For Boris Frankel, however, as for Habermas,[9] a genuine postmodernism remains a project rather than an already achieved reality. Critical though his paper is of the post-industrial 'utopianism' of writers such as Bahro and Toffler, he rejects also much of postmodernist thought and seeks to establish what might be termed a type of 'scientific post-industrialism', in which the Enlightenment narrative of emancipation is still realizable within some form of post-Marxist socialism.

But if postmodernism can be understood in such epochal terms, it can also be viewed, very differently, as a moment within modernity. This is the stance adopted by Lyotard both in his 1982 essay 'Réponse à la question: qu'est-ce que le postmoderne?' and in his 1983 'Règles et paradoxes et appendice svelte'.[10] Julian Pefanis's paper hints at such a view in its discovery in Bataille's 'heterology' of a heterogeneous element at the heart of the modernist project, which decisively influenced subsequent French post-structuralisms. But both David Bennett and John Rundell argue the case much more explicitly. For Bennett, all periodizing logics project as a unilinear trajectory what is in fact an oscillation within modernizing thought, an oscillation between what he terms the modernist 'moment of resistance' and the postmodernist 'moment of complicity'. For Rundell, too, postmodernity is internal to but also inimical to modernity and it is present even in the work of Marx, who is for Lyotard the most modernist of thinkers. While Bennett and Rundell both understand postmodernity as a moment within modernity, they nonetheless differ radically about the exact nature of each. If Bennett defines the postmodern moment, in Jamesonian terms, as a moment of complicity, Rundell by contrast understands the postmodern in a fashion much closer to the later Lyotard, but even more so to Marshall Berman,[11] as the heterogeneous and open-ended element both within Marx's marxism and within modernism in general.

This difference between a view of postmodernism as fundamentally complicit with the socio-political status quo, as a culture of incorporation, and that of postmodernism as open-endedly subversive and paralogistic, also recurs within those contributions which attempt periodizing accounts. For Fehér postmodernism is exactly the cultural mood of being after modernity: it represents the final attainment for art both of complete autonomy from external constraints and of complete emancipation from internal aesthetic constraints. While Fehér quite understandably declines Andreas Huyssen's open invitation to the role of the Georg Lukács of postmodernism, his insistence both that art must render meaning to life and that postmodernism must be reduced to an intermezzo if art and literature are to be revived, nonetheless serves to remind us of his Budapest intellectual antecedents. For Frankel, too, postmodernism is essentially an impasse, although one constituted within politics as much as within art: nihilistic and relativistic by turn, its rejection of meta-narratives opens the way to a privatized cynicism and pseudo-toleration which Frankel views as both naive and dangerous. For Pefanis, whose detection of the ghost of anti-production as the possible true end of Marx's productivism is reminiscent of Rundell, Bataille's anti-Durkheimian and anti-rationalist sociology of the sacred and of sacrifice, permits precisely that criticality which will enable us to see both capitalism and communism as mere instances of societies of production, each counterposed equally to paleolithic abundance and the sacred economy of sacrifice. For Roberts, Felski, During and Holloway postmodernism is neither necessarily complicit nor necessarily critical. For Roberts, rather, it is necessarily both: Peter Weiss's *Marat/Sade*, which he analyses as a paradigmatically postmodern work, is both a revolutionary play and the play of the imprisonment of the revolution within the institution. For Felski, During and Holloway there is no one postmodernism as such: there are postmodernisms, some complicit and some critical. Heller alone of the contributors refuses anything other than an entirely provisional statement of the problem: postmodernist pluralization might perhaps render impossible any meaningful rational politics, but on the other hand it might also permit more democratic and more rational forms of political action.

However interpreted, whether as complicit in or as adversarial to the structures of social power, postmodernism presents at least as central a theoretical challenge to contemporary radicalism as did earlier modernisms to older radicalisms. Much of Jameson's disquiet in the face of postmodernism echoes the earlier Lukácsian Marxist antipathy to modernism – despite his declared intention to grasp postmodernity 'dialectically', that is, in both its negative and its positive moments. Bürger's sense of the post avant-gardist impasse has a similar origin. Lyotard's celebration of the postmodern, on the other hand, arises in part from his own personal rejection of the Marxist grand narrative of emancipation (he is, of course, a former member of the *Socialisme ou Barbarie* group). The rival claims of art and politics here become apparent. For Bennett and Roberts in particular, that rivalry has been resolved or, rather, dissolved in postmodernist art: there is no political space outside postmodernity from which to criticize it, just as there is in turn no aesthetic space outside the institution of art from which to criticize it. For Fehér the claims of politics (and religion and philosophy) over art and literature are presumptuous and archaic; but postmodernity remains nonetheless at an impasse because the claims of life over art (which some might argue are perhaps also political, religious and philosophic) are not. Heller, as we have seen, remains uncertain as to the political implications of postmodernism, but she also registers the absolute centrality to it, as to earlier post-war cultural movements, of one particular form of radical politics, that of feminism. Feminist politics are similarly central for Felski and Holloway, for both of whom postmodernism is neither a style nor a form, but rather a site of conflict where incorporative but also adversarial cultural modes are at work. For both, oppositional cultural politics are feminist, although they differ as to the extent to which such politics are necessarily embedded in alternative cultural forms. Felski, in an argument which might prove a suitable epilogue for earlier debates within Marxism as much as a contribution to those within contemporary feminism, insists on the relative political neutrality of form in the postmodern epoch, and argues for the strategic priority over art of a feminist politics—but one which will require no normative political aesthetic. Holloway does insist on the politically and culturally radical properties of particular postmodern artistic practices, but these remain, not coincidentally, the practices of an engaged feminist art. During's political preoccupations are those neither of Western Marxism nor of contemporary feminism, but rather of the post-colonial encounter with western cultural imperialism. For During, postmodernist art *can* resist postmodernity in its guise as multinational capitalism, and it does so most promisingly in the recovery of pre-colonial languages. His own prognoses for the future of Aotearoa, but not for Australia, suggest a cautious optimism as to the political efficacy of post-colonial nationalism. In very different ways, Pefanis's social theoretical concerns also lead to a relativization of the European experience, both capitalist and communist, and to a theoretical recovery of the anthropology of difference. Whether such relativisms will lead to a politics of post-colonized resistance or to an aesthetics of multinational consumption remains to be seen.

Of all our contributors Frankel and Rundell remain those most clearly concerned with the classical Marxist narrative of emancipation. Both appear to combine a respect for Marx with a deep suspicion towards orthodox communism; both take much comfort from Habermas; and both aspire to an emancipatory political practice, embodied in some kind of libertarian socialism. This leads Frankel to an almost fully Habermasian rejection of postmodernism in favour of the continuation of the Enlightenment project of emancipation. It leads Rundell, by a very different route, to a surprisingly positive reading of Lyotard and to an attempt to rediscover the heterogeneous within Marx himself. For both, however, such questions are primarily matters of politics and only secondarily of art and literature. Frankel's essay, at least, seems to echo Felski's view that politics takes priority over art, and if art is entitled to its autonomy, then this is so only because artistic form has indeed been politically neutralized. The socialist project in the west remains today as much at an impasse as do the remnants of the historical avant-garde. But if postmodernity is a moment within capitalism, as Jameson argues, and if multinational capitalism is as destructive in its socio-cultural consequences as many of our contributors appear to believe, then the question may indeed still turn out to be *socialisme (féminisme?) ou barbarie?* Only a postmodernist politics and a postmodernist art can reasonably aspire to provide an adequately postmodern answer to a question such as this. The essays collected here are not simply the record of an occasion, but are also preliminary contributions to a cognitive mapping of our several postmodern conditions.

NOTES

1. Cf. Ernst Bloch et al., *Aesthetics and Politics* (London: Verso, 1980).
2. See the 'Select Bibliography' for full references for these three texts.
3. Peter Bürger, *Theory of the Avant-Garde*, p.34.
4. Jean-François Lyotard, *The Postmodern Condition*, p.xxiv.
5. Ibid., p.5.
6. Fredric Jameson, 'Postmodernism, or the Cultural Logic of Late Capitalism', p.65.
7. Ibid., p.92.
8. Jochen Schulte-Sasse, 'Modernity and Modernism, Postmodernity and Postmodernism: Framing the Issue', *Cultural Critique*, 5 (1986–7), p.6.
9. Cf. Jürgen Habermas, 'Modernity versus Postmodernity', *New German Critique*, 22 (1981).
10. The 1982 essay is included as an appendix to *The Postmodern Condition* (see 'Select Bibliography'); the 1983 article appeared in translation as 'Rules and Paradoxes and Svelte Appendix', *Cultural Critique*, 5 (1986–7), pp.209–19.
11. Cf. Marshall Berman, *All That is Solid Melts into Air* (London: Verso, 1983).

CHAPTER 1

Existentialism, Alienation, Postmodernism: Cultural Movements as Vehicles of Change in the Patterns of Everyday Life

Agnes Heller

The term 'culture' or 'civilization' was invented in the West as one universal among many. Yet, in comparison to other universals such as 'science' or 'freedom', the universal termed 'culture' has always had a pluralistic connotation. One discussed science or freedom, for example, and not 'Western science' and 'Western freedom', because the general understanding was that these good things were one and indivisible. On the other hand, one discussed 'Western culture' because it has always been assumed that there were many other cultures alongside the Western one, whether inferior or superior to it, or even simply different from it. Irrespective of whether those cultures were regarded as superior or inferior, the relationships among cultures were always temporalized as well as historicized. Cultures follow one another, for example, and there is no way back to a previous one except via a nostalgic trip which is only open to the single individual. In this understanding, cultures were regarded as closed universes which either remained closed or, if they eventually did open up, were then thought to lose their distinctive features and would thus be vulnerable to subversion by the latest, i.e. Western, culture. This view of 'alien' cultures coincided structurally with the cultural divisions within particular countries in the period of early capitalism. Aristocratic, gentry, grand- and petty-bourgeois and peasant forms of life were strictly distinct from one another. The debate on cultural inferiority versus superiority occurred unremittingly with the contenders consisting of the aristocracy, the gentry (in England) and the bourgeoisie.

Class culture in the nineteenth century was more than a mere figure of speech. Disraeli's famous dictum mentioned two nations which were not even in communication with one another. Early working-class movements, the trade unions and later the parties, whether or not they explicitly advocated the creation of a special working-class culture, all nevertheless strongly contributed to the emergence of such a culture. Class cultures as a rule were almost hermetically sealed with individuals only occasionally able to cross the borders between them. This crossing of cultural borders was extremely difficult, and not only for those at the bottom aspiring upwards. Henry James, for example, was a great chronicler of the immense difficulties encountered even by people of enormous wealth once they ventured to cross the cultural barriers which divided them from 'the ancient families'.

The modern division of labour, with its capacity to stratify society along functional lines, began to break down the strict segregation of class cultures as early as the end of the nineteenth century. Freelance intellectuals, artists in particular, were the first 'splinter groups'. These artists created 'Bohemia' with a specific cultural flavour, a form of life all their own, which was neither aristocratic, nor bourgeois nor for that matter working-class, but simply different. The culture of 'Bohemia' gradually broke up the hermetic closure of various cultures on a global scale by virtue of the fact that 'Bohemians' of one country regularly borrowed artistic material, elements, themes and motifs from the so-called aliens of other countries. Gauguin's islanders no longer resemble the 'noble savage'; they are like us with a difference.

Yet it was only after the Second World War that the erosion of a network of class cultures became visible and cultural relativism unmistakably gained momentum. Forms of life and cultural patterns could now be freely chosen, particularly by the younger generation, and cultural habits which had previously been exclusively class-related were now becoming generally available. In addition, in this epoch, one also sees 'other cultures' begin to borrow lavishly patterns of behaviour, habits, etc. from Western fashions. Of course, such an obvious conspicuous parallel development begs for a multi-causal explanation. I have already mentioned the emergence of the functional division of labour as one factor in this development. Factors such as the birth of mass production, the rise of the mass media, decolonization, and the decrease in working hours in the centres of Western and Northern Europe, could also be mentioned.

Rather than focus on causes, however, I would like to discuss briefly what might be termed imaginary *institutions of signification* (to borrow the phrase of Cornelius Castoriadis). In my view, there have been three distinct waves in which new imaginary significations of ways of life have been created since the Second World War. I will deliberately disregard those theoretical tendencies (for example structuralism) which have deeply influenced our vision of the world. Instead, I will focus on those world-views and philosophies which were carried by cultural movements. For it was in the movements themselves that life-patterns were changed and that a new group of cultures in everyday life began to be slowly created. Needless to say, we are not at the end of this trend, but sufficiently in the midst of it to be able to watch the main tendencies of its unfolding.

As a rule, each new generation of young men and women has taken the initiative from the previous generation, since the time of the French Revolution. However, the distinct patterns of action, aspiration and imagination amongst post Second World War youth have been sharply dissimilar to those of former generations. More precisely, the patterns have been becoming increasingly different from generation to generation. Although intellectuals, philosophers, sociologists, writers and artists have had their share in launching these movements and in articulating their aspirations, the youth whom they address and the aspirations and self-perceptions to which they give voice are widely dissimilar to those of the earlier bourgeois splinter group, 'Bohemia'. Post Second World War movements did not warm up the old clichés about the aesthetic life; their extravaganza was not aesthetic, but existential. To an even lesser extent did they regard themselves as the cohort of a new political elite. Whether or not they were politically oriented, these movements were not involved in attempts to change elites.

In a society increasingly characterized by a functional division of labour, the term 'young' becomes equivalent to 'pre-functional'. In other words, everyone who is not yet absorbed by a function within the division of labour, is young. Movements of the young start to attract and embrace youth from extremely different social milieus, irrespective of whether their later function is to be that of academic or social worker, self-employed or industrial worker, etc. The tendency for the social 'absorbing power' of movements to widen is clearly in evidence. The cultural trend of 'punk' is a strong case in point.

However, pre-functional existence is at the same time pre-stratification existence. As such, it allows for forms of life to develop which no longer have the characteristics of class cultures. Institutionalized function performance no longer suffices for preforming ways of life, as 'being a bourgeois' or 'being a worker' once did. This is why people cannot shed the vestiges of a particular 'youth culture' once they are settled in a social function. Certain elements of their own youth culture will continue to shape their lifestyles as adults. It is easy to ascertain that this is indeed the case. The transition from traditional class cultures to modern culture was destined to give birth to the most violent generation conflict modern men and women have ever known, and this dramatic process repeats itself wherever there are still traditional class cultures. However, once fathers and mothers themselves have been shaped by a modern movement, generation conflict between them and their children will be relatively mild, even if they disapprove of each other's values and ways of life. The softening of the generation conflict is but one sign among many of the structural changes in which new cultural movements are embedded.

Three consecutive generations have appeared since the Second World War: the *existentialist* generation, the *alienation* generation and the *postmodernist* generation, to employ the terms of their own self-description. Modern cultural movements appeared in waves, and this happened for the simple reason that each new generation had to 'come of age' in the sense of creating a new 'imaginary institution' before it could take over the torch from the former generation. The First Wave began its career immediately after the war and reached its zenith in the early fifties. The Second Wave was launched by the events of the mid-sixties and reached its peak in 1968, but continued to expand until the mid-seventies. The third movement arose in the eighties and has not yet reached its zenith. The second movment grew out of the first, and the third from the second, both in the sense of continuation but also in the sense of reversing the signs of the previous movement. In responding to one another, *each wave continues the pluralization of the cultural universe in modernity as well as the destruction of class cultures.* Furthermore, *each wave gives a new stimulus to the structural change in intergenerational relationships.* The latter is not quite independent from the former, for structural change in intergenerational relationships is yet another pattern of everyday life which points towards cultural relativism.

'Waves' and 'generations' are more precise terms than 'movement'. Although waves consist of cultural and social movements, certain movements continue through generations in a direct line instead of appearing in waves; feminism is the prime example. At the peak of the waves, movements which are 'fellow travellers' of the main trend tend, as a rule, to merge with the former, only then to be disconnected from them in an intermediary standstill. In addition, a wave is broader than the sum total of movements which emerge with it and which merge into one another at their peak. As a rule, movements meet with resistance, they provoke countermovements, but even the countermovements themselves display the characteristics of the waves which have brought them to the surface. And perhaps more interestingly, even those people, those forms of social action and those institutions which apparently have nothing to do with the 'waves', still have something in common with them. For they too participate in those changes in the social 'imaginary institution' of which the wave is an expression. It may seem far-fetched to associate the Falklands War and its *modus operandi* with postmodernism. And yet the war – the behaviour of the marines, the press reports and the like – seemed to be a deliberate quotation from the First World War. It was as if the participants were purposefully quoting Renoir's celebrated movie, *La Grande Illusion*, as they imitated the valiant and chivalrous officers fighting duels of honour in the age of modern technology.

The *existentialist* generation was the first and the narrowest. The rapidity with which Sartre's message, though not necessarily his philosophy, caught the minds of the young in Western Europe, and to some extent in Central and Southern Europe, was in itself not completely unprecedented. The Romantic movement had spread just as swiftly, over a century ago. What was unprecedented, however, was the character of the movement, namely the *circumstance*, realized only in retrospect, that the existentialist wave was the first in a series of the most striking phenomena of Western history in the second half of our century. The unprecedented character of the movement was due to its historical setting. This movement, like Romanticism, initially appeared as a *revolt of subjectivity* against the ossification of bourgeois forms of life, against the normative and ceremonial constraints rooted in this way of life. The rebellion of subjectivity did have a political implication but one no more explicit than in previous Romantic movements. But prior to its emergence there had been the cataclysmic experience of totalitarianism, which made the life experience of contingency, so typical of modernity, an experience of personal freedom as well. However, the freedom of the existing, contingent person no longer sufficed in its capacity as *the* notion of freedom. Freedom had to be politicized. To this we must add the guilt of colonization and the experience of de-colonization. In this experience, the politicization of freedom and the relativization of (Western and bourgeois) culture were combined. All this swept though Europe in a series of cultural practices. 'Shocking the bourgeois' is precisely the gesture that makes men and women in revolt dependent on the bourgeois. But in the extentialist wave this famous *épater* was no longer present. What mattered now was doing things in our own way, practising our own freedom. Young men and women, intoxicated by the atmosphere of unlimited possibilities, began to dance existentially, love existentially, talk existentially, etc. In other words, they were intent on breaking free.

The alienation generation, which reached its peak in 1968, was both a continuation and a reversal of the First Wave. Their formative experience was not the war but the post-war economic boom and the consequent widening of social possibilities. Their experience, furthermore, was not the dawn but the dusk of subjectivity and freedom. While the existentialist generation, despite its discovery of alienation, the lifelessness of modern institutions and the senselessness of contingency, had nevertheless been a rather optimistic breed, the alienation generation, on the contrary, began in despair. Precisely because this generation took seriously the ideology of plenty, it rebelled against the complacency of industrial progress and affluence, as well as claiming for itself the sense and the meaning of life. Freedom remained the main value, however, and unlike the existentialist generation the alienation generation has remained committed to collectivism. The quest for freedom was a common pursuit.

Though an outgrowth of despair, the alienation generation became affirmative by virtue of the process in which different movements merged in the peak of this wave. In this merger literally nothing was left as it had been before. One movement made a plea for the extension of the human experience into taboo areas (and promoted the 'radical' cult of drugs, causing untold damage); the other made a claim for expanded families; yet another advocated the return to the simplicity of rural life; while still others supported sexual, or gay, liberation. Some movements raised concrete political objectives, while others were involved in experimental theatre, happenings, permissive education or in the advocacy of the slogan 'small is beautiful'. It is practically impossible to list all the issues and practices through which the second wave of the cultural movement made inroads into the perception and self-perception of modern Western civilization.

As a social theory, postmodernism was born in 1968. In a manner of speaking, postmodernism was the creation of the alienation generation disillusioned with its own perception of the world. It can be argued that the defeat of 1968 was the reason for this disillusionment (if there was such a defeat, which remains an open question). However, one can also maintain that postmodernism had already appeared in the very beginnings of the 1968 movements, particularly in France, and that it therefore should simply be regarded as the continuation of the former. But whatever happened on the theoretical scene, the movements themselves seemed to disappear. The very same theorists who continued to relay the message of the alienation generation made speeches about the final defeat of social movements. Meanwhile, something else occurred. While the external signs of the movements vanished, there was still a movement; or rather, there were several, but they were invisible because they were essentially psychological and interpersonal. These movements increasingly saturated human relationships with their message to such an extent that they altered the social fabric from which they had emerged.

Postmodernism as a cultural movement (not as an ideology, theory, or programme) has a simple enough message: anything goes. This is not a slogan of rebellion, nor is postmodernism in fact rebellious. As far as everyday life is concerned, there are many and various things and patterns of life against which modern men and women can or should rebel, and postmodernism indeed allows for all sorts of rebellion. However, there is no single great target for collective and integrated rebellion. 'Anything goes' can be read as follows: *you* may rebel against anything you want to rebel against but let *me* rebel against the particular thing I want to rebel against. Or, alternatively speaking, let me not rebel against anything at all because I feel myself to be completely at ease.

For many, this boundless pluralism is the sign of conservatism: are there not crucial, focal issues which demand rebellion? And yet the truth is that postmodernism is neither conservative nor revolutionary nor progressive. It is neither a wave of rising hope nor a tide of deep despair. It is a cultural movement which makes distinctions of this kind irrelevant. For whether conservative, rebellious, revolutionary or progressive, all can be part of such a movement. This is so not because postmodernism is apolitical or anti-political, but rather because it does not stand for a particular politics of any kind. Cultural relativism, which began its rebellion against the fossilization of class cultures as well as against the 'ethnocentric' lionization of the 'only-right-and-true', which is to say the Western heritage, has succeeded. Indeed, it has succeeded so completely that it is now in a position to be able to entrench itself. Those who are now in the process of entrenching themselves are the members of the youngest generation who have learned their lessons and have drawn their own conclusions. Postmodernism is a wave within which all kinds of movements, artistic, political and cultural, are possible. We have already had several brand-new movements. There have been movements with a focus on health, anti-smoking, body-building, alternative medicine, marathon-running and jogging. A movement of sexual counterrevolution has been developing. We have had and still have peace or anti-nuclear movements. Ecological movements are in full bloom. We witness the expansion of feminist movements, the movement for educational reform and much else. The fashion magazines are perhaps the best indicators of the pluralist character of postmodernism. 'Fashion' as such no longer exists, or more precisely everything is, or many things are, fashionable at the same time. We no longer have 'good taste' or 'bad taste'. (Of course, one still might refer to having taste or not in the sense of being able to distinguish between the better and the worse within the same genre.)

If postmodernism, then, is going to be absorbed by our culture as a whole, we will finally reach the end of the transformation which began with the existentialist generation after the Second World War. This is not a prophecy about the end of movements, rather the opposite. What this statement does forecast is a situation in which concrete cultural transformations will take place in so far as such transformations are carried by one or another movement; however, the movements themselves will not occur in generational waves. These movements, finally, will not be the 'movements of the young'; they will not only be cross-class, but also cross-generational movements.

By way of introduction to the short story of the three generations which have created our present cultural 'imaginary institutions of signification', I have pointed out two decisive developments. I have stated that each wave continues the pluralization of the cultural universe in modernity as well as the destruction of class-related cultures. I have added that each wave has given a new stimulus to the structural change in intergenerational relations. I will now return to these fundamental questions in some detail.

What the three waves of cultural movements have achieved thus far and what can be expected to happen in the near future, will be discussed in the same breath. The transformation is uneven, for the present of one country is the future of another. No one factor can account for all of the differences in speed and character of the transformation. In matters of cultural transformations traditions of different provenance may accelerate or slow down a process. For example, traditional bourgeois forms of life are more entrenched in Germany than in Scandinavia. Yet even where the transformations are most spectacular, they are far from being close to completion. Class cultures are still very much in evidence. The European feeling of superiority has not evaporated and serious forms of generational conflict still exist. The bottom line is therefore a tendency rather than a *fait accompli*. A tendency is a possibility, and the latter can be regarded as less than 'reality'. But one could also agree with Aristotle that possibility stands higher than reality, that poetry is more true than history. The possibility mentioned here entails a small dosage of poetry, but it is based on the extrapolation of contemporary socio-economic features which have been discovered, discussed and corroborated through empirical data by sociologists such as Touraine, Offe and Dahrendorf.

The demise of class-related cultures can be explained in terms of the increase in consumerism. Previously, both bourgeois and working-class ways of life were centred on work performance. However, in what is termed these days 'post-industrial society', the centre of crucial life activities has become leisure time. As Dahrendorf has recently pointed out, not more than twenty-five per cent of the populace of the countries in the European Common Market perform socially necessary labour, which means holding a job or owning a business. Furthermore, function performance no longer provides the sufficient 'matter' from which a way of life can be constituted. In relation to life activity as a whole, function performance can be seen as fairly contingent, and is thus hardly the centrepoint of cultural identification. Rather, it is the *level* of consumption (the amount of money spent on consumption) that becomes the source of cultural identification. Cultural identification is therefore a quantitative rather than a qualitative issue. It was the deep conviction of the alienation generation that the *type* of preferred consumption had been socially generalized under the impact of the manipulation of tastes and desires by the mass media. In terms of this conception, everyone was manipulated into enjoying, being pleased with, and having a need for 'the same', irrespective of whether 'the same' referred to objects, products, forms of art, practices or whatever.

Although the growth of consumerism came to an abrupt halt with the advent of economic crises and depressions, and although the 'affluent society' proved to be far less affluent than the 'alienation generation' had previously assumed, the patterns which gave birth to the 'manipulation paradigm' have themselves not disappeared. But the outcome of general manipulation no longer assumes as gloomy a forecast as in earlier predictions. As so often happens, the prediction itself has changed the course of what was predicted. It seems an exaggeration, but in fact is not, that the wave of the alienation generation was, in this respect as well, the forerunner of the postmodernist generation. The spectre of 'mass society' in which everyone likes the same, reads the same, practises the same, was a short intermezzo in Europe and North America. What has indeed emerged is not the standardization and unification of consumption, but rather the enormous pluralization of tastes, practices, enjoyments and needs. The quantity of money available for spending continues to divide men and women, but so do the kinds and types of enjoyment, pleasure, practices which they seek. Instead of becoming the Great Manipulator, the media have become rather a catalogue for highly individualized tastes. More importantly, the different patterns of consumption have become embedded in a variety of lifestyles, 'each according to his or her preference', and of course, the means available to satisfy that preference.

At this point, I have to return to the general problem of cultural relativism. Non-Western cultural patterns were first discovered by 'Bohemia'; the taste of the Bohemians was literally exotic. Today, 'alien' cultures are present at each and every level of everyday life. They have become embedded in our cultural practices; they have been assimilated, and they have become 'commonplace', as it were – from Chinese restaurants to Indian dresses, from African hairdos to Latin American novels. However bizarre it may sound to associate Chinese cuisine, African hairdos, herbal tea and sex movies with the alienation generation, it nevertheless remains a fact that this generation introduced the paraphernalia of exotic novelties into the menu of our daily life, in which every taste can find its own satisfier. A varied menu does not add up to a lifestyle, however. Rather, certain practices, tastes and preferences constitute *patterns*. One can easily identify several such patterns in which 'this goes with that', but not with something else.

However, a problem presents itself with respect to this infinite variety, this pluralization of the ways of life, this demise of self-complacent and ethnocentric class cultures. Hannah Arendt, and others, have stressed that social classes are necessary for the conduct of rational politics. Classes can give birth to institutions (political organizations which represent their interests). Representative governments grow out of class society. If classes are on the wane, if cultures are becoming pluralized to the degree of total particularization, is a meaningful, rational decision-making process still possible? We are left only with corporations organized according to functions, and corporations do not represent the interests of ways of life as a whole, but rather the interests of particular functions. Thus, societies based on corporate decision-making can easily be described as 'mass societies', despite cultural pluralization. The 'alienation generation' made a case for 'grassroots politics', for a kind of politics embedded in communities and ways of life on all levels of social stratification. It remains uncertain at this stage whether cultural relativization and pluralization will lead to the demise of rational policy-making or whether they will rather be the prelude to a more democratic and more rational form, or forms, of political action, a combination of the parliamentary system with a type of direct democracy. At this point we do not have sufficient data for extrapolation.

Let me now turn to the change in the intergenerational relations. All three waves of movements were carried by the younger generation. However, the term 'young' requires clarification. In a functional society, 'the young' are those men and women (and not just those boys and girls) who do not perform a 'function' that locks them into one stratum or another within the social division of labour. Thus students are young even when they are thirty years of age, which meant 'middle age' in the generation of our grandparents. Precisely because of this functional connotation, I will in what follows avoid the distinction between 'young' and 'old'. (In any case, old people or 'senior citizens' do not have a job these days. They are, in other words, the 'postfunctional ones'.)

The present changes in the relationship of prefunctional and functional generations are so obvious that one can read them from quite external signs. In class-related cultures young men tried hard to look older than their age. After the Second World War, however, the pattern gradually transformed to the point where it was, finally, totally reversed. Those who are mentally and physically fully grown up now make sometimes desperate efforts to look like youngsters and behave accordingly. 'Looks' have different social meanings. Looking older than one's age expresses the aspiration to be treated as a responsible adult, as someone who has been settled or at least who is ready for being settled. Looking younger than one's age expresses the aspiration to be treated as someone who is still open to every option, who is not yet a 'bureaucrat', who is not yet fossilized by his or her function. At the peak of generational waves, it has become a common practice that members of the 'functional generation' look for the favours of their children in order to be regarded as 'honorary youth'. The term and the practices of 'mid-life crisis' were invented in this world of the functional division of labour; it is the exclusive production of functional society. In a class culture, be it bourgeois, working class or gentry, being middle-aged lends one a dignity which is the representative quality of the fully-fledged adult. It is *qua* adult, as someone who is *still* able-bodied and -minded but *already* the repository of a great amount of experience, that one becomes a *persona* in a given culture. Men in mid-life crisis wish to be immature and not-yet-settled again, bald teenagers looking for a new identity.

The functional division of labour is attended by a very complex and ambivalent combination. Function performance requires identification, particularly in business, and in public institutions. The stronger the identification with function performing, the greater the temptation for a person to become a self-complacent bore or an arrogant bureaucrat. The function-performer is almost inevitably driven to lock out young people because they are competition. Function-related self-complacency is often nothing more than a psychological cover-up for the fear of competition. It follows from this that fathers of this kind have no major conflict with their own children, as had typically transpired in the dramatic period of generation conflict, but rather with the children of others. Looking young has therefore a double function: it helps the adults to be 'accepted' by the young in their own milieu and it lends them weight in their competition with the children of others. It is precisely this conflict that is normally solved in mid-life crisis when the middle-aged person resigns from competition and dons the costume of the young. The world after the Second World War is no longer œdipal. What other kinds of neurosis it will develop is another matter. Lasch's thesis on narcissism is a significant attempt at exploring our new diseases.

Let us make one final observation about the three waves of cultural movements after the Second World War. In all the ups and downs of their continuities and discontinuities, one feature has remained stable. Feminist movements have constituted a major trend in all three, and this is the trend which, despite some minor setbacks, has totally changed modern culture. Feminism was, and has remained, the greatest and most decisive *social revolution of modernity*. Unlike a political revolution, a social revolution does not break out: it takes place. A social revolution is always a cultural revolution as well. The relativization of cultures and the inroads made by 'alien' cultures into Western cultures have been repeatedly mentioned above. The feminist revolution is not just one contribution to this enormous change, but the single major one. For female culture, hitherto marginalized and unacknowledged, is now well on its way to articulating a final statement on its own behalf, to claim its half of the traditional culture of humankind. The feminist revolution is not just a novel phenomenon of Western culture, *it is a watershed in all hitherto existing cultures.*

The feminist revolution could not have been brought about by the new form of the division of labour alone. Democratic institutions, the value ideas of freedom, equality and rights had to be present in the global 'imaginary institution of signification' for feminist movements, these carriers of the revolution, to come about. For previously women, just like men, could be incorporated into the functional division of labour, and yet women could also remain subjected to male domination. But without a functional division of labour, the objective of the feminist revolution would have remained unattained for the simplest of reasons: women would not have achieved the opportunity to make a living of their own, to acquire the minimal precondition of an independent life.

Why is it such a widespread belief that 'movements have disappeared', that the past forty years was a period in which 'nothing has happened'? Perhaps because we are too much used to history as political history. And yet history is, first and foremost, social and cultural; it is the history of the daily lives of men and women. Placed under close scrutiny, this history will disclose changes which include a social revolution. The three waves of cultural movements analysed above were the main stewards of this transformation. They did not alter the vessel, but they did change the ocean on which the vessel navigates.

CHAPTER 2

Wrapping up Postmodernism: The Subject of Consumption Versus the Subject of Cognition

David Bennett

The socialist Greater London Council having apparently resigned itself to its promised abolition by the Thatcher government on April Fools' Day, 1986, it was being rumoured in London's alternative press in October 1985 that the G.L.C.'s leader, Ken Livingstone, was planning to balance his Council's books by spending what remained in its kitty on a Christmas present for Margaret Thatcher. The rumour had it that County Hall (soon to be vacant) was to be gift-wrapped at a cost of several million pounds by the expatriate Bulgarian artist Christo Javacheff and presented to Thatcher in a parodic gesture of political compliance. If Eagleton is right in suggesting that 'What is parodied by postmodernist culture, with its dissolution of art into the prevailing forms of commodity production, is nothing less than the revolutionary art of the twentieth-century avant garde'[1] – an avant-garde which spurned the notion of aesthetic 'representation' for an art which would be a direct, material intervention in social praxis – then such a gesture on the G.L.C.'s part would have amounted to politics parodying postmodernism's parody of a political art. (The rumour, of course, proved apocryphal; the Council threw a quarter-million pound farewell party for itself instead, and Livingstone embarked on the career of a parliamentarian.)

Meanwhile, in Paris (one of the incubators of what Peter Bürger in his *Theory of the Avant-Garde* has termed the 'historical avant-garde'), Christo himself had just added another package to an *œuvre* which, spanning some twenty-seven years, had begun modestly with projects like *Wrapping a Girl* (London, 1962) and progressed to such bolder and bigger parcels as *Packed Medieval Tower* (Spoleto, 1968), *Packed Museum of Contemporary Art* (Chicago, 1969), *Wrapped Coast* (Sydney, 1969) and *Surrounded Islands* (Greater Miami, 1980–3). Completed on September 23, 1985, after a decade of planning, the new work was *Le Pont-Neuf Empaqueté*. For fourteen days the double span of France's most photographed bridge stood wrapped with seventy-five miles of rope and 444,000 square feet of sewn-to-measure nylon fabric whose sandstone tones reflected those of the weather-washed facades of the Ile de la Cité buildings and concealed the smog-blackened surfaces of the bridge without obstructing the flow of commuter and tourist traffic either over or under its upholstered arches. Handbills distributed to pedestrians by the artist's uniformed assistants gave an explanation of this latest *empaquetage*:

> *Le choix d'empaqueter le Pont-Neuf est né il y a dix ans, de ses références historiques, urbaines et artistiques exceptionelles et de sa situation privilegiée qui réunit la rive droite, la rive gauche et l'Ile de la Cité, cœur de Paris depuis plus de deux mille ans. La construction du pont a débuté en 1587 sous Henri III et a été terminée sous Henri IV en 1606.*
>
> [The decision to wrap up the Pont-Neuf was born ten years ago, because of its exceptional historical, urban and artistic points of reference and because of its privileged position uniting the Right Bank, the Left Bank and the Ile de la Cité, the heart of Paris for more than two thousand years. The construction of the bridge was begun in 1587 under Henry III and was completed under Henry IV in 1606.]

While Christo supervised the five hundred-strong team of helpers (including frogmen, tree surgeons, rockclimbers, bargees, electricians, engineers, builders and students) needed to execute this '*œuvre d'art temporaire et publique*', not far away, on the Left Bank, Michael Cachoux's commercial gallery was preparing for a *vernissage*, its shop window eye-catchingly dressed with a five-foot non-figurative bronze packaged in transparent polythene and rope and bearing the legend: '*CECI N'EST PAS UN CHRISTO*'. Cachoux's own handbills announced: '*CHRISTO emballe le Pont-*

Neuf / *CACHOUX déballe ses Cristaux*' [*CHRISTO* wraps up the Pont-Neuf / *CACHOUX* unwraps his Crystals].

II

That the logic of commodification has come to structure every aspect of contemporary life, not least the cultural-aesthetic, is now a commonplace of periodizing theories of postmodernism. Displacing the use values of objects and practices with an exchange value which erases immanent qualities and differences, this universal commodification of our object world is said to have drained things of their independent 'being' and reduced them to so many means for their own consumption, so many instruments of commodity satisfaction.[2] In *Society of the Spectacle* Guy Debord has argued that the ultimate form of commodity fetishism in contemporary consumer society is the image or spectacle itself ('the spectacle is the *main production* of present-day society'[3]). The familiar example, as Fredric Jameson explains, is that of tourism:

> The American tourist no longer lets the landscape 'be in its being' as Heidegger would have said, but takes a snapshot of it, thereby transforming space into its own material image. The concrete activity of looking at a landscape – including, no doubt, the disquieting bewilderment with the activity itself, the anxiety that must arise when human beings, confronting the non-human, wonder what they are doing there and what the point or purpose of such a confrontation might be in the first place – is thus comfortably replaced by the act of taking possession of it and converting it into a form of personal property.[4]

Given the other-directed nature of contemporary conspicuous consumption, such reifying images (by which 'we consume, less the thing itself, than its abstract idea'[5]) serve in turn to 'speak' their owners for others. Like designer clothes, Cachoux's crystals, or the latest-model car, our tourist snapshots of Parisian bridges, medieval towers or Sydney beaches become images for others to have of us, their owners or 'takers'. Obsessively packaging such thoroughly 'mythologized' objects or spectacles as if for consumption, purchase or mailing back to the tourist's hometown, Christo's *empaquetages* (not least his re-wrappings of those institutional pre-packagings of art and history called galleries) seem monstrous parodies of the universal commodification which fetishizes history and nature, reducing cultural and natural objects to so many reified images for consumption. In so far as they eclipse the pretext or occasion of art, Christo's parcels seem bold postmodernist negations of a 'representational' aesthetic. Teasingly masking the object from the camera's reifying eye, they simultaneously erase all its distinctive intrinsic features, rendering it just one more anonymous package on the equivalence principle of commodity exchange. Read parodically, Christo's *empaquetages* reactivate the strategies of alienation familiar from the historical avant-garde, repeating on a grotesquely inflated scale such *gestes* of surrealistic defamiliarization as Duchamp's ready-mades or Man Ray's *The Enigma of Isadore Ducasse* (a packaging in sackcloth and cord of the sewing machine of Lautréamont's celebrated image of alienation: 'the chance encounter of a sewing machine and an umbrella on a dissection table'). Works of 'temporary and public' art, commercially value-less in themselves since ephemeral and freely accessible to the most casual passer-by, Christo's *empaquetages* are clearly the political gestures of an avant-garde refusal of the commodification of art, and of what Benjamin called the 'aura' of the 'authentic', unique and possessable art-work.

What ought to be powerful and critical political statements, however, seem to have lost their disturbing charge. It is as if the quantitative principle of exchange value (as opposed to the qualitative one of use value) had definitively determined that the new and the different — once the very hallmark, now perhaps merely the trademark, of the avant-garde — had become purely a matter of proportion: a sheer size or scale which in Christo's case attests to the complicity of neo avant-gardist art with those bureaucracies that the early avant-garde had, precisely, targeted. If modernism, in exalting the unique as the resistive element amidst the universal sameness of things (the homogenizing effects of mass production), ultimately played into the hands of a culture industry for which novelty, fashion and fad are the very stuff of marketability, then Christo's postmodernism will assert its own distinction by exalting quantity. The spectacular scale of his projects, in attesting to spectacular, 'wasteful' cost and bureaucratic organization, would seem to lay claim to a value which is paradoxical in proportion to its apparent irrelevance to means-end or value-for-money rationality (a value which literally lesser spectacles or works cannot, by definition, claim).

What would seem to distinguish the postmodernist *geste* from its Dadaist or Surrealist counterpart, then, is its changed relation to its socio-economic context. To describe Christo's cultural practice as simply subversive of commodification would be misleading. Just as Leonardo, Vasari and Rubens made preparatory oil sketches of the elaborate 'triumphs' they designed for Renaissance patrons, so Christo makes preparatory drawings, maquettes and photo-collages for his projects, the sale of which through the private gallery system (whose dependence on the 'original' art-work as commodity his populist works of 'street' art would seem to bypass and parody) generates the multi-million dollar budgets of his parcels. (The budget of *Le Pont-Neuf Empaqueté* was conservatively estimated at 2.6 million dollars.)

It was not until the poster, paperback, record and gallery culture of the 1950s that the densely-textured, self-regarding artefacts of high modernism and the anti-art gestures of the avant-garde became institutionalized, canonized and made available for mass cultural consumption. But what took several decades to achieve for high modernism and the avant-garde takes postmodernism a matter of moments. For within hours of Christo's tying the final knot of *Le Pont-Neuf Empaqueté*, mass-reproduced photographic images of the spectacle and its designer's preparatory sketches were available for mailing back to the tourist's hometown in the form of postcards for sale in the Left Bank souvenir shops, all such images 'copyright Christo'. Postmodernism's putative parody of commodification is itself commodified and transformed into its own consumable image. Gone, it seems, from postmodernist art are not only the interventionist or revolutionary ambitions of the early avant-garde, but also its scandalous spontaneity and irrationality. After a decade of intricate negotiation, organization and cooperation between Christo and the French civic and political bureaucracies, it was no less an authority than François Mitterand who overrode any lingering official objection to the Pont-Neuf's wrapping and paid the package a visit in his capacity as President of the Republic. *The Secret Life of Salvador Dali* (1948) detailed its author's plans for the universal demoralization of instrumental reason through staging the appearance, at strategically timed intervals, of freshly-baked French loaves, from 15 to 45 meters long, in prominent public spaces in the capital cities of Europe and the U.S.A. ('If such an act could be successfully carried through', Dali thought, it 'would be capable of creating a state of confusion, of panic and of collective hysteria . . . [and] of becoming the point of departure from which . . . one could subsequently try to ruin . . . systematically the logical meaning of all the mechanisms of the rational practical world'.[6]) What distinguishes Christo's projects from such unrealized Surrealist *gestes* of comparable scale is, precisely, their realization.

III

Whatever intrinsic or stylistic features postmodernist art may share with modernism or the avant-garde, it would seem, in Jameson's words, that 'the two phenomena ... still remain utterly distinct in their meaning and social function owing to the very different positioning of postmodernism in the economic system of late capital ....'.[7] 'What has happened', Jameson says, 'is that aesthetic production today has become integrated into commodity production generally ...'.[8] The projects of both modernism proper and the avant-garde have foundered. Where the modernists sought to affirm the relative autonomy of the 'cultural' sphere – asserting its traditional constitutive values (of creativity, imagination, individuality, autonomy, etc.) against the values of the marketplace – the avant-garde sought to undermine the ideology of aesthetic autonomy, to collapse the cultural back into the socio-economic, in order to translate such values into social praxis.[9] (Hence Eagleton's wry suggestion that what postmodernism parodies is the revolutionary programme of the avant-garde.) The historical failure of both projects is, we are told, the determinate condition of postmodernism as a period. Contemporary aesthetic innovation and experimentation have lost their oppositional or subversive potential and are themselves stimulated and catalysed by the culture industry's reliance, for the reproduction of its market, on generating fresh waves of ever more novel-seeming commodities, from clothing to cars to artistic movements – and no less, we might want to add, their situating cultural theories.

Such, at least, is how Jameson, Eagleton and a growing number of American and European commentators have undertaken to define the distinctive cultural logic of the new 'period'. Jameson's own successive attempts to unravel this logic – attempts characterized in his seminal essay 'Postmodernism, or the Cultural Logic of Late Capitalism' as essays toward the 'cognitive mapping' of postmodernism – represent only the most subtle and powerful limbs of this swelling body of periodizing theory which takes its bearings from the work of the Frankfurt School theorists and their successors such as Habermas and Peter Bürger. But if such critics are right to ground their period definitions of postmodernism in an altered relation between cultural production and its socio-economic context, then it would seem a properly dialectical strategy to reflect on the relation between such cultural criticism (or production) itself and its putative object of analysis – in other words, its own positioning in the terrain it would map. Including as it does the production of new period definitions, the re-reading of history, and the development of interpretative strategies said to be appropriate to the texts of postmodernity, such cultural criticism is itself an instance of cultural production. If the adversarial potential of the 'cultural' sphere has been lost through its penetration by the logic of the commodity, then the question arises: from where and in whose name can oppositional criticism of Jameson's and Eagleton's own kind be conducted? Among other things, this is a question about the implied subject of their critical discourse, the subject of the knowledge it undertakes to produce – what I refer to in the subtitle of this paper as the subject of cognition as opposed (both epistemologically and politically) to the subject of consumption.

Echoing critics as diverse as Ihab Hassan, Hal Foster, Norman Holland and Eagleton, Jameson himself has argued that what he calls 'contemporary theory – or better still, theoretical discourse – is also . . . itself very precisely a postmodernist phenomenon'.[10] The theory of 'expressive causality'[11] which underwrites this equation (but which, as I shall suggest, Jameson doesn't invite us to employ in situating his own theoretical discourse) hinges largely on the fate of the individual subject in the postmodern era. Of the two ways of viewing this once scandalously decentred subject, Marxist commentators like Jameson and Eagleton prefer to see it as less the discursive effect of a demystifying literary, linguistic and psychoanalytic theory, than as the 'objective' effect of a socio-economic process of which this theory is a mere epiphenomenon. The process in question is the social transition from 'the classic age of competitive capitalism' ('the heyday of the nuclear family and the emergence of the bourgeoisie as the hegemonic class') to an age of 'consumer' or 'corporate' capitalism ('of the so-called organization man'),[12] a transition which has fractured the autonomous social subject of the bourgeois era into what Eagleton describes as 'a dispersed, decentred network of libidinal attachments, emptied of ethical substance and psychical interiority, the ephemeral function of this or that act of consumption, media experience, sexual relationship, trend or fashion'. Technology and consumerism, Eagleton suggests, have 'scattered our bodies to the winds as so many bits and pieces of reified technique, appetite, mechanical operation and reflex desire'; 'it is surely arguable that late capitalism has deconstructed . . . [the monadic] subject much more efficiently than meditations on *écriture*'.[13]

If we were provisionally to accept such a reflexion model of the relation between 'contemporary theory' and its social context, and look for an 'expression' of the logic of consumerism within literary theory, for example, we might find it in those radically 'subjectivist' accounts of reading which have emerged in the wake of a once equally fashionable structuralism. What I have in mind are those forms of reader-response and reception theory which, in representing what we call 'texts' as simply the epiphenomena of reading – as the projects or productions of reading subjects, either individual or collective – would seem to represent something in the nature of a consumers' revolution in the sphere of interpretative theory.[14]

Among the critics associated with this broad tendency in postmodern literary criticism are Roland Barthes, Hans Robert Jauss, Norman Holland, Stanley Fish and Tony Bennett. Methodologically and ideologically diverse though they are, the problems their reading practices pose for the discerning consumer of literary theories have generally been addressed as problems of epistemology. What I want to do is temporarily to suspend epistemological questions and consider such theories of reading, which privilege the act of reception/consumption over the act of production, within the perspective of the Marxist historical narrative of modernism and postmodernism currently being elaborated by Jameson and other critics, a narrative to which the category of the commodity would seem central. What I shall be suggesting is that such models, which at once construct and deconstruct the reader as an autonomous subject, have, like Marxist criticism's own discourse of knowledge, both their 'modernist' and their 'postmodernist' moments. In other words, the ideal of aesthetic autonomy which modernism reputedly entertained for itself, and which postmodernism is said to have deconstructed, is not only perpetuated in contradictory forms in certain kinds of supposedly postmodernist criticism, but such an ideal is in fact inherent in any self-reflexive discourse. The moments I am calling 'modernist' and 'postmodernist' respectively are the moment of imaginary autonomy, transcendence or emancipation, and the moment of knowing complicity, subjection or determination.

To tell the story of the consumer revolution in literary theory is, precisely, to construct *as* narrative a logic whose conclusion will also appear as an historical destiny. ('Construct and deconstruct', we say – rarely the other way round.) But what such narratives historicize or project as a unilinear trajectory in time is, I would suggest, a necessarily incessant oscillation in all interpretative theory between what I have termed its 'postmodernist' and its 'modernist' moments.

IV

What Marx called the fetishism of commodities is the process by which the products of labour come to appear as an independent and uncontrolled reality apart from the people who create them. Commodity production (i.e., production for exchange, not for use by the producer) creates the social division of labour, as a result of which labour appears as private – expended to meet private needs and wants through exchange on the market – rather than as real, complex social relations with other people. Commodity production constitutes a social relationship between producers, but this relationship appears to the latter not as a social relationship between themselves, but as one between the products of their labour. This confusion of relations between people with relations to things is the fundamental contradiction of commodity production.

The moment of this 'reification of social relations' (Marx) within literary theory – a transitional moment in its consumer revolution – is the concept of 'intertextuality', a promiscuous concept whose twentieth-century alliances include Russian Formalism, New Criticism, Eliot's 'tradition', and classical structuralism. For the 'intertextualist', the determinate social relations in literary interpretation (and production) are those between texts themselves – apprehended, like the circulation and exchange of commodities, as an independent reality, uncontrolled by their producers. The progressive attrition, in modern criticism, of Romanticism's 'author' – his/her demotion to structuralism's 'scriptor', Wolfgang Iser's 'implied author', Stanley Fish's 'necessary fiction', and finally to Barthes's dispensable trope of reading – corresponds to a progressive alienation and reification of the social relation of writing and reading: a reification of the symbolic act, the praxis or production, of writing signalled in the now pervasive displacement of the concept 'work' by that of 'text'.

Where the 'work' was grounded in history (the history of its labour of production) to which it thus 'referred', the concept 'text' has the power to suspend both historical and generic definitions. Like commodification itself, the concept 'text' erases the intrinsic heterogeneity of objects, dissolving distinctions between the 'literary' and the 'non-literary', the 'high' and the 'low', the 'aesthetic', the 'cultural' and the 'social', even the written and the non-written. Marking the moment of culture's opacity to history, the Text signals the repudiation of Authority, and with it, of the œdipal charge that might once have typified the reading experience. With the author's demotion to 'a paper-*I*' (Barthes), the reader can no longer bring paternity suits against the 'only begetter' of a text: the author who, fathering something on the mother tongue, previously provided a chromosomal key or guarantee of identity to the 'work' and a patronymic label for that legal relation of ownership, the copyright or *droit d'auteur* which is the relatively recent invention of capitalist publishing.[15] The identity of the text, as distinct from the work, lies in its destiny not its origin, in the moment of its consumption not of its production.

No sooner reified and so freed from any intrinsic determination by the mode of its production, however, the text (this reified symbolic act) is itself dematerialized, becoming no more than an image of itself, an 'object-effect' of the consuming subject, the reader of whose autonomy *qua* consumer Barthes was the most eloquent exponent. In 1971 Barthes offered his theory of the *scriptible* as not so much the promise as the record of an historical reparation of the social division of labour between writing and reading, a division which he described as itself a comparatively recent historical phenomenon.[16] In pre-capitalist cultures, according to Barthes, reading and writing were the equal privileges of a single class. Just as in the history of music there was a period when for the numerous class of practising amateurs ' "playing" and "listening" formed a scarcely differentiated activity' – i.e., before the delegation of playing to the professional 'interpreter' and the relegation of the amateur to passive listener – so also in literature, Barthes says, 'the coming of democracy' introduced a new social division of roles between producer and consumer.[17] The *scriptible* or modernist text heals over this division and restores the literary commodity – the alienated product of labour – to its producer for consumption. Barthes is the least ingenuous of reader-champions, but his defence in the rhetoric of utopian socialism of the notion of the *scriptible* text as a 'genuinely democratizing' effort to reverse 'the reduction of reading to a consumption' seems a postmodernist parody of Walter Benjamin's prediction in 1936 that with the expansion of the press, 'the distinction between author and reader is about to lose its basic character ... At any moment the reader is ready to turn into a writer'.[18] What Benjamin envisaged as a reversible social relation, Barthes envisages as a non-alienated privatized act of simultaneous production and consumption. Acknowledging that consumption has its pleasures, Barthes contrasts these with the pleasures of co-production, not the co-production of the writer and the reader, however, but of the reader and the 'writerly' text.

Illustrating what he calls the 'abolition of critical distance' in the postmodernist period, Jameson argues that the aesthetic of 'expression', which is 'closely linked to some conception of the subject as a monad-like container, within which things are felt which are then expressed by projection outwards', is one which dominated much of what we call high modernism, but which has disappeared in the world of the postmodern.[19] As in the reception theories of Iser, Jauss, Holland, Fish and Bennett, so in Barthes's theory of the *scriptible* text, there is a moment when this expressivist aesthetic resurfaces in the poetics of postmodernism. As for Romanticism (and if we believe Jameson, modernism), the 'expression' in question is still for the postmodernist critic the 'text', but what it is an 'expression' *of* is the subject of reading (consumption) not of writing (production).

Stanley Fish, the coiner of 'affective stylistics', is at once the most radical and conservative exponent of the reader's emancipation as an autonomous subject from determination by its object or other, the text. In *Self-Consuming Artefacts* (1972) Fish still wrote of reading a work 'correctly', which was to say as the writer intended, but in 'Interpreting the *Variorum*' (1976) and his subsequent work, Fish rejected as 'positivist' the notion that there could be a correct reading of a text or even 'the assumption that there *is* a sense, that it is embedded or encoded in the text . . .'.[20] Affective stylistics begins its de-reification of the text by substituting questions of experience for those of knowledge, questions of response for those of meaning. What we call 'text' is no more than a temporal sequence of mental operations or experiences of which the reader is the subject: strategies of anticipation and readjustment, experiences of unbalancing, reassurance, disappointment, surprise. What the Fishian consumer responds to, however, is not a structure objectively 'there' or inscribed by the producer in the work, as it might be for the merely *semi*-autonomous subject of Iser's and Jauss's reception aesthetics. For Fish, as for Wittgenstein, interpretation is not a two-stage process, a matter of *adding* an identity or response to some neutral sense-datum. What is perceived in or as the text is itself always already an interpretative product. There are no raw materials – whether of meanings, grammar, letters, or marks on the page – given before the interpretative labour.

If it is not an immanent structure of the work that structures the reading experience, then the determinants and constraints of that experience are immanent in the interpreting mind. What, then, is the other of this reading subject? Affective stylistics liberates the interpreter from determination by the work, only to deprive its transcendent subject of its sovereignty. Having dematerialized literature, Fish's criticism dematerializes the reader, turning him/her into an imaginary subject, a mere image of itself, a 'subject-effect' of the codes and conventions which constitute what Fish calls the 'interpretive community' in which the individual reader is inscribed. 'Subjectivist' or 'consumerist' criticism can be divided into two kinds: that which constructs the subject of reading as essentially collective and public, and that for which it is essentially individual and private. To move from one to the other is to shift interpretation from the axis of the reality principle to the axis of the pleasure principle, to move from questions of knowledge and signification to questions of pleasure and desire. As an exponent of the collective subject's autonomy, Fish attributes sovereignty over the work to the 'interpretive community' whose norms, codes and conventions speak through its members' reading experience.[21]

Fish's theory of the transcendent 'interpretive community' is a consensual one, seemingly predicated on the imaginary insulation of a monastic academy against the multiple, potentially conflicting interpretative communities in which any individual participates, either serially or simultaneously, as a gendered social being. If the critical community is still able to fall out with itself and produce new, revisionary or contradictory readings of *Paradise Lost*, this, for Fish, is only because one of the unbending rules of the academic institution of literary criticism is that which requires interpretative originality of the reader for the latter's professional survival. Like the scholarly journals on whose acceptance or rejection of articles professional appointments often depend, the academies themselves depend on the acquisition or production of new and different intellectual commodities for the reproduction of their markets: in the case of journals, a professional readership; in the case of the universities, a student population and corporate or state endowments. As an essentially epistemological project, Fish's deconstruction of the individualist reader has yet to pose any perceptible threat to the institutional boundaries within which it is conducted. In other words, his reading subject remains unified and autonomous, albeit collective.

The more *engagé* and refractory historical and ideological analyses of interpretative communities to which Fish's theory of the institutional subject of reading would seem to point (and which would presuppose a political theory of textual production/consumption) have been the concern of the Marxist theorist of consumer autonomy, Tony Bennett. Bennett's 'reading formations' are as autonomous and transcendent of the so-called 'texts' they construct in their own images as is Fish's interpretative community.[22] How Bennett's or Fish's own texts could therefore be regarded as 'saying' anything to the reading-formations whose interpretative autonomy they postulate is a question still in need of a satisfactory answer. Another criticism which could be levelled at such theories is the one frequently made of Jauss's insistence that it is the 'horizon of expectations' (cultural, ethical and literary) that the public brings to a literary work which determines how it is read:[23] namely, that such models fail to allow for sufficient diversity both *among* the various publics by which a text is consumed at a given moment in time and *within* any single group of consumers.

From the perspective of the consumers' revolt in literary theory, the radical moment of collective subjectivism no sooner arrives than it passes. Suggesting that the capitalist culture industry has effectively eroded the whole notion of an autonomous art, Habermas has argued that when the laws of the market which govern the sphere of commodity exchange penetrate the sphere of art and discourse about art, then critical judgement transforms itself into consumption and into acts of individualized reception, rather than public communication.[24] The valorizing theory of this privatized response in the case of literature is Norman Holland's 'transactive criticism', which he describes as abandoning 'the Cartesian craving for objectivity' and 'restor[ing] stories to their rightful owners – you and me . . .'.[25] The transactive critic celebrates 'the obvious truth that we each read differently', and counters those 'more orthodox critics' who try to suppress 'that embarrassing fact by using differences in response as an occasion for eliminating difference', that is, 'subtracting readings so as to narrow them down or cancel some'.[26] (Robert Crosman, incidentally, has re-cast this hermeneutic point in the rhetoric of consumerism when he insists that 'in order to serve the various needs and desires of various readers, texts *ought* to have plural meanings'.[27])

For the transactive critic, the text is the private property of its individual consumer – 'you and me'. 'Much as a musician might play out an infinity of variations on a single melody', Holland's individual lives out variations on an 'identity theme' which, as the 'primary identity' imprinted on the infant psyche in its relations to its 'mother-person', is structurally unchanging though capable of infinite 'variations' or transformations.[28] All interpretations, according to Holland, 'express the identity themes of the people making the interpretations . . . each reader, in effect, re-creates the work in terms of his own identity themes', shaping 'the text to match his own characteristic defences, fantasies, and coherences'.[29] (Holland's habitual use of the masculine pronoun would seem to help prove his theory.)

> First, he shapes it so it will pass through the network of his adaptive and defensive strategies for coping with the world. Second, he re-creates from it the particular kind of fantasy and gratification he responds to.[30]
> . . .all of us, as we read, use the literary work to symbolize and finally to replicate ourselves . . . .[31]

Re-reading 'The Purloined Letter' in 1980 in the light of Lacan's and Derrida's readings, Holland rejected as both epistemologically and empirically untenable those dualistic theories of reading, such as Iser's, Jauss's and Riffaterre's, which concede only a relative autonomy to the reader, attributing certain inherent features to the text, which the reader is then said to re-construct in his/her own image.[32] Radically subjectivist and consumer-oriented though it is, Holland's criticism could be viewed as an attempt to repair, at the level of interpretation or consumption, that self-alienation and *anomie* of the individual subject which preoccupied so much of literature during the high modernist period but which, Jameson and Eagleton tell us, has symptomatically ceased to be a source of anxiety in the postmodernist period, either for literature or for interpretative theory. Simultaneously producer and consumer, Holland's unalienated reader is a subject of pleasure, rather than knowledge, of the text. Similarly, it is as an 'aristocratic', semi-autonomous subject of pleasure that Barthes seeks to re-constitute the subject in *The Pleasure of the Text*: a subject whose dispersal among the codes and discourses of which it is an imaginary effect has denied it any cognitive relation to its object. ('Thus, what I enjoy in a narrative is not directly its content or even its structure, but rather the abrasions I impose upon the fine surface: I read on, I skip, I look up, I dip in again'.[33])

Like most subjectivist or consumer-oriented theories, Holland's and Barthes's have both their 'modernist' and their 'postmodernist' moments: moments of imaginary autonomy and transcendence, and moments of knowing subjection and complicity. Holland's 'transactive criticism' might be characterized in Lacanian terms as a 'mirror stage' or narcissistic criticism. The textual object, according to Holland, reflects back at the reader an image of the reading subject; but this subject is restored to itself, recentred or de-alienated, only to lose itself again, turning into an 'imaginary' self, a subject caught in the realm of simulacra, of imaginary identifications. In his 1983 essay 'Postmodern Psychoanalysis', Holland reiterates the 'modernist' moment of this theory when explaining that 'transactive criticism in America asks the critic to build his [sic] essay from his own response rather than from a work of art imagined as having a being all its own';[34] but this moment of autonomous, unalienated production proves illusory when the critic tries to identify the response in question without mediating it with a 'meta-response'. The 'identity theme' of which every reading of a text is a 'variation' is, by definition, unknowable, since every attempt to interpret it merely produces a further variation.

> In other words, this theme-and-variations concept of identity decenters the individual in a distinctly Postmodern, metafictional way. You are ficted, and I am ficted, like characters in a Postmodern novel.[35]

Remote as Holland's nutting out of the problem is from the mercurial self-reflections of Barthes, their discourses rehearse analogous movements of vertigo. The reader for *jouissance*, in *The Pleasure of the Text*, is the subject which knows itself as 'ficted' and seeks a sensation of freedom from its subject-ion, its imaginary selfhood, by dissolving itself into the forces and codes of which it is an imaginary effect, or in which it is unconsciously constructed.

V

Emancipation and subjection, autonomy and complicity, production and consumption – what I have called the themes of 'modernism' and 'postmodernism' respectively – oscillate throughout the radically relativistic or 'subjectivist' theories of reading which have displaced the structuralist dream of scientificity. Privileging consumption over production (reading over writing) only to unmask the one as a covert form of the other, such theories can be read as instances both of resistance to, and complicity with, what Jameson terms the 'cultural logic' of the postmodernist period. Objective cognition having been demystified as an imaginary effect of the structures and forces which unconsciously inhabit the subject, such theories return the decentred subject to an imaginary autonomy and transcendence, either by constructing it as a subject of consumption and pleasure rather than of knowledge, or by re-constituting it as a collective autonomous subject. Viewed from one angle, these 'postmodern' theories can be seen as quintessentially 'modernist' strategies within contemporary criticism to resist the reduction of art/literature to the status of an exchangeable commodity, and the reduction of reading (or the interpretation of any cultural text) to a passive consumption. Commodity production is production for exchange, not for consumption by the immediate producer; 'subjectivist' criticism re-constitutes the reader-consumer as the text's producer, and when I produce the text for my own, immediate consumption, the critical labour is no longer alienated.

My usage of the terms 'modernist' and 'postmodernist' in this paper is, of course, essentially arbitrary, and as the prefix 'post-' entails, it projects as a temporal distinction (and a recent one at that) what I have tried to suggest are coexistent moments in any self-reflexive discourse. Perhaps equally plausibly, we might call these two moments (the moment of 'imaginary' autonomy and the moment of 'knowing' subjection) those of Realism and Modernism respectively, or again, those of Romanticism and Realism respectively.[36] It seems an invariable property of any modernizing poetics that having defined itself (its own disillusionment) against the mystifications of an earlier period's poetics, it then colonizes the past – its defining historical other – with its own preoccupations, its own truths. The 'classic realist' or 'Balzacian' work against which Barthes set the modernist or *scriptible* text turns out on close inspection, in the case of *Sarrasine*, to be more modern than might have been expected. In the preface to his recent book on Shakespeare, Terry Eagleton suggests that 'though conclusive evidence is hard to come by, it is difficult to read Shakespeare without feeling that he was almost certainly familiar with the writings of Hegel, Marx, Nietzsche, Freud, Wittgenstein and Derrida'.[37] This has happened before; *Shakespeare Our Contemporary* and *Shakespeare: An Existential View* are the titles of two other modernizing constructions of the bard.[38]

One of the functions of the production of new period definitions like that of 'postmodernism' is a renewal or defamiliarization of our cultural milieu, an up-dating of the present by locating its distinctive origins in the more recent past. Theories of postmodernism as 'period' rather than as aesthetic genre or style typically entail a notion of cultural *coupure*, ·a decisive break with 'modernism', generally (though by no means universally) dated in the late 1950s or early 1960s.[39] Yet to re-read Balzac's anatomy of early nineteenth-century French culture in *Illusions perdues* in the light of Peter Bürger's, Jameson's or Eagleton's definitions of the distinctive cultural conditions of our own period is to be reminded that the penetration of commodity-logic into the failing heart of the cultural sphere (i.e., the alienation and reification of writing as a commodity for exchange, the structural subjection of the publishing, reviewing, theatre, poetry-writing and paper-making industries to the profit motive) has typified capitalist society at least since the 1820s. And while it is argued that the historical failure of the early avant-garde's interventionist ambitions is one of the determinate conditions of 'postmodernist' culture, it might equally and perhaps more plausibly be argued that the feminist avant-garde of the past two decades has come closer to realizing such ambitions than was ever latent in the programmes of Surrealism or Futurism. The holistic concept of 'period' depends upon the taxonomical privileging of one ensemble of cultural practices – identified as the distinctive or definitive one – over a plurality of others within the so-called 'period'. The homogenizing effects of such privileging – which subsumes a multiplicity of cultural practices with potentially non-synchronous or relatively autonomous histories under a single 'cultural dominant' – resembles the homogenizing effects of commodification. (While my own self-consciously 'tropical', quasi-parodic reading of certain instances of 'subjectivist' criticism within the problematic of consumerism rejects the assumption that such theories are simply complicit with postmodernism's supposed disempowering of the subject, it also clearly elides significant differences which inform those diverse theories in their various national and institutional contexts. Any adequate historical critique of reader-oriented hermeneutics would need to take account of the different ideological formations in which Fish's professionalism and Bennett's Marxism, Holland's ego psychology and Barthes's Lacanianism, are inscribed in their respective North American, English and French academic and cultural contexts.)

In so far as the institutions of the capitalist culture industry and market (including those of education, publishing, art galleries, theatres and the media) depend for their intelligibility and survival on the canonization or privileging of certain cultural products over others, the enterprise of periodization – identifying, as it does, what is new or newly 'dominant' – is complicit with that industry's interests. The recent massive production of monographs, journals, art shows, conferences, T.V. and radio programmes devoted to defining the phenomenon of postmodernism clearly participates in that reification and commodification of culture which is said to be a defining feature of the period itself. If the culture industry relies on generating new or oppositional movements for the continuous reproduction of its markets, however, this is not so much in order to displace as to defamiliarize the 'classics' of a (previously) dominant movement – to renovate the images we have of them. This defamiliarization is now happening with respect to 'high modernism' and the avant-garde as Anglo-American critics (rediscovering their debt to the Frankfurt School) review the artefacts of a now 'old' period in the waning light of the cultural sphere's submergence beneath the horizons of the marketplace.

Participating willy-nilly in the logic of the culture industry, then, the oppositional criticism of period-theorists like Jameson and Eagleton has its moment of complicity as well as its moment of resistance, and it may be the former which is unavoidably the more enduring moment. Jameson's essays toward the cognitive mapping of postmodernism promise to restore to us in the form of a knowledge the cultural text we inhabit or which inhabits us. But how does the self-transcending subject of cognition differ from the 'imaginary' autonomous subject of consumption? Like ideology itself in its Althusserian definition, the commodity (or the advertising industry which invests the object with its symbolic value and, thus transforming it into an image of itself, constructs the object *as* commodity) interpellates the consumer as an autonomous subject: the subject of *choice* and as such a self-determining, self-defining subject. But if what we are consuming is (as Debord suggests) not so much an object as an image of the object, one which is in turn an image of ourselves as consuming subjects, this closing of the gap between object and subject simultaneously opens up a gap within the subject. The subject of consumption can never be self-identical; there is always *différance* or slippage in consumption. The desire to consume (the consuming desire) is predicated on lack: precisely a lack of the subject-identity of which the commodity is an image. Without such difference and deferral, commodity consumption would come to an end. And this is no less true of the consumer of cultural criticism than it is of the consumer, say, of the huge array of perfumes manufactured to meet each woman's image of herself – made, as the advertising says, 'for the kind of woman you are'.

A loss of coordinates, both spatial and conceptual, is for Jameson, Eagleton, Baudrillard and others a defining feature of postmodernism as a new period. Thus Jameson explains his own efforts to map the postmodernist terrain as essays toward an 'as yet unimaginable new mode of representing' the 'world space of multinational capital', a representation 'in which we may again begin to grasp our positioning as individual and collective subjects and regain a capacity to act and struggle which is at present neutralized by our spatial as well as our social confusion'.[40] Always cast as a prolegomenon to (and thus a deferral of) a genuine knowledge, Jameson's essays in cognitive mapping finally make no ingenuous claims to faithful 'reflexion' of their terrain; and the self-reflexive moment in his work, the moment at which it refuses any artless claims to mimesis of its object, is also the most explicit statement of the kind of subject that oppositional criticism projects. Recalling Althusser's redefinition of ideology as 'the representation of the subject's *Imaginary* relationship to his or her *Real* conditions of existence', Jameson says: 'surely this is exactly what the cognitive map is called upon to do . . .'.[41] Promising no more than imaginary (if as yet unimagined) knowledge of its object, cognitive mapping is, in other words, a confessedly ideological project, founded on the Althusserian assumption that ideology, if not the poor, will always be with us – its explicit aim being to constitute individuals as (albeit 'imaginary') autonomous subjects, the subjects of choice and thus of history. Jameson's own habit of referring to this subject as 'the bourgeois ego', however, is a reminder that the project is less one of constitution than of re-constitution: something like trying to squeeze the toothpaste of the socially deconstructed subject back into the tube of ideology – surely a Sisyphean labour by the logic of Jameson's own base-superstructure analysis of the postmodern period. In confessing to its ideological motive, cognitive mapping announces its moment of resistance: resistance to the disempowering fragmentation of the self under late capital. Since there can be no politics without a subject (nor anything for that politics to envisage emancipating) and no praxis without a knowledge, then it would seem, for Jameson, that the subject of knowledge *is* the subject of politics. But if the fragmented subject of 'contemporary theory' is a mere epiphenomenon of the decentred *social* subject of consumer capitalism, then the project of reconstructing this subject at the level of critical discourse (i.e., as a discursive effect) would seem at best a self-contradictory undertaking, doomed always to fail in its aim of repairing within theory what is an 'objective' effect of socio-economic process.

There is certainly a pleasure of consumption for the reader of Jameson's own texts: the continual pleasure of discovering unexpected homologies, novel resemblances and differences, vertigos of self-reflexion – above all, the pleasure of always knowing that there will always be more to know. But that the desire for knowledge (and thus for the transcendent subjectivity of cognition) does not in or of itself give rise to the desire to act, was signalled by Marx in the hiatus which he marked with a semi-colon in his eleventh thesis on Feuerbach: 'The philosophers have only *interpreted* the world, in various ways; the point is to *change* it'. In the *Critique of Pure Reason* Kant distinguishes between 'theoretical cognition' as one through which we come to know '*what there is*' and 'practical cognition' as one through which we imagine '*what there should be*'. The deconstructive reading of Marx is to interpret his master-narrative of human progress toward emancipation as the expression of a desire, rather than of a knowledge. Yet as the Kantian definition of 'practical cognition' suggests, such a deconstruction might in itself serve as an emancipation into politics or practice of the otherwise self-divided subject of an always deferred, since always incomplete, knowledge. Like any self-reflexive art (Christo's *empaquetages*, say), the discourse of the oppositional wrapping-up of 'postmodernism' as a 'period' is always in varying degrees complicit with what it opposes. How this critical discourse is to be judged must depend on the kind of desire we allow it to generate for us: the desire to know, for example, or the desire to act. A deconstructive reading of Jameson's own totalizing theories of postmodernism might ask whether the implied subject of his cognitive discourse can afford to know itself as white, First World, probably male, middle-class and academic – without, that is, its transcendent knowledge being recognized as the 'imaginary' effect of particular institutional, social, economic and ideological determinants.

I began this paper by asking from where and in whose name can adversarial criticism of Jameson's and Eagleton's kind be conducted. Clearly, the oppositional consumer which their texts interpellate is no more a universal subject than the knowledge which they promise and withhold is universally desired. Jameson is the most self-reflexive of postmodernist theorists (and it is perhaps for this reason that his texts may generate more of a desire to know, less of a desire to act, than those of a critic such as Eagleton). But the question of what kind of representation or 'imaginary' knowledge would be politically most useful for a Third World factory worker, for example, as distinct from a First World academic is one which his texts never pose. The 'modernist' moment of oppositional postmodernist theory is that in which it mistakes the liberal academy as the collective subject of a universally useful knowledge. And on that, regretfully 'postmodernist' moment of my reflections, I must give up the pleasure of my own text.

NOTES

1. Terry Eagleton, 'Capitalism, Modernism and Postmodernism', *New Left Review*, 152 (1985), p.60.
2. See Fredric Jameson, 'Reification and Utopia in Mass Culture', *Social Text*, 1 (1979), p.131.
3. Guy Debord, *Society of the Spectacle* (Detroit: Black and Red, 1983), paragraph 15.
4. Jameson, op. cit., p.131.
5. Ibid., p.132.
6. Salvador Dali, *The Secret Life of Salvador Dali* (London: Vision Press, 1973), pp.310–11.
7. Fredric Jameson, 'Postmodernism, or the Cultural Logic of Late Capitalism', p.57. See 'Select Bibliography'.
8. Ibid., p.56.
9. Peter Bürger, *Theory of the Avant-Garde* (1984). See 'Select Bibliography'.
10. Jameson, 'Postmodernism, or the Cultural Logic of Late Capitalism', p.61. Cf. Ihab Hassan, 'The Culture of Post-modernism', *Theory, Culture and Society*, 2:3 (1985), pp.119–31; Hal Foster, '(Post)Modern Polemics', *New German Critique*, 33 (1984), pp.67–78; Norman N. Holland, 'Postmodern Psychoanalysis', in Ihab Hassan and Sally Hassan (eds), *Innovation/Renovation: New Perspectives on the Humanities* (Madison: University of Wisconsin Press, 1983), pp.291–309; and Eagleton, op. cit., p.71.
11. Cf. Fredric Jameson, *The Political Unconscious: Narrative as a Socially Symbolic Act* (Ithaca: Cornell University Press, 1981), p.28. In explanations of cultural process which employ what Althusser terms a theory of 'expressive causality', 'a sequence of historical events or texts and artifacts is rewritten in terms of some deeper, underlying, and more 'fundamental' narrative, of a hidden master narrative which is the allegorical key or figural content of the first sequence of empirical materials'.
12. Fredric Jameson, 'Postmodernism and Consumer Society', in Hal Foster (ed), *The Anti-Aesthetic: Essays on Postmodern Culture* (Port Townsend: Bay Press, 1983), p.115.
13. Eagleton, op. cit., p.71.

14. Cf. Terry Eagleton, 'The Revolt of the Reader', *New Literary History*, 13:3 (1982), pp.449–52.
15. See Roland Barthes, 'From Work to Text', in *Image-Music-Text* (New York: Hill and Wang, 1977), pp.160–1.
16. Ibid., p.162.
17. Ibid., pp.162–3.
18. Walter Benjamin, 'The Work of Art in the Age of Mechanical Reproduction', in Hannah Arendt (ed.), *Illuminations* (New York: Schocken Books, 1969), p.232.
19. Jameson, 'Postmodernism, or the Cultural Logic of Late Capitalism', p.63.
20. Stanley Fish, 'Interpreting the Variorum', in *Is There a Text in This Class? The Authority of Interpretive Communities* (Cambridge, Mass.: Harvard University Press, 1980), p.158.
21. Ibid., pp.303–55.
22. Tony Bennett, *Formalism and Marxism* (London: Methuen, 1979), Ch.8, and 'Text, Readers, Reading Formations', *Literature and History*, 9:2 (1983), pp.214–27. See also Bennett's contribution to 'The Text in Itself: A Symposium', *Southern Review*, 17:2 (1984), pp.118–24.
23. See Hans Robert Jauss, 'Literary History as a Challenge to Literary Theory', in Ralph Cohen (ed.), *New Directions in Literary History* (Baltimore: Johns Hopkins University Press, 1974), pp.11–41.
24. Jürgen Habermas, quoted in Peter Uwe Hohendahl, *The Institution of Criticism* (Ithaca: Cornell University Press, 1982), p.165.
25. Norman N. Holland, 'Unity Identity Text Self' (Abstract), *PMLA*, 90:5 (1975), p.809, and 'Re-Covering "The Purloined Letter": Reading as a Personal Transaction', in Susan R. Suleiman and Inge Crosman (eds), *The Reader in the Text: Essays on Audience and Interpretation* (Princeton: Princeton University Press, 1980), p.370.
26. 'Re-Covering "The Purloined Letter" ', p.370.
27. Robert Crosman, 'Do Readers Make Meaning?', in *The Reader in the Text*, p.162.
28. Holland, 'Unity Identity Text Self', p.814.
29. Ibid., pp.816, 818 and 809.
30. Ibid., p.818.
31. Ibid., p.816.
32. 'Re-Covering "The Purloined Letter" ', pp.365–7.
33. Roland Barthes, *The Pleasure of the Text* (London: Jonathan Cape, 1976), pp.11–12.
34. Holland, 'Postmodern Psychoanalysis', p.296.
35. Ibid., p.304.
36. Where realism places the individual subject at the centre of its fictional world, asserting the primacy of individual experience, modernism explores this subject's self-alienation and *anomie*. Where romanticism affirms subject autonomy, positing an un-socialized subjectivity, realism explores the socialization of the subject, the formation of the self by the other.
37. Terry Eagleton, *William Shakespeare* (Oxford: Basil Blackwell, 1986), pp.ix–x.

38. Jan Kott, *Shakespeare Our Contemporary* (London: Methuen, 1967); David Horowitz, *Shakespeare: An Existential View* (London: Social Science Paperbacks, 1967).
39. For a discussion of generic and historical definitions of literary postmodernism, see my 'Parody, Postmodernism and the Politics of Reading', *Critical Quarterly*, 27:4 (1985), pp.27–43.
40. 'Postmodernism, or The Cultural Logic of Late Capitalism', p.92.
41. Ibid., p.90.

CHAPTER 3

Marat/Sade, or the Birth of Postmodernism from the Spirit of the Avant-Garde

David Roberts

Peter Bürger's *Theorie der Avantgarde* (1974)[1] drew its critical energy from the failure of the May 1968 revolt in Paris and the collapse of the student movement in West Germany at the beginning of the 1970s. The year 1968 became the historical vantage point which sharpened Bürger's perception of the connexions between the avant-garde movements of the 1920s and the revolutionary impulses of the 1960s. The momentary fusion of surrealist slogans and political action in May 1968 pointed to the renewed actuality of the Surrealists' call to 'pratiquer la poésie' at the same time as the proclamation of the 'end of art' in West Germany articulated a deep dissatisfaction at the impotence of art to change the world. If the revolts of the late 1960s failed and the utopia of cultural revolution faded, the old question about the end and the ends of art remained. And this is the question posed by Bürger: what is the function of art in contemporary society, given that the avant-garde's project of cancelling the separation, the alienation of art from life has become doubly historically viewed through the prism of 1968? In his most recent book, *On the Critique of Idealistic Aesthetics*,[2] Bürger has retreated from the impasse of his position in *Theory of the Avant-Garde*. Just as for Adorno the moment of practising philosophy had passed, for Bürger the moment for practising poetry – the historical moment of the avant-garde in the 1920s – was behind us. If this left

Adorno with nothing but the hibernation of negative dialectics, it left Bürger in the situation of a suspended aesthetics. The end of art which was no end had revealed art as the prisoner of its impotent autonomy, safely neutralized within the 'institution of art', as Bürger termed it. Bürger's argument went as follows: the historical process of differentiation – the immanent logic of development – of autonomous art had run its course by the end of the nineteenth century. The subsequent reaction of the avant-garde movements, impelled not least by the impact of the World War and revolution, led not to the overthrow of autonomous art but to the laying bare of the 'institution of art' itself. This paradoxical result is reflected in the paradox of Bürger's position. On the one hand the avant-garde challenge created the possibility, indeed the inescapability, of a system-transcending criticism which invalidates the categories of the autonomous work of art, enshrined in idealistic aesthetics (the internalization of the institution 'art'). On the other hand, this very system-transcending criticism is incapable of proceeding beyond the theory of the historical avant-garde. The caesura of the avant-garde is pronounced the decisive historical event in the development of art in bourgeois society, but what Bürger presents as a consequence is purely negative. Post avant-garde art is characterized by a plurality of styles and tendencies in the face of which aesthetic theory can offer no valid aesthetic norms (122). In this sense art has entered, for Bürger, the stage of post-history with the laying bare of the institution. The legacy of the failure of the avant-garde is thus the imaginary museum of modernity, in which the free disposition over all the elements of tradition defines the playground of post avant-garde art. Accordingly, Bürger is led to the following resigned conclusion to his *Theory of the Avant-Garde*:

> Whether this condition of the availability of all traditions still permits an aesthetic theory at all, in the sense in which aesthetic theory existed from Kant to Adorno, is questionable, because a field must have a structure if it is to be the subject of scholarly or scientific understanding. Where the formal possibilities have become infinite, not only authentic creation but also its scholarly analysis become correspondingly difficult. Adorno's notion that late-capitalist society has become so irrational that it may well be that no theory can any longer plumb it applies perhaps with even greater force to post avant-gardiste art. (94)

The impasse of Bürger's theory can be stated most succinctly in his own words: 'The meaning of the break in the history of art that the historical avant-garde movements provoked does not consist in the destruction of art as an institution, but in the destruction of the possibility of positing aesthetic norms as valid ones' (87). The alternative open to theory, which Bürger raises but does not exemplify, is that of functional analysis:

> the normative examination is replaced by a functional analysis, the object of whose investigation would be the social effect (function) of a work, which is the result of the coming together of stimuli inside the work and a sociologically definable public within an already existing institutional frame. (87)

The purpose of such empirical analyses, which could be multiplied indefinitely, is far from evident. It is not even clear that functional analysis is the necessary consequence of the abandonment of normative aesthetics, if its purpose is simply to accumulate historical specifications of the social effects of art within existing institutional frames, since these historically given frames already determine in Bürger's view the production and reception of works of art. The pre-emptive meta-norm of the institution replaces aesthetic norms. Functional analysis does not appear to be the way out of the impasse, which Bürger now defines in *On the Critique of Idealistic Aesthetics* as the abstract alternative of either reviving the avant-garde project of reuniting art and human practice or confirming the ruling institution of art. The critical task as he now sees it is to find a way between these abstract alternatives by seeking out the potentials of contemporary art. In *The Theory of the Avant-Garde* Bürger had already spoken of the need for concrete investigation through the analysis of individual works. In *The Critique of Idealistic Aesthetics* he proposes a specific work, Peter Weiss's novel *Die Ästhetik des Widerstands* ('The Aesthetics of Resistance'), but without the analysis required to substantiate his claim that it offers a way out of the impasse. The claim is this: Weiss's novel indicates the possibility (if only in fictional form) of a non-auratic reception or use of works of art through its presentation of a group of anti-fascist proletarian youths, whose appropriation of works of the past is significant for their social practice. The novel goes beyond the false alternatives outlined above, because it is neither completely removed from everyday life nor completely absorbed by it. By assimilating avant-garde intentions in altered form *Die Ästhetik des Widerstands* can serve as both a sensuous and conceptual medium of experience and interpretation of the world.

As we can see, Bürger has modified his original radically negative diagnosis. On the one hand he seeks a way forward by a critical reconsideration of idealistic aesthetics and their categories of autonomy (the genius, the auratic concept of the work of art and of contemplative reception), on the other he turns tentatively to contemporary art for alternatives to the abstract alternative opened up by *The Theory of the Avant-Garde*.

The appeal to *Die Ästhetik des Widerstands* cannot of course take the place of either theory or analysis. It remains a pointer in the direction of a concrete theory of post avant-garde art, or, as I would prefer to call it, postmodernist art. (The reason I prefer to speak of postmodernism is not simply that this spectre haunts contemporary consciousness, as Hans Robert Jauss has observed,[3] but that Bürger's theory is the product of a post-1968 horizon of perception, and shares with 'postmodernism' the sense of the historicity of modernism.[4] That is to say, if the beginnings of modernism can be identified – and here it is indifferent whether it be 1848, the 1880s or the years prior to the First World War – the end of modernism can only be dated from the consciousness of its end. In this sense postmodernism defines itself negatively as the yet indeterminate consciousness of a paradigm change. It is a consciousness in search of a content, for which Bürger's search for a post avant-garde position is symptomatic.) What is significant for Bürger – or for Jürgen Habermas[5] – in Weiss's novel is the thematization of a life-altering reception of art works. But as this is already the explicit theme of *Don Quixote* this can hardly be a sufficient condition for defining the possibilities of post-avant-garde art, for, if the avant-garde inaugurates the stage of the self-criticism of art through its exposure of the 'institution of art', then the question must be (given that art is still with us since the avant-garde): in what way can or does the self-criticism of art, as the altered consciousness of the institution, enter into the contemporary work of art? This is the question which is not posed by Bürger and which cannot be answered by *Die Ästhetik des Widerstands*, or only indirectly by means of a detour.

Peter Weiss's novel presents, Bürger argues, the possibility of a non-auratic reception of works of art – but only in fictional form. Bürger's proviso precisely misses the point. That this or any novel can only explore the possibilities of reception in fictional form is self-evident and needs no apology. Rather the apology should be turned around to focus on the fact that Weiss's novel, like so many novels since Cervantes, discusses the reception of works of art.

Indeed we owe the birth of the novel to the spirit of reception. Don Quixote (like his author) is first of all a highly impressionable reader of romances before he can become the quintessential figure of the novel, the 'problematic individual' (Lukács) seeking to overcome the gulf between the soul and the world, between art and life. At this point we may recall Bürger's definition of the 'institution of art' as the art-producing and distributing apparatus and the given ruling conceptions of art which determine reception (22). Despite the sociological gesture inherent in the term 'institution' Bürger's interest is confined in practice to the concepts or norms, e.g. the doctrine of autonomy, which govern reception. Cervantes and his successors – Fielding, Sterne, Wieland – owe their importance for the history of the novel to the fact that their reflexions on the conditions of production and reception are integral to the constitution of this new genre. But already 2,000 years earlier Aristophanes, by placing Euripides on stage, had given not only a practical criticism of a fellow artist but a criticism of the institution of the theatre. Similarly, from Shakespeare to Tom Stoppard the play within the play has remained a favourite device for the exposure of the conventions, the 'fictionality' of the stage action. What all such critical and self-critical reflexions on the status (production and reception) of the literary work of art have in common is not only the awareness of the artifice of art, i.e. its non-identity with life, but more significantly, for the purposes of our argument, the awareness contained therein of the institution of 'art'. The point here is that literature as an institution, understood not as individual works but as the norms governing their production and reception, has always possessed its own self-criticism in the form of parodistic self-reflexion. The function of parody may be defined as the critique of the representation of life in literature and as such as the immanent self-consciousness of literature as institution, for parody must necessarily foreground and estrange both the forms of production and the norms of reception. It is not surprising that idealist aesthetics, which privileges the autonomy of the work of art, has remained indifferent or blind to the practice of parody as the critique of 'authenticity' and aura. What is surprising is that Bürger's *Theory of the Avant-Garde* should be so blind to the parodistic impulse – the assault on the autonomous work and the provocation of the norms of reception – in Dada and Surrealism. Parody as the self-criticism of the institution 'art' is identical, however, neither with Bürger's system-immanent criticism nor with the self-criticism realized by the avant-garde:

Examples of system-immanent criticism would be the criticism the theoreticians of French classicism directed against the Baroque drama, or Lessing's of the German imitations of classical French tragedy. Criticism functions here within an institution, the theatre. . . . There is another kind of criticism and that is the self-criticism of art: it addresses itself to art as an institution and must be distinguished from the former type. (21)

As opposed to the exclusive alternatives set up by Bürger – the conforming or negating of the institution – the estrangement of the work of art undertaken by parody is dialectical, because it involves the *simultaneous* negation and affirmation of the specific status of art. This applies as much to a 'conventional' *Virgile travesti* of the seventeenth century as to the provocations of Dada or Duchamp's celebrated *Urinoir*, to which Bürger refers (52). In this sense Dada and Surrealism do not inaugurate the 'imaginary museum' of post avant-garde art, they signal rather the moment when the creative possibilities of parody are released in the energy of destruction, which sets free all the elements of tradition. The avant-garde thus becomes the extreme against which the parodistic symbiosis of 'authenticity' and 'inauthenticity' in modernism, in which the stylistic consciousness of non-identity plays out its Endgame, may be measured.

Bürger's resigned conclusion to his *Theory of the Avant-Garde* stems from the loss of aesthetic norms, that is, the loss of the criteria for determining the paradigmatic work of art – the essential theoretical function of Lukács's and Adorno's aesthetics. The dialectic of authenticity and inauthenticity, of the autonomous work of art and its parodistic *Aufhebung*, offers, I suggest, an alternative to Bürger's abstract alternative of the affirmation or negation of the 'institution of art', in that parody *practises* the simultaneous negation and affirmation of the institution, a practice whose significance for a theory of modernism (Picasso, Stravinsky, Joyce, Brecht, Beckett, etc.)[6] finds an additional critical focus through Bürger's theory of the avant-garde. Nevertheless, this only partially answers the question as to how the self-criticism Bürger sees effected by the avant-garde challenge to the institution can be taken into the post avant-garde work of art. In proposing *Die Ästhetik des Widerstands* as one answer Bürger is implicitly granting Weiss's novel paradigmatic status, without sufficiently acknowledging the retrospective quality of this work, a testament and process of '*Er-innerung*', which appears to me more adequately accounted for by the aesthetic theories of Lukács and Herbert Marcuse than by the caesura of the avant-garde. This is not an objection to Peter Weiss's novel but to its relevance for the problem posed by *The Theory of the Avant-Garde*, which I believe can be addressed concretely in terms of Bürger's own premises. Bürger is on the right track when he turns to Peter Weiss, whose early work stands in a direct line of descent from Surrealism, but it is not Weiss's novel which provides a way out of the impasse, but his play *Marat/Sade*. If Beckett's *Endgame* marks the limits of Adorno's aesthetic of modernism, then *Marat/Sade* represents in relation to Bürger's theory of the avant-garde the paradigmatic work of the post avant-garde (which can be assimilated to neither Adorno's nor Lukács's aesthetics), in that it poses the central question of the function of art in bourgeois society since the French Revolution and the possibility of the self-transcendence of art. It must be added, however, that the postmodernist dimensions of *Marat/Sade* have become apparent only in the light of a post-1968 consciousness. In the context of the 1960s the play was received as the revolutionary renewal of the avant-garde of the 1920s, and as an important contribution to the repoliticization of the public sphere in West Germany. The anarchic 'revolutionary' impact of *Marat/Sade* prior to the student revolt calls now for another reading, for we can now see that it was the pre-1968 answer to questions posed only in the wake of 1968. The play has now acquired a different kind of actuality, which is revealed in its contradictory *fusion* and *suspension* of the avant-garde impulse to abolish the gulf between art and life – a suspension (*Aufhebung*) which is paradigmatic for the postmodernist situation in that the question of the ends and the end of art has found an as yet unsurpassed aesthetic objectification.

II

Above I suggested that the practice of parodistic self-reflexion escapes Bürger's exclusive alternatives of system-immanent or system-transcendent criticism, which reproduce what he now sees as the abstract alternative of affirmation or negation of the institution of art. The theatre as institution has not simply produced system-immanent aesthetic and ideological debates (e.g., Lessing or Brecht), but also since Aristophanes a practical self-reflexion, whose object is the critical examination of the representation of life in the drama and whose effect is the simultaneous exposure and acknowledgement of the institutional parameters of the theatre.

Marat/Sade is no exception. The remarkably complex representation of the interferences and interactions between art and life makes this play, in Bürger's terms, a functional analysis, an analysis, that is, of the social effect 'which is the result of the coming together of stimuli inside the work and a sociologically definable public within an already existing frame' (87). The stimuli *inside* the work and the public *within* an institutional frame are foregrounded in a particularly significant fashion in *Marat/Sade*, for this is a play in which institutional containment is demonstrated on a double level: not only the theatrical institution itself – e.g., 'art' (the play within the play) as aesthetic illusion – but also the social institution of the asylum. Behind the audiences within *Marat/Sade*, the invited audience of the play written and directed by Sade and performed by inmates of the asylum who are also its primary audience, are the audiences of Peter Weiss's play, who in turn form within an already existing institutional frame the spectators of this theatre within the theatre. A play which is at the same time a functional (self-)analysis necessarily operates on the level of the 'institution of art': stimuli and public come together for each of the three audiences as three versions of the containment of social effects within the institution.

Common to all self-reflexions of the theatre since Aristophanes is the unmasking of the production of illusion to reveal the (institutional) nexus between production and reception. On one level *Marat/Sade* repeatedly destroys illusion by insisting on the non-identity of actor and role in Sade's play. The 'actors', that is the asylum inmates, constantly fall out of their roles, forget their lines, require prompting, physical support or coercion in order to produce the dramatic illusion for the benefit of the invited audience. But all these devices of estrangement (*Verfremdung*), which are multiplied by Sade's own sadistic dramaturgy of *interruptus* and punctuated by the spoken interventions of the master of ceremonies and the sung commentaries of the 'people's' chorus masquerading as *commedia dell' arte*, are compounded by the uncertainty as to what is within the 'play' – are for instance Roux's outbursts part of Sade's script or an effect of it? The institutional containment of Sade's play as aesthetic illusion, as a closed representation – i.e. as the re-presentation of Marat's persecution and assassination – is impossible, precisely because we are not allowed to forget that it is presented within a closed institution. The constantly reinforced estrangement of the production within the setting of the asylum serves to destroy one level of illusion by creating a second level of illusion: not Sade's play *qua* play but the actuality of its location and *performance*. On this level Roux, Coulmier and Sade are *identical* with their roles outside the 'play', whereas the paranoic patient who plays Marat or the erotomaniac who plays Duperret are not. Location and performance take on a presence, a reality of illusion which uncovers the patient behind the role but not the actor behind the patient. All the devices of estrangement thereby become 'stimuli' which transfer our attention from production to reception. By making the performance itself the reality of the illusion *Marat/Sade* actualizes the institution of the theatre as an act of representation and reception, in which the three unities of the performance, place, time and act, are those of the theatre itself and its audience. The dialectic of art and life on stage – as a process of functional analysis – is not confined, however, to the location of the asylum, with its repeated interventions and eruptions of the 'real', but involves of course a third level of reception, the audience of each performance of *Marat/Sade*, for whom the location is not the asylum but the theatre. But this third level of reception only acquires its full significance by virtue of the second level of reception, which juxtaposes the two institutions of asylum and theatre (a juxtaposition in which the metaphors of the world as a stage or a madhouse regain their social reference). The refraction of the institution of the theatre through the second level of the closed institution of the asylum brings the institution of 'art' into focus in a way which goes beyond the traditional self-criticism of the theatre, whether in its general form of the play within the play or in the specifically 'revolutionary' form of the tension of play and reality to be found in dramas of the revolution, a tradition which is of course relevant to *Marat/Sade*.[7] That is, *Marat/Sade* as a functional analysis provides not only the unity of demonstration and objectification, particular to the critical self-analysis of art and its effects, but at the same time the objectification of the *social* institution itself which contains art and its effects. The decisive new dimension introduced by Weiss is that the play within the play has become a play within an institution of coercion. Sade's play is thus only a 'play' of the Revolution because of its confinement within the institution, but by this very token a 'play' which threatens to explode its containment. Art is presented here literally as a product of repression: Sade's play is not only a product of imprisonment (as of course historically Sade's work was born of his imprisonment) but is also transformed by its location into an *enforced* representation. Just as his play remains precariously poised between repression (censorship) and revolt, so too its author becomes the director of an experiment which necessarily provokes a contradictory reception. The ensuing interplay between stimuli and public (the inmates, the asylum authorities and their invited guests) necessarily provokes the confrontation of art and life, revolt and repression. The dynamic of this confrontation *enacts* a functional analysis, in which on the one hand art within the institution is revealed as the enforced non-identity of art and life, i.e. a representation, whose function is to transmute the reality of the *performance* into the closed aesthetic autonomy of the *play*, while on the other hand the inescapable estrangement of the play as aesthetic illusion draws attention to the reality of the performance, thereby unmasking the (repressive) non-identity of art and life as the *conditio sine qua non* of reception. This provokes and excites in turn in the inmates (the primary audience) the desire for the violent realization of the identity of art and life through the breakout from the institution. The play of the Revolution within the institution thus lives, through its dual realization as play (representation, repetition) and performance (difference), from the explosive tension of 'aesthetic' sublimation and 'revolutionary' desublimation.

Against this interference of art and life the impulse to 'pratiquer la poésie' takes on all the urgency of the drive to 'pratiquer la révolution'. The *form* this interference is given derives from the model Weiss discerns in Sade's writings: 'analytical and philosophical dialogues set against a scenery of bodily excesses'. The relation between philosophical and political debates and their violent stage commentaries, between reason and the drives, defines the thematic of *Marat/Sade* and at the same time the contradictions of reception explored by Peter Weiss. The interaction between 'philosophical dialogues' and 'bodily excesses' means that what is at issue is the relation between words and their effects, above and beyond the debate between Marat and Sade. In the part of Marat Sade explores his own response to the Revolution, as the idea and reality of liberation, with the advantage of fifteen years' historical hindsight. Marat is the object of the Marquis's demonstration and the projection of his self-analysis. This is not a real debate but the dramatic presentation of two possibilities of the same consciousness. We must therefore look to what Sade and Marat have in common rather than to their obvious differences. Both are outsiders, persecuted and driven into isolation for their radicalism in analysing man and society. Cut off from the world, they pursue with ruthless logic the consequences of their thought. If Europe's history since the French Revolution provides the larger backdrop to their ideas and their consequences, it is the stage action itself which provides the commentary on their words. That is to say, the action onstage is the projection and realization of the fantasies of Sade ('There is nothing I could not do and everything fills me with horror' (40))[8] and of the revolution within Marat's head ('There is a rioting mob inside me' (24)). Inner and outer reality form the one phantasmagoria, in which the political and psychological spheres meet in terms of the one complex: the relationship and interference between ideas and action, theory and practice, mind and the body. Both Sade and Marat are rationalists and materialists who seek to free man from his determination by nature, human and social. Marat's most important work was the treatise of 1773, *De l'homme ou des principes et des lois de l'influence de l'âme sur le corps et du corps sur l'âme*. In the play Roux refers to this work when he says of Marat:

> You wondered how forces can be controlled
> So you studied electricity
> You wanted to know what man is for
> So you asked yourself What is this soul
> This dump for hollow ideals and mangled morals
> You decided that the soul is in the brain
> and that it can learn to think
> For to you the soul is a practical thing
> a tool for ruling and mastering life.. . . . (77)

The Marquis too sets out to conquer nature by bringing the instinctual drives to consciousness and by uncovering the processes of repression which turn the revolutionary ideal into bloody reality (Marat, Corday, the revolutionary crowd). He loses control of his experiment to this end – his play produced for the asylum inmates – and stands the mocking spectator of the anarchy he has released and its brutal suppression. The Four Singers say the same of Marat:

> Poor old Marat you lie prostrate
> While others are gambling with France's fate
> Your words have turned into a flood
> Which covers all France with her people's blood.. . . . (91)

Why is this so? Why can neither control the forces they release? Is it because man's nature is such in this mad world, because 'a man is a mad animal'? If this is the case it applies to Sade and Marat as well. They who want to bring enlightenment bow to the blind force of nature. They who want to enlighten, to liberate, also want to destroy. The Marquis's experiment in psychotherapy and Marat's belief in the powers of reason defeat themselves. The two succeed, consciously and unconsciously, through their knowledge and their 'art' (as excitement and as rhetoric), in setting free the irrational and destructive in man. These two versions of the same contradiction in each figure – between ideas and reality, words and their effects – reveal the identity of the extremes, but with the one vital difference that Sade understands Marat but Marat does not understand himself. Sade analyses his figures; Peter Weiss analyses the audience.

The 'dialectic of the enlightenment' inherent in this dialectic of the rational and the irrational manifests itself in the contradictions of reception. Weiss sets out to influence the audience simultaneously in two diametrically opposed ways – through the spoken word and through the stage action. *Marat/Sade* is both analytic, epic theatre, which continues Brecht's project of enlightenment, and a play of sensation and shock, which continues Artaud's 'theatre of cruelty' and ends in chaos and uproar. The connection between Weiss and Artaud is much older than Weiss's interest in Brecht.[9] The influence of Strindberg, whom he has translated, his acknowledgement of the importance of Artaud's theatre manifestos, his admiration for and indebtedness to the surrealist cinema, especially the work of Buñuel, confirm that Weiss was originally drawn to a fantasy world of violence and dream, as his early play *Die Versicherung* ('The Insurance'), written in 1952 but only published in 1967, makes clear. *Die Versicherung* is a spectacle of sex and sadism, absurd, obscene, anarchic (its refrain is 'catastrophes, revolutions'), presented as a series of film-like sequences. The first scene, for instance, very soon turns into an orgy, the second shows an operation during which all present undress, and so on to the final catastrophe.

The confrontation of Brecht and Artaud is undoubtedly central to the disturbing power and fascination of *Marat/Sade* and has been widely acknowledged by critics. What has not been recognized, however, is that Weiss is confronting here the two most radical theatrical forms of the avant-garde project of cancelling the split between art and life. The rationalist theatre of didactic estrangement and the theatre of madness, crime and revolt are each intended as practical critiques of the autonomous, closed representation and of the theatre as institution, for each seeks to break out of the institutional containment of art by crossing the boundaries separating representation and reality, stage and audience. But of course in sharply opposed ways, for their conceptions of the ends of art derive from mutually exclusive anthropological premises. Thus, for instance, the function of the play within the play in Brecht's *Caucasian Chalk Circle* is to demonstrate rational liberation from 'natural' prejudice, just as the practically desirable social effects are displayed in the reception by the play's 'audience', the decision of the peasant collective to depart from tradition. Artaud chooses the other path of liberation: not cool distance but sensuous immediacy. The logical and rational intentions of discourse are to be subordinated to the living presence of the body. This concept of the theatre as incorporation and not representation (Derrida)[10] finds its most telling moment in *Marat/Sade* in Sade's presentation of Charlotte Corday to Marat. Behind the role, behind the sleep-walking patient, behind the actor is the other reality of the *body*. This other reality is the goal of Artaud's theatre, life itself as the unrepresented before and beyond discourse: the Dionysian intoxication behind all Apollonian individuation (the latter being what Derrida calls the humanist representations of man in the metaphysics of classical theatre).[11]

The two genealogies of the avant-garde – Marx and Freud, Brecht and Artaud – through which we read the Marat and Sade of Weiss's play, are confronted as the two versions of the interference of art and life which subvert the closed ideology of classical representation. But in turn we can only read Brecht and Artaud through the dialectic of revolutionary liberation incorporated in Marat and Sade. The avant-garde project can only unfold its full significance, intensity and complexity through the historical perspective of Weiss's play. Art as liberation and the liberation of art: this is the 'avant-garde' question which has been on the agenda of bourgeois society since the French Revolution. Just as Sade's and Marat's revolutionary challenges lay bare the repressive institutions of society, so parallel to this the avant-garde challenge lays bare the repressive institution of art by setting the avant-garde 'revolution in the theatre' against the play of the Revolution. That is, *Marat/Sade* replays an unfinished history: it is this tension of historical repetition and living difference which enables Peter Weiss to pose the question of the ends and the end of art in a dialectical confrontation which goes beyond the abstract alternatives of Bürger's impasse.

Through the foregrounding of performance and location, Weiss can present Sade's play as an act between repetition and difference: the *historical* predetermination of the script calls forth the dimension of the aleatory.[12] This field of interferences becomes the testing ground of the radical and radically opposed projects of the avant-garde. The result is *Aufhebung* in the threefold form of negation, preservation and suspension:

Negation: Art cannot escape the containment of the institution, neither the 'rational' agitation of Marat nor the 'irrational' incitement of Sade leads to liberation. Brechtian 'philosophical dialogue', with its clash of thesis and antithesis, and the 'bodily excess' of Artaud cancel each other. The voice of reason – Roux's 'When will you learn to see/When will you ever understand' – is engulfed by the blind hysteria of the marching and chanting inmates. Liberation collapses into a prison revolt. The Revolution and its reenactment degenerate into an orgy of unfreedom, a sadistic compulsion to repetition ('revolution, copulation') which reverses the Revolution into re-volution, as the inmates march in circles in ever greater frenzy, while Sade triumphs at the 'success' of his aesthetic experiment.

Preservation: The very failure of liberation from the institution preserves art as the expression of needs (Freud) and the need to change the world (Marx). Just as the failure of the Marxian *Aufhebung* of philosophy in praxis preserves the need for radical philosophy, so the failure of the avant-garde preserves the need for radical art. In this sense the revolutionary potential of Brecht and Artaud is preserved within the institution in *Marat/Sade*. The art of liberation and the liberation of art remain the project and the passion of an unfinished history, opened by the French Revolution.

Suspension: The simultaneous negation and affirmation of the project of the avant-garde opens up a new dialectic between art and its institutionalization, which is integral to the *Aufhebung* of the avant-garde in *Marat/Sade*. It is on this level – the self-reflection of the 'institution of art' through the medium of the repressive institution of the asylum – that the status and function of art in bourgeois society can be made *explicit*. This demonstration of the institutional containment of art not only translates Bürger's self-criticism of art into a concrete functional analysis, it transforms the alternatives of Bürger into the dialectic of the 'institution of art' itself. More exactly, Bürger's alternatives, the containment of art within the institution and the break out from the institution, are the ground from which the post-avant-garde (postmodernist) dialectic of *Marat/Sade* arises.

The *manifest* dialectic of art and the institution (whose internalized form is 'art', autonomy, the non-identity of art and life) raises the question of the ends of art (its function) to the level of the question of the end of art. The possibility of the cessation of Sade's play poses in concrete form the question of the end of art – and so *Marat/Sade* plays through the alternative endings of the 'play'. The end of 'art' (the play within the institution) can be (1) revolution as the liberation from external *and* internal imprisonment; (2) anarchy and desublimation – the return of the repressed, as the liberation from all external and internal norms, not least the repressive norms which institutionally define and enclose madness, in an orgy of destruction; (3) the collapse of liberation into the reinforcement of the institution (Napoleon's order as the outcome of the Revolution). All these endings are 'contained' in *Marat/Sade* as an historical reality – (2) and (3) – or as unfinished history, that is, as utopian possibility – (1). But of course the *true end* of art can only be utopia, that alone would be the real end of the play, the real breakout of history, the cessation of the repetitions of revolt and repression. It is for this reason that the utopian end of art can only be expressed in art – and that means within the institution. Between and beyond the alternatives of the destruction of the institution (the desublimation of art) and its reinforcement (the re-enforced 'autonomy' of art) is the dialectic held in suspense by Peter Weiss. *Marat/Sade* as 'work' hovers therefore on the edge of self-destruction. The avant-garde's attempt to cross the boundary between the institution and life is held in suspension through the contradictory tension of representation and its deconstruction, with its dramatization of simultaneous estrangement and shock. This suspension shows art as definable only in relation to the institution. It is both the product and the negation of the institution, just as the institution defines the necessity and the impossibility of the self-transcendence (*Aufhebung*) of art. If, as I have suggested, parody serves as the *immanent* self-criticism of art – the simultaneous negation and affirmation of the aesthetic sphere in relation to life – then the level of consciousness of the *explicit* self-criticism of art is attained in *Marat/Sade* by means of the social institution (the asylum) as the 'dramatic' mediation which objectifies the contradictory status of art.

By means of this mutual interference of Brecht and Artaud, *Marat/Sade* is able both to actualize and historicize the avant-garde's programme. Just as the avant-garde challenge only gains its full significance through its revolutionary pre-history, so this historical framework reveals at the same time the parameters of art in bourgeois society. This historicization has a double consequence: firstly, the self-reflection of the 'institution of art' (made explicit as the dialectic of art and the institution) permits, as we have seen, the functional analysis of the possibilities of art in bourgeois society; secondly, this analysis of art within the institution provides in turn the setting and testing ground for the replaying of the avant-garde project of the *Aufhebung* of art. This replaying is simultaneously actualization and historicization, i.e. a suspension between representation and cessation, repetition and difference.

If we consider the possibilities of art within the institution, *Marat/Sade* presents us with a *Gesamtkunstwerk* of words, mime and music, a phantasmagoria of tableaux and happenings, philosophical discourse and political rhetoric, improvisations and interventions, commentary and pantomime. It is oratorio, passion play, *commedia dell'arte*. It is psychodrama and 'scientific' experiment, sadistic incitement and excitement – a complex totality, actualized through the setting and the dynamics of performance, which stands, we must recall, under the sign of the Enlightenment. As Coulmier informs us in his welcoming address:

> To one of our residents a vote
> of thanks is due Monsieur de Sade who wrote
> and has produced this play for your delectation
> and for our patients' rehabilitation.. . . .[13]

The Director's 'enlightened' view of the function of art takes the form of an experiment in aesthetic education. Schiller's programme, designed to open the path to freedom between the Scylla of despotism and the Charybdis of anarchy (the antinomy of the Revolution), is entrusted to the less than disinterested intentions of Sade. His play of aesthetic therapy, which is at the same time the self-interrogation of the revolutionary, is a psychotherapy, which unchains the impulses it is supposed prophylactically to discharge. The programme of aesthetic education and the cynical manipulations of 'enlightened' reason (Coulmier) are mutually exposed by the experiment which runs out of control, uncovering in the process through its effects the interests bound up in the work of art. This, then, is the experimental setting and testing ground for the avant-garde challenge, *rationalized* in the theatre of estrangement and *embodied* in the theatre of cruelty.

Brecht and Artaud, as we have seen, both constitute a revolutionary critique and practice directed against the classical theatre of representation. *Marat/Sade* 'suspends' their critique not only by revealing the antagonistic one-sidedness of each but by intensifying it to the point that their method becomes its own critique. Thus Artaud's attack on the *logic* of representation (that it is division, the separation of mind and force, the exclusion of the spectators and the actors from the creative act) serves as Brecht's contrary starting point. His techniques of estrangement set out to foreground and make transparent this logic of representation in order to liberate the spectator and actor from identification. The epic theatre is precisely *not* an act of presence but the unmasking of representation as re-presentation in order to transform it into the experimental specification of the laws of social behaviour, subject to the scrutiny of 'scientific' investigation. This one-sided rational division by means of estrangement is estranged in its turn, however, by the presence of its suppressed other, the difference of the unpresentable. This estrangement is both the objectification of Brecht's method and its critique, for the process of objectification demonstrated in *Marat/Sade* – the patient behind the actor behind the role – opens up a transparency which reverses into its opposite: the opaqueness of the body and its drives. But by the same token Artaud's project – the assertion of living presence against representation, where representation is to be understood in all its institutional and ideological dimensions as absent authority and power – is realizable only by virtue of *its* other. That is to say, *difference* can only be actualized as a process of interference. Pure difference is impossible. Here too, *Marat/Sade* is the simultaneous objectification and critique of Artaud's dream of difference. Life, the aleatory and unpresentable, is glimpsed as the threatening other of representation. Thus paradoxically and necessarily, *Marat/Sade* becomes the only possible *incorporation* of Artaud's theatre of cruelty at the same time as it remains the critical objectification of Brecht's *rationalism*. It is this confrontation of Brecht and Artaud which defines the paradigmatic status of Peter Weiss's play, for this confrontation is a true *Aufhebung* – negation, intensification and objectification – of the avant-garde's critique of representation and its two opposed poles of overcoming the separation of art and life.

III

The question which follows is what does *Marat/Sade* 'represent'? The answer, I suggest, is the 'institution of art', for the objectification of the avant-garde's critique of representation is accomplished by laying bare the institutional frame of representation. It is from this point, the self-criticism of art, that we can briefly reconsider (following Bürger's trajectory) the categories of idealistic aesthetics – organic work, subject, illusion (*Schein*), reception – through the prism of deconstructed representation. Since *Marat/Sade* constitutes a functional analysis, reception becomes a central category, and, as we have seen, it is split into the sharpest contradictions through the juxtaposition of the immediacy and presence of the performance and the distance of historical mediations. The ideal spectator is called upon to be both Dionysius and Socrates. This tension is not resolved. Peter Weiss's play permits neither resolution nor integration, for his subject matter is unfinished history and this history has no subject. The identity and autonomy of the work and of the subject are decomposed into the tensions of conflicting levels. The utopia of liberation is confronted by its other, the pathology of bourgeois society since the French Revolution. The locus of this pathology is the lunatic asylum and its topology repeats the Freudian drama of the super ego (Napoleon, Coulmier, the law, the censor, the institution) and the id (the patients), between which the alter egos Sade and Marat conduct their altercation. Their scene of reason and rationalization is the narrow sphere of discourse menaced from below by the obscene, in its double sense of the repressed and the unrepresentable, and from above, by the interventions of the censor, who is not God presiding over this passion play, but the representative of the state as inheritor and liquidator of the Revolution. Instead of the teleological integration of the organic work of art we have vertical conflict (the simultaneity and interference of the conflicting levels). This vertical structure of the institution (Freud's topology) relates representation not only to the institution but also to its other – excluded and incarcerated madness. That is, the unveiling of the institution behind representation calls forth at the same time the other of representation. This is the very logic of the avant-garde's project of 'practising poetry', whose complementary and split halves are the Brechtian unmasking of the institution and Artaud's dream of the pure difference of life and 'madness'. *Marat/Sade* yokes the antagonistic halves together in an act of *Aufhebung*, which is at the same time the subversion and decomposition of the categories of aesthetic autonomy into their conflicting elements; the traditional idealistic categories are thus polarized within the field of forces set up between the poles of institutionalized representation and its other. The unity of the autonomous work is dissolved into the interferences and contradictions of play and performance, representation and difference, determination and chance. The identity of the subject is split into the conflicting classes of the social subject, which are confronted at every level – state institution, revolutionary reason (Sade, Marat, Roux) the people's chorus, the agitation of the inmates – by their other. Illusion (*Schein*) presents itself as its own negation in the form of the play within the play. Reception is split into the effects of simultaneous attraction and repulsion, immediacy and estrangement, rational and irrational responses. Similarly, the historical mediations of the time levels of the play are constantly broken through by the actualizations of the performance. In *Marat/Sade* all the traditional aesthetic categories stand under the contradictory sign of the institution and its other as the post-avant-garde (postmodernist) paradigm of the situation and status of art.

This polarization of the categories defines the situation of art which can choose neither institutional 'autonomy' nor its own destruction, but lives in their contradiction, a contradiction which suspends the project of the avant-garde in the 'total' contradiction of actualization and historicization.

The vertical axis of time is of the greatest importance for this 'totalization', for the interference of the time levels presents us with the paradox of an unfinished history: that *Marat/Sade* is both the future of the past and the past of the future. The dialectic of revolution and repression, liberation and pathology is played through *once again*, for the 'subject' of the play is unfinished history. And it is at this point that we can define what constitutes the post-modernism of *Marat/Sade*. In so far as it is a revolutionary play, not only a debate on but a continuation of the Revolution, it is part of the project of modernity. This was the face of the play which was turned to us in the 1960s, this was the project that Peter Weiss himself espoused. *Marat/Sade* is postmodern, however – and this is the post-1968 face of the play – in that it imprisons the Revolution within the institution, in that the confrontation of the theatre of reason and the theatre of the body can find no issue. And above all, it is postmodern in that the unfreedom of an unfinished history is the compulsion to repetition which compels the return to the origins, the replay of the Revolution *as a passion play*. As the unfinished history, which is behind us and which repeats itself and yet is always actual, always threatening the other, living from the possibility of cessation, it is the complement and opposite of the absurdity of the endless last act of Beckett's *Endgame*. *Endgame* is the endgame of modernism and the terminal focus of Adorno's aesthetics, *Marat/Sade* is the new stage of postmodernism: the paradoxical presence of the past, the unfinished history contained within the institution, which poses once again the question of the ends and the end of art in a rich and explosive act of self-criticism.

If the 'institution of art' marks a new level of historical reflection, which is given concrete form in *Marat/Sade*, Weiss's play makes it clear that the caesura of the avant-garde must be seen within the context of bourgeois art since the French Revolution. If for Bürger the situation of post-avant-garde art is defined by the end of normative aesthetics from Kant to Adorno, this end also remains that of an unfinished history, which now is to be reviewed under the sign of the institution, that is, from the perspective of the self-criticism of art. This self-criticism involves the silenced other of idealistic aesthetics: historically it has taken the form of parody as the critique of identity and representation. By foregrounding the non-identity of art and life, parody is the critical practice of difference, the 'differential' of art and life, which allows the possibility of the full differentiation of the categories of idealistic aesthetics which would uncover their repressive unity. The dialectic of representation and its other in *Marat/Sade* offers a concrete model for this contradictory 'differentiation'. The failure of the avant-garde to cancel the gap between art and life points not only to the significance of the 'institution' but also to the need for revision of the synthetic categories of traditional aesthetics in the search for the paradigmatic work of postmodernist consciousness.

NOTES

1. See the 'Select Bibliography'. Numbers in brackets in the body of this essay refer to page numbers in the Manchester University Press edition of *Theory of the Avant-Garde* (1984).
2. Peter Bürger, *Zur Kritik der idealistischen Ästhetik* (Frankfurt/Main: Suhrkamp, 1983).
3. Hans Robert Jauss, 'Der literarische Prozeß des Modernismus von Rousseau bis Adorno', in Ludwig van Friedeberg and Jürgen Habermas (eds), *Adorno-Konferenz 1983* (Frankfurt/Main: Suhrkamp, 1983), pp.95–132.
4. See Peter Bürger, 'Das Altern der Moderne', in *Adorno-Konferenz 1983*, pp.177–97.
5. Jürgen Habermas, 'Modernity versus Postmodernity', *New German Critique*, 22 (1981), pp.12ff. For a more critical view of *Die Ästhetik des Widerstands* see Ferenc Fehér, 'The Swan Song of German Krushchevism', *New German Critique*, 30 (1983), pp.157–70.
6. Cf. Arnold Hauser on Picasso, Stravinsky, Dada and Surrealism in the chapter 'The Film Age' of his *Social History of Art* (London: Routledge and Kegan Paul, 1962).
7. Reinhold Grimm, 'Spiel und Wirklichkeit in einigen Revolutionsdramen', *Basis*, 1 (1970).

8. Quotations are from the English translation of *Marat/Sade* by Geoffrey Skelton and Adrian Mitchell (London: Calder and Boyers, 1969).
9. Cf. Marianne Kesting, 'Verbrechen, Wahnsinn und Revolte. Peter Weiss' Marat/de Sade Stück und der französische Surrealismus', in Walter Hinck (ed.), *Geschichte und Schauspiel* (Frankfurt/Main: Suhrkamp, 1981), pp.304–21.
10. Jacques Derrida, 'La théâtre de la Cruauté et la clôture de la représentation', in his *L'Écriture et la différence* (Paris: Seuil, 1967), pp.341–468.
11. The Nietzschean strain in Artaud's *Le théâtre et son double* points back to the opposition in *The Birth of Tragedy* of the Dionysian and the Socratic (Aeschylus and Euripides), which Reinhold Grimm sees as adumbrating the polar possibilities of drama since Nietzsche, e.g., Strindberg and Shaw, or Artaud and Brecht. See R. Grimm, 'The Hidden Heritage: Repercussions of Nietzsche in Modern Theatre and Its Theory', *Nietzsche-Studien*, 12 (1983), pp.355–71.
12. Cf. Peter Weiss's comment: 'One theme is the sober clarifying description of universally valid events, the counter theme: the indeterminate and fluid nature of all events and the autistic dream world. . . . One theme is the absolute moment . . . in which something unexpected, unpredictable arises through improvisation (psychodrama, happening, role playing).. . . .' Quoted from Karlheinz Braun (ed.), *Materialien zu Peter Weiss's Marat/Sade* (Frankfurt/Main: Suhrkamp, 1967), p.91.
13. On *Marat/Sade* as a revolutionary passion play see Fehér, 'The Swan Song of German Krushchevism', p.162:

> What is the fundamental world-view which generates the passion play as something distinct from habitual drama or dramatic parable? Its main tenet is the emphatic and explosively contradictory conviction that cast, plot, and final outcome have already been inalterably set by a superior power (God or History). In this sense fate reigns supreme over the protagonists. Nevertheless, they have to act out their roles (their martyrdom) as if they were free agents, while in fact they are mere ornamental representatives of an order higher than their autonomy. This is how both of Bach's Jesus-figures, the *citoyen* (in *St. John's Passion*) and Man (in *St. Matthew's Passion*) appear before us with serene dignity and in 'bound freedom' as Kierkegaard would say. This is how both Marat and Sade, these sublime captives of an already miscarried history, struggle against a situation which offers them only the imitation of action, not action itself.

CHAPTER 4

Feminism, Realism and the Avant-Garde

Rita Felski

Recent discussions in feminist theory on the question of a feminist aesthetic have tended to polarize around a typology of realist versus avant-garde art: advocates of realism argue the importance of texts which can authentically communicate the quality of female experience, while critics insist upon the inherently conservative and ideological nature of a realist style, and argue for an experimental feminist aesthetic which will subvert existing codes of representation. The point at issue is the question of whether some literary and artistic styles can be defined as more 'advanced', more radical than others and therefore more suited to the interests of feminism as a progressive social movement, or whether it is in fact impossible to construct any necessary relationship between feminism and any particular aesthetic or linguistic form. I indicate below some of the contradictions which emerge from any attempt to construct an abstract model of a normative feminist aesthetic in order to suggest an alternative model of a feminist cultural politics situated in relation to the heterogeneous publics constituted within the feminist public sphere.

A naive defence of realism played an important part in early theories of feminist aesthetics, exemplified in the assertion: 'to win feminist acclaim, a literary work by a woman must first of all be authentic ... a realistic representation of "female experience", "feminine consciousness" or "female reality".[1] This belief that women's writing could simply mirror a pre-given subjective experience was based on an inadequately theorized reflectionist aesthetic which failed to take into account either linguistic, ideological or intertextual determinants of textual production and which remains incompatible with contemporary theories of signification. It has consequently been largely discarded by feminist theorists who have sought to develop more sophisticated theories of literary meaning and alternative models of feminist cultural production. One influential source has been Barthes's opposition between the 'readerly' and the 'writerly' text, which sets up a dichotomy between realist forms which are passively consumed by the reader and experimental forms which problematize signification and involve the reader's active co-operation in the construction of meaning.[2] Another influence has been the Althusserian theory of the subject as interpellated within ideology, which has inspired a hostility towards realism and a celebration of modernist texts which foreground their own conventional status and thus by implication the constructed nature of reality.[3] Irrespective of actual content, the realist novel is perceived to be irredeemably compromised. It generates the illusion of transparency, of showing things as they really are, rather than drawing attention to its own signifying practice and the workings of ideology in the construction of meaning and the unified subject.

This critique of realist narrative has gained wide-spread support. Thus Catherine Belsey asserts that 'realism is a predominantly conservative form'[4], while Rosalind Coward, in an influential essay which addresses the question of a feminist aesthetic, argues: 'Nor can we say that the structures of the realist novel are neutral and that they can just be filled with a feminist content'.[5] The development of an anti-realist aesthetic has been significantly encouraged by the influence of Lacan and Derrida on feminist theory. The function of a feminist art is perceived as primarily negative and subversive, a critical dismantling of existing ideological and discursive positions which can liberate a non-specific textual plurality often described in terms of a notion of feminine desire.[6] Consequently a conservative realism is counterposed against a modernist or avant-garde art perceived to challenge rather than affirm dominant modes of representation, liberating an indeterminate plurality of meaning considered more appropriate to a subversive feminist art.

This assertion that modernist art can be counterposed to realism as a more advanced form which disrupts ideological closures has an initial plausibility but offers a number of theoretical difficulties which make it a tenuous basis for the development of a feminist cultural politics. To begin with, the proposition that realism is a 'closed' form which imposes single and transparent meanings upon the reader, in which, as McCabe argues, 'everything becomes obvious,[7] can easily be challenged by pointing to the large numbers of realist novels – including virtually the whole canon of nineteenth-century realism – which continue to generate a multiplicity of different and contradictory readings. Polemically one could in fact argue that realist works frequently allow for a *greater* plurality and richness of interpretation than modern experimental texts which are interpreted with monotonous regularity as self-reflexive statements on the nature of language.

The belief that the realist novel constitutes a closed ideological form which presents itself as a reflection of the real is based, as Macherey notes, upon a confusion of the difference between fiction and illusion.[8] As a fictional construct governed by aesthetic conventions and bearing a highly mediated relationship to social reality, the realist novel cannot be meaningfully accused of deception. It is neither intended nor interpreted as a literal transcription of the real, but rather contains within it a formally mediated distance to its own substantive content. The basis of this confusion lies in the equation of the language of realism with language *per se* as ideological discourse; it is thus assumed that only a style which ruptures linguistic conventions can offer any form of resistance to ideology. This conclusion however ignores the fact that the crucial distinction between texts is not constituted by stylistic differences – experimental vs. non-experimental, literary vs. non-literary language – but is rather a result of the difference of social function as constituted in the context of reception. As Macherey points out: 'The writer's language is new, not in its material form, but in its use'.[9] It is in being read as literature that the formal dimension of the text becomes the primary object of the reader's attention, allowing for a receptivity of textual ambiguities and the possibility of multiple re-readings. It is, in other words, because of the prior existence of prevailing ideologies of art that certain texts are read as containing a formally mediated distance to the ideological positions which they represent, not because of the uniquely privileged status of any particular linguistic or artistic form as such. Consequently an analysis of the social construction of the category of art as the product of a particular historical conjuncture must play a crucial role in attempting to assess the question of the relationship between aesthetic form and political effect. For example, a text which subverts language is not in itself necessarily 'revolutionary' if such subversion has become established as a typical feature of literary works which is perceived to bear no relationship whatsoever to everyday life. Both realism and modernism are aesthetic conventions, and as such need to be examined within the broader context of the institutionalized status of art in modern society.

Sociological objections to theories of a 'revolutionary' experimental art thus centre on the failure to deal with art and literature as socially constructed categories which mediate the response to a particular text. The implications of this are significant in suggesting that the modernist view of art as the self-problematization of signification is itself grounded in a particular ideological position. The conception of the specificity of literature as expressed in the idea that the formal properties of the literary text negate, transcend, deconstruct or otherwise problematize its substantive content is revealed as the product of the modern understanding of art and needs as such to be critically examined in relation to the ideological functions which it serves. Thus entire academic industries are based upon the exegesis of the experimental literary or artistic text, which acquires an enigmatic aura that can only be deciphered by the expert: 'in a way analogous to religion, the work of art alludes mysteriously to a superior but now essentially opaque and unknowable order'.[10] Consequently, a feminist aesthetic theory must take into account this institutionalized status of art as exemplified in existing ideological and discursive frameworks. How does this status influence the potential social effect of any particular work? To what extent can a political maovement such as feminism influence the function and reception of literary and artistic texts?

From a historical perspective, it may be argued that while modernism, and indeed realism itself, once possessed a subversive function, the revolutionary status of formal techniques is no longer self-evident. No form of art can hope permanently to escape the constraints of signification; the text's defamiliarizing effect is inevitably exhausted as it in turn comes to embody the new norm of artistic production. The historical avant-garde, however, according to Peter Bürger, constitutes a fundamental caesura in this historical succession of aesthetic styles by its iconoclastic protest against the status of art itself in the form of a disruptive and nihilistic 'anti-art'.[11] Contemporary art can only either repeat its acts of provocation – which thus no longer shock by their novelty – or reappropriate more traditional forms; neither option appears in itself to offer a convincing solution to the problem of a radical art in a post-avant-garde era. The belief in the oppositional function of experimental aesthetic techniques is further undermined by their acceptance and institutionalization in contemporary culture; the avant-garde celebration of the new as the most advanced can be seen in this context as offering a parallel to the fetishization of novelty which is the hallmark of a capitalist consumer culture built upon immediate obsolescence. As Andreas Huyssen suggests, the theory of a subversive textual politics reveals an over-emphasis on the transgressive function of the experimental text in modern society.

> To insist upon the adversary function of *écriture* and of breaking linguistic codes when every second ad bristles with domesticated avant-gardist and modernist strategies strikes me as caught in that overestimation of art's transformative function for society which is the signature of an overly modernist age.[12]

Finally, objections to the assertion of any necessary relationship between feminism and a modernist or avant-garde aesthetic can be made from a political and strategic position. Firstly, there is the obvious question of accessibility: the subversion of conventions of representation invariably places severe limitations upon the nature and size of any potential audience. Experimental art often assumes a sophisticated knowledge of the significance of formal techniques which constitutes a language accessible only to the expert. To argue that avant-garde form embodies the privileged site of a feminist aesthetic is to categorize intellectuals as the only legitimate practitioners and recipients of feminist art, and to leave the question unanswered as to the means by which this elitist culture is to be transmitted to the women's movement as a whole.

Secondly, there is the question whether feminist cultural activity can be adequately defined by a formal model which lays exclusive stress on the disruption of existing styles and conventions. Certainly feminism contains within it a negative moment which seeks to expose the illusory nature of patriarchal discourses; it also however goes beyond a strategy of negation to the development of alternative cultural and political positions. As Jochen Schulte-Sasse argues: 'discourses aimed at criticising or organising social praxis may be unable to avoid working with metaphysical closure'.[13] A limitation of a modernist aesthetic from a feminist standpoint is its frequent dismissal of the category of content as an illusion to be deconstructed by the 'progressive' text, and the consequent inability to account for the inescapable semantic function of literature (e.g., as a medium of social criticism). The modernist equation of stylistic innovation with political radicalism is called into question by a social movement such as feminism; the specific interests of women cannot be encompassed in terms of a notion of linguistic indeterminacy and free play. Consequently, feminism needs to circumvent the kind of dualism which opposes a 'progressive' avant-garde to a 'conservative' realism in order to work towards a more sophisticated understanding of the relationship between art and feminist politics.

As such criticisms make clear, it is difficult to offer any satisfactory account of the necessary relationship between feminism and modernist/avant-garde art. Adorno's advocacy of modernism, it must be remembered, springs from a social pessimism which is unable to identify any contemporary agent of political change: given the prevailing technocratic logic of an administered society, the dissonant, fragmentary nature of modern art offers a passive resistance to the commodification of experience. Adorno does not assign this art any direct social function or political effect; rather it embodies a form of critical negativity whose autonomy is guaranteed by its esoteric and difficult character. Modernist art, in other words, possesses a redemptive function as the sole authentic site of critical resistance in a reified social world in which any notion of collective action has become problematic.

Feminism, however, rejects any such pessimism in its identification of women as an oppressed class which embodied a potential force for social change, and consequently pursues a political approach to literature and art in relation to women as gendered social subjects. As a result feminist criticism is able to offer the main convincing alternative to current formalist textual theories, since it can ground its analysis in relation to an active political agent. Given that existing discussions of the question of feminist aesthetics are only *possible* because of the recent re-emergence of the women's movement, it is surprising that socially based theories have not played a bigger role in determining the relationship between feminist politics and art.

A feminist cultural politics thus needs to incorporate an analysis of feminism as a social movement and to develop a theoretical position which is not open to the kind of critical objections listed above. A useful starting point here is Peter Bürger's *Theory of the Avant-Garde* which specifically addresses the question of the historical development of aesthetic form and the status of art as a social institution. Bürger stresses that the meaning of literature or art cannot be adequately understood through either internal formal analysis or a model of individual reader response, but demands consideration of the ruling ideologies and discourses of art in a given society: 'works of art are not received as single entities, but within institutional frameworks which largely determine the function of the work'.[14] While Bürger himself does not draw any explicit political conclusions from his arguments, his assertion that the quest for a progressive aesthetic is historically invalidated by the avant-garde's revolt against tradition and needs to be replaced by a sociological analysis of the function of individual texts, whether realist or avant-garde, in relation to particular audiences, is one which can be usefully adapted to the specific interests of a feminist cultural politics.

Bürger summarizes the development of art as a distinct sphere within bourgeois society, the division of labour and increasing specialization which accompanies the growth of capitalism leading to the detachment of art from other aspects of social and cultural life, and its transformation into a marketed commodity. Deprived of any obvious use value or social purpose, artistic activity is compelled to provide its own legitimation, with the consequent emergence of the notion of art as a privileged and autonomous realm of experience. This detachment of art from any immediate social function has a double-edged significance: the artist's emancipation from a system of patronage makes it possible for art to reflect critically upon society; at the same time, however, this criticism is consumed as art and can thus be seen to possess a compensatory rather than critical function. Irrespective of its actual content, in other words, the social framework within which the work of art is received places limits on the direct political effectivity of any critical intervention.

The historical avant-garde, however, is the first movement in art which both recognizes and opposes this autonomous status of art in bourgeois society. Unlike modernism which is primarily concerned with an attack on conventional formal techniques, the avant-garde movements (Dada, Surrealism) direct their attack at the social category of art as such. Their manifestos and demonstrations seek to break down the barriers which surround the work of art as a hallowed cultural object. This protest is, however, unsuccessful; rather than dismantling the category of the aesthetic, the works of the avant-garde themselves become exhibits in the museum, assimilated into the infinitely flexible 'institution art'.

While failing to abolish ruling ideologies of aesthetic autonomy, the protest of the avant-garde does, however, have significant implications for the future understanding of art by revealing its institutionalized status as a major factor determining the degree of political effectiveness of any particular work. 'All art that is more recent than the historical avant-garde must come to terms with this fact in bourgeois society', argues Bürger;[15] it is no longer possible to ignore the social mediation of the work of art and to assume that it can have any direct political effect. Two important implications follow from this. Firstly, it becomes clear that the problem of the social ineffectiveness of art cannot be resolved by a more 'revolutionary' style, but is rather determined by ruling ideologies of reception resulting from the separation of art from social life within bourgeois society. Simultaneously, however, the very concept of a 'radical' form is itself revealed as historically invalidated. The avant-garde does not constitute a specific style in art, but rather employs a montage of past and present techniques in its revolt against tradition, and thus makes it possible to recognize artistic forms and procedures as such, a freely available range of styles no longer bound to any teleological model of historical development.

From this vantage point Bürger can assess the limits of the theories of Lukács and Adorno, both of whom continue to cling to an idealist aesthetic based in a philosophy of history. Adorno's belief that the modernist work constitutes the most advanced state of artistic technique is merely the mirror image of the Lukácsian understanding of modernist art as decadence. In a post-avant-garde era, however, it becomes fundamentally problematic to attribute a fixed social or political meaning to any particular aesthetic style. The contemporary artist is no longer bound by the conventions of a particular school which perceives itself as the most advanced, but is, rather, free to choose from a variety of forms the one which is most appropriate to any particular purpose. Consequently the present era exemplifies an end to the historical periodization of art as a succession of styles; no form can be defined as inherently more radical or conservative than any other.

The value of Bürger's argument for the development of a feminist cultural politics thus lies in its exposure of the antithetical opposition of realism and modernism as based in an outmoded conception of progress in art which fails to come to terms with the free circulation of styles characteristic of a post-avant-garde era. Emancipated from their historical origins, aesthetic modes are revealed as *conventions* whose meaning is contingent and contextually produced. It thus becomes impossible for feminists to deduce the political value of a text from an analysis of its formal properties. The question of a radical art is not a formal but rather a social and ideological issue which demands an analysis of *reception* in relation to the prevailing ideologies of artistic function. Thus the central question here is: how does a social movement such as feminism influence the way we think about art and the framework of textual reception?

Bürger's analysis is significant in offering a theoretical articulation of the sense of unease with modernist theories of 'progressive' art which permeates much of Western cultural production in the

1970s and 80s: 'the familiar ideas of what constitutes a critical art . . . have lost much of their explanatory and normative power in recent decades'.[16] One reason for this increasing scepticism regarding the relationship between aesthetic and political progress may be the sense of the 'death of the avant-garde', the ease with which the iconoclastic gestures of experimental art have been accepted and neutralized within the cultural institutions of modern society. Another reason is the emergence of new social movements such as feminism which have questioned the validity of theories which ignore the representational and political dimensions of texts in relation to readers. The emancipatory significance of a subversion of aesthetic codes is not necessarily self-evident to marginalized groups attempting to define an oppositional cultural identity through the medium of literature or art. Consequently the once clear-cut theoretical distinctions between oppositional and conservative forms lose much of their authority when faced with the current diversity of cultural activity.

Bürger's *Theory of the Avant-Garde* can be understood in this context as the articulation of a postmodern response to the theory of modernism which calls into question the self-understanding of experimental art as possessing a critical or redemptive social function. The question of postmodernism and its relationship to feminism is a complex issue which I cannot fully explore here. However, a brief summary of some recent discussions of this issue may be useful in helping to elucidate potential points of affinity between feminism and a postmodern aesthetic.

Postmodernism is a term which has acquired a wide range of differing and often contradictory meanings and which has proved resistant to any systematic definition; there has been little agreement either as to its actual referent (art, philosophy, culture) or as to its significance and value (a populist, pluralistic, revitalized modernism on the one hand, a nostalgic, affirmative, neo-conservatism on the other). Andreas Huyssen argues the theoretical poverty of any such dichotomy, and of any attempt to reduce postmodernism to an ironic and self-reflexive style in art (e.g., Borges, Calvino) or to a mere variant on the theme of post-structuralism. Rather, he argues, postmodernism is most appropriately understood as an historical condition, a collection of varied and often contradictory responses to the aporias of modernity and of modernist thinking, which cannot thus be assigned any coherent and unified meaning or value. As a 'slowly emerging cultural transformation within Western societies',[17] postmodernism thus embodies a shift in perception and sensibility which is necessarily still marked by the continuing influence of modernist thought; consequently it cannot be understood as either a simple extension of modernism or its antithetical opposite. Rather, Huyssen argues:

> it operates in a field of tension between tradition and innovation, conservation and renewal, mass culture and high art, in which the second terms are no longer automatically privileged over the first; a field of tension which can no longer be grasped in terms of categories such as progress vs. reaction, Left vs. Right, present vs. past, modernism vs. realism, abstraction vs. representation, avant-garde vs. kitsch.[18]

Huyssen argues that postmodernism contains within it an important critical moment as an historical response to the contradictions generated by modernist thought, in particular the rigid separation of high and mass culture. Against the fetishization of novelty and the exclusive concentration on formal innovation, postmodernism contains within it a greater openness to tradition and an interest in questions of content in relation to the self-differentiation of oppositional communities. Against the modernist claim to a universally valid progressive art, postmodernism raises the problem of cultural elitism and the need to consider the question of reception in relation to the needs of different audiences. Postmodernism does not, in its better moments, embody a rejection of the critical and oppositional impetus of modernism, but rather can be seen as constituting the criticism of a modernism aware of its own institutionalization. Thus postmodernism offers a more differentiated understanding of the possibilities of an oppositional culture in relation to the social and historical specificity of particular publics.

In this context it can be argued that the feminist reintroduction of political questions into cultural analysis, its stress on heterogeneity and difference, and its eclecticism in the exploration of cultural forms have played a crucial role in the revision of the tenets of modernism and the questioning of rigid oppositions between high and mass art which has become apparent in contemporary culture.[19] Against the experimentation with formal innovation for its own sake, feminism has re-asserted the importance of the representation of difference, whether through experimental texts or the reappropriation of existing realist forms such as the *Bildungsroman*. The interest in tradition and the exploration of women's history has played an important part in feminist activity, inspired by a search for cultural identity and a critical response to the alienation and rationalization of modernity, and to modernist texts often complicit with such alienation in a fetishization of the modern and a negation of tradition. Equally, the feminist interest in texts written and read by women, many of which have traditionally been excluded from the realm of high culture, has blurred many of the distinctions between high and low art and encouraged creative interaction between a variety of forms. The practice of feminist criticism has in turn reflected and interwoven with many of the preoccupations of feminist art. By insisting upon the fact of gender as a fundamental political category in the production and reception of texts, it has challenged the self-understanding of 'progressive' formalist literary theories which detach the text from all outside influence, and has consistently sought to relocate art within a broader social and cultural framework.

As is intimated by Bürger's analysis, changes in the social function of art are not set in motion through internal changes in textual form, but necessarily involve a shift in the cultural and ideological framework which determines existing conceptions of the significance of art. In attempting to define the influence of the women's movement upon theories of artistic function, the model of a feminist public sphere is a useful one. This concept has been recently discussed by several critics, most notably by Terry Eagleton,[20] and is developed in analogy to the model of the bourgeois public sphere analysed in Habermas's *Structural Changes in the Public Sphere*.[21] There Habermas argues that the public sphere is an historically determined formation which emerges for the first time from the specific conditions of seventeenth- and eighteenth-century bourgeois society, its participants male property-owners and the enlightened aristocracy. It represents the first emergence of a critical and independent public domain which perceives itself as distinct from state interests, a discursive community bound by shared assumptions which define its boundaries. Primary among these is the belief in rationality which serves to equalize all participants within the discourse; it is critical reason which henceforth provides the legitimation for argument on politics and culture, not tradition, religious dogma, or social privilege. 'Access is guaranteed to all citizens'.[22] At the same time participation in this discursive community is of course determined by such factors as gender and class; the eighteenth-century public sphere which perceives itself as grounded in rational and universal principles is in reality limited to an educated male bourgeoisie. Neverthless, according to Habermas, this emergence of the bourgeois public sphere historically represents an emancipatory moment which, while linked to a class interest, is nevertheless important in generating the first relatively autonomous discursive space which can define itself critically against state power.

This consensual basis and critical function of the bourgeois public sphere slowly disintegrates under the dynamic of capitalist growth and the development of an industrialized and increasingly anonymous mass society. The resulting intervention of the state in the regulation of economic affairs and the growth of ever more powerful state bureaucracies leads to a blurring of the distinction between civil society and the state upon which the bourgeois public sphere depends. While on the one hand a rapid expansion takes place in education, literacy and communication, the extension of the public sphere into ever larger sectors of society is accompanied, Habermas argues, by a decrease in critical function as its institutions become integrated into late capitalist society. The commodification of the mass media and the increasing influence of state bureaucracies on individual life-experience make it impossible to identify any independent arena for the critical and informed formation of public opinion.

Political developments since the writing of Habermas's work in 1962 - most notably the radicalization of student groups in the '60s and the growth of new social movments in the '70s - have since inspired theorists to posit the growth of counter public spheres, understood as critical oppositional forces within late capitalism which voice needs which the public sphere of the 'culture industry' fails to meet.[23] The women's movement has offered one of the most dynamic examples of a counter ideology in recent years which has generated an oppositional public arena. Like the original bourgeois public sphere, the feminist public sphere constitutes a discursive space, here exemplified through women's centres, political literature, film and art, feminist journals, etc., which defines itself in terms of a common identity. Here it is the shared experience of gender-based oppression which provides the mediating factor uniting all participants beyond their specific differences. 'As with the classical public sphere, distinctions of class are temporarily suspended, though not ignored, within this new domain; the shared fact of gender works to equalise all participants within it'.[24] At the same time, of course, the feminist public sphere differs in important ways from Habermas's model of the bourgeois public sphere, some of these differences stemming from the specific needs and interests of the women's movement, others from the changed relationship between state and civil society within late capitalism.

Within the feminist public sphere gender is the equalizing factor which is perceived to unite all participants and which in theory allows for the possibility of a temporary suspension of other differences based in race, nation or class; the consciousness of membership of an oppressed group engenders a solidarity based in collective identity and grants all participants equal status. The 'we' of feminist discourse represents all women as collective co-subjects. As a consequence the women's movement can accommodate disparate and often conflicting theoretical and political positions, because membership is not conditional upon the acceptance of any specific theoretical framework, but rather on the shared consciousness of oppression as a woman. Hence the importance which literature has assumed in the development of an oppositional women's culture, the feminist novel focusing upon areas of personal experience which women are perceived to share in common beyond their cultural and political differences.

Unlike the bourgeois public sphere, then, the feminist public sphere does not claim a representative universality but rather offers a critique of cultural values from the standpoint of women as a marginalized group. In this sense it constitutes a *partial* or counter public sphere. Yet in so far as it is also a *public* sphere, its logic is directed towards a dissemination of feminist arguments through society as a whole. The tension between universality and particularity in a feminist public sphere here becomes apparent. On the one hand it is gender-specific, appealing to the experiences of women who find their interests distorted or excluded through patriarchal ideology and discourse. Yet at the same time it is a public discursive arena which disseminates its arguments through such generally accessible channels of communication as books, journals, the mass media, the education system, and does not allow for any *a priori* exclusion of men from its domain. One can make a distinction here between the women's movement as such, which has for obvious reasons restricted its membership to women, and a feminist public sphere, which is by definition potentially accessible to all members of a given society. This gradual expansion of feminist arguments from their roots in the women's movement through society as a whole is a necessary corollary of feminism's claim to be a catalyst of social and cultural change. The feminist public sphere, in other words, serves a dual function: it demarcates a discursive space which is oppositional and gender-specific, enabling a consciousness of community and solidarity among women, yet it also disseminates feminist arguments throughout society, its logic thus tending ultimately to its own dissolution through a transformation of society which seeks in the final analysis to render its own oppositional functional redundant.

A further tension endemic to the operation of a public sphere is the disparity between ideal and real status. The ideal of a free discursive space which equalizes all participants is an enabling fiction which engenders a sense of collective identity but can only be attained by a suspension of other forms of difference, an erasure felt most painfully by those whose unequal status and particular needs are suppressed by the fiction of a unifying identity. bell hooks claims that the white middle-class bias of much feminist activity has ignored the specific problems of black women:

> white women who dominate feminist discourse today rarely question whether or not their perspective on women's reality is true to the lived experiences of women as a collective group. Neither are they aware of the extent to which their perspectives reflect race and class biases.....[25]

At the same time hooks's own critique would not be possible if it were not for a public sphere which claims to represent all women and can thus be made answerable for its failure to do so. The notion of a collective identity remains a necessary condition for the operation of a public sphere; feminist theorists who reject any notion of a unifying identity as a repressive fiction fail to specify how diversity and fragmentation can be harnessed to collective and goal-based political activity. It is precisely because of the varied life-experiences of women that their self-differentiation through a notion of communal identity provides the necessary means through which women as an oppositional group can define themselves. Feminism thus necessarily oscillates between the ideology of a unified collective subject drawn from the primary distinction of male versus female, and the actual activities and self-understanding of women, in which gender-based divisions frequently conflict with other alliances such as those based around race or class. Consequently any attempt to construct a notion of female identity is necessarily both empowering *and* constricting, and will be continually subject to critical revision by specific groups who find their own experiences and interests excluded.

This diversity of interests is in turn exemplified in the institutional locations of the feminist public sphere. On the one hand the women's movement offers one of the main forums for political activity which operates on a grass-roots level outside of existing institutional frameworks and which has generated an infrastructure of decentralized collectively-based projects, while another important site of feminist activity has also been within such institutions as bureaucracies and universities. There exists furthermore a range of feminist activities such as women's refuges and advisory centres which often function with a degree of autonomy but within the framework of existing social welfare bureaucracies. Thus Ferree and Hess discuss bureaucratic and collectivist modes as interweaving 'strands' within feminism rather than distinct branches, and refer to the increasing 'blurring of distinctions between self-help collectives and the bureaucratically organized lobbying organizations' within the women's movement.[26] Equally, feminist cultural activity has developed on a number of distinct but often interconnecting levels, from the small autonomous writers' or film-makers' group through to the dissemination of feminist ideas through mass publishing.

As such examples make clear, the present influence of the women's movement cannot be adequately accounted for by the notion of a unified and autonomous counter public sphere which operates exclusively outside of existing state and social institutions. In this context it is important to clarify the fundamental differences in the operation of the feminist and the bourgeois public spheres. Given the complex interpenetrations of state and society in late capitalism, it is no longer feasible to postulate the ideal of a counter public sphere which can remain outside of existing institutions and which can at the same time claim an influential and representative function as a forum for feminist activity and debate. Instead of adhering to a nostalgic model of an autonomous political community which cannot provide a feasible source of critical opposition in the mass culture society of late capitalism, it is necessary to rethink the conception of a public sphere in terms of a series of cultural strategies which can be effective across a range of levels both inside and outside of institutions.

The multiplicity of audiences constituted within a feminist public sphere thus invalidates any attempt to develop any one normative political aesthetic based on a notion of woman as unified collective subject, and suggests the need for a pragmatically based cultural politics which can be effective on a range of levels. Consequently, it is no longer possible to argue, for example, that realism is antithetical to feminism, given that the realist novel has constituted a significant instrument of social criticism within an important section of the women's movement. Issues of form and technique cannot be abstractly determined, but need to be based upon the needs and interests of specific groups at particular historical conjunctures. As Terry Lovell says: 'Feminism does not carry imperatives as to form. Feminist intervention is possible and necessary at all levels of cultural production and in most genres'.[27]

It is in this context that feminism needs to re-examine its relationship to the mass media, and to acknowledge the importance of feminist influence in channels which can potentially reach vast audiences. Feminist theories have at times embraced a 'purist' position which assumes that the only legitimate feminist cultural activity renounces all popular and established conventions and is situated outside of existing commercial cultural institutions, resulting in an exclusive focus on an esoteric modernist art – as in the case of Kristeva – which is problematic in its elitism and in its inability to offer any convincing account of the relationship between this kind of art and the broad base of the women's movement. This is not to devalue feminist exploration of complex or experimental forms, which, even if they do not possess any inherent 'revolutionary' value, can nevertheless play an important role in the development of a feminist presence in high art. The point is rather that the *political* significance of such art cannot be located in any inherent formal properties, but only in relation to the social phenomenon of a feminist public sphere. Consequently feminism needs to balance the value of aesthetic innovation against the importance of communicating a degree of political awareness to large audiences of women: 'a small popular change is relatively just as significant as a large minority change. There may be at least as much potential for change in a T.V. soap opera as in agit-prop theatre'.[28]

The actual diversity of the feminist public sphere thus provides the justification for a cultural pluralism which seeks to address the needs and interests of a range of audiences. Rather than a unified community, this public sphere includes women from diverse class, racial and cultural backgrounds and operates both within and outside of existing social and state institutions. Given this fundamental heterogeneity, any abstract notion of a 'subversive' or 'feminine' aesthetic is rendered invalid, and needs to give way to an analysis of the function of a range of cultural forms in relation to specific and historically constituted publics. Consequently, feminism needs to explore the political potential of both realist and avant-garde forms, of both 'high' and mass culture, and cannot assign absolute priority to any particular aesthetic mode or textual strategy.

NOTES

1. Cheri Register, 'American Feminist Literary Criticism: A Biographical Introduction', in Josephine Donovan (ed.), *Feminist Literary Criticism: Explorations in Theory* (Lexington: University Press of Kentucky, 1975), p.12.
2. See Roland Barthes, *S/Z* (New York: Hill and Wang, 1974).
3. For a critical account of the influence of Althusser on English cultural studies, see Simon Clarke et al., *One Dimensional Marxism* (London: Allison and Busby, 1980).
4. Catherine Belsey, *Critical Practice* (London: Methuen, 1980), p.51.
5. Rosalind Coward, 'Are Women's Novels Feminist Novels?', *Feminist Review*, 5 (1980), p.60.
6. See, among others, Alice Jardine, *Gynesis* (Ithaca: Cornell University Press, 1985); Ann Rosalind Jones, 'Towards an Understanding of *L'Écriture féminine*', *Feminist Studies*, 7:2 (1981).
7. Colin McCabe, 'Realism and the Cinema: Notes on Some Brechtian Theses', *Screen*, 15:2 (1974), p.16.
8. Pierre Macherey, *A Theory of Literary Production* (London: Routledge and Kegan Paul, 1978), pp.61–5.
9. Ibid., p.55.
10. Blaine McBurney, 'The Post-Modern Transvaluation of Modernist Values', *Thesis Eleven*, 12 (1985), pp.100–1.
11. Peter Bürger, *Theory of the Avant-Garde* (1984). See 'Select Bibliography'.
12. Andreas Huyssen, 'Mapping the Postmodern', *New German Critique*, 33 (1984), p.41.
13. Jochen Schulte-Sasse, 'Foreword: Theory of Modernism versus Theory of the Avant-garde', in Bürger, *Theory of the Avant-Garde*, p.xxiii.
14. Bürger, p.12.
15. Ibid., p.57.
16. Huyssen, p.9.
17. Ibid., p.8.
18. Ibid., p.48.
19. See also Craig Owens, 'The Discourse of Others: Feminists and Postmodernism', in Hal Foster (ed.), *Postmodern Culture* (London: Pluto Press, 1985).
20. Terry Eagleton, *The Function of Criticism* (London: Verso, 1984).
21. Jürgen Habermas, *Strukturwandel der Öffentlichkeit* (Darmstadt: Luchterhand, 1962).
22. Jürgen Habermas, 'The Public Sphere: An Encyclopaedia Article', *New German Critique*, 1:3 (1974), p.49.
23. See Oskar Negt and Alexander Kluge, *Öffentlichkeit und Erfahrung* (Frankfurt/Main: Suhrkamp, 1972).
24. Eagleton, op. cit., p.118.
25. bell hooks, *Feminist Theory: From Margin to Center* (London: Southend Press, 1984), p.3.

26. Myra Marx Ferree and Beth B. Hess, *Controversy and Coalition: The New Feminist Movement* (Boston: Twayne, 1985), p.49.
27. Terry Lovell, 'Writing like a Woman: A Question of Politics', in Francis Barker et al. (eds), *Politics of Theory* (Colchester: University of Essex, 1983), p.24.
28. Michèle Barrett, 'Feminism and the Definition of a Cultural Politics', in Rosalind Brunt and Caroline Rowan (eds), *Feminism, Culture and Politics* (London: Lawrence and Wishart, 1982), p.54.

CHAPTER 5

The Pyrrhic Victory of Art in its War of Liberation: Remarks on the Postmodernist Intermezzo

Ferenc Fehér

Perhaps no modern work in the philosophy of art and literature emphasizes the centrality of, and the need for, the liberation of artistic activity from all kinds of alien hegemonies so emphatically as *The Specificity of the Aesthetic* written by Georg Lukács in his old age. The chapter dealing with the 'war of liberation' targets religion as the chief of these alien hegemonic forces and musters supporting argumentation in a manner which is not always convincing.[1] Moreover, in one way or another, the idea of 'liberation' runs through all six decades of Lukács's life and activity as a theorist.[2] Lukács is certainly the most emphatic though not the only advocate of the thesis of artistic and literary self-liberation among his contemporaries. Adorno's cryptic remark, crucial to his theory, that music has always been a city-dwelling art and, above all, *bürgerlich*, thus curtly dismissing Palestrina as well as centuries of church music from the history of the subject, also finds its explanation in the 'liberation thesis'. It simply means that as long as music had been subjected to external expectations and postulates, it had not yet reached 'the level of its notion', to use a Hegelian term. Only when foreign occupation ended and music was abandoned to the exclusive task of rationalist self-organization did it become 'music for itself', a liberated art with the commitment to living up to its own destiny. The emphasis on artistic and literary self-liberation can be, and often has been, traced back to the great period of German classical idealism, to its fight against the Enlightenment reduction of the artistic to a level of *perception confuse*. Both this emphasis and this fight can, moreover, be evaluated in several different ways.³ But for my present purposes it is perhaps sufficient to link this trend with Weber's pathbreaking morphology of modernity. Weber conceived *the progressive separation of spheres* (religious, legal, political and economic) from one another as the *differentia specifica* of modernity. In a sense, Lukács and Adorno, both deeply influenced by Weber, do nothing but provide an ontological foundation for this progressive separation, using as their example one sphere: the aesthetic. Let me anticipate the final conclusion of this paper. Many of the apparently unresolvable difficulties confronting the professional critic and uninitiated recipient alike in their attempts at rendering meaning to the elusive category of 'postmodernism' can be resolved in a relatively straightforward manner if we follow the progressive separation (or 'self-liberation') of the artistic and literary sphere up to its final stage. But for this to be achieved, we must first distinguish between the two meanings of liberation: *autonomy* and *emancipation*.

Autonomy means the self-liberation of art and literature from the hegemony, or even the influence, of other spheres. The striving for autonomy has been a clearly identifiable trend for centuries, one borne initially by the artists and writers themselves but which gained increasing support from their audiences as well. It is also an extremely 'legitimate' tendency provided that we accept Weber's characterization of modernity. The main battle fought for the autonomy of the aesthetic sphere was that between religion on the one hand, art and literature on the other. In this respect, Lukács's diagnosis was correct. There is a straightforward explanation for the distinguished place which religion has occupied among the forces which have dominated the aesthetic domain: religion and aesthetics were doubly enmeshed. Religion's domination involved a *cultural and institutional hegemony*, so that its control was therefore external and internal at the same time. However, for centuries the cultural influence of religion was incomparably more than one of mere domination. It also provided a vital stimulation, it supplied its maidservant with a universally comprehensible subject matter (it was the *Biblia pauperorum*), with a zealous inspiration, and with a well-defined objective for art and literature's sublime vocation. The secularization of art and literature between the High Renaissance and the second half of the nineteenth century is a phenomenon discussed so often that it hardly bears repetition. One point, however, needs to be added: whilst a revival of religion, and with it that of religious art, can never be entirely excluded as a possibility, for the time being at least, Dostoevsky can be regarded as the last Christian writer, the last man of art and literature for whom religion is not just the personal piety of the author but also the very principle of aesthetic creation. Devotion, for him, guides the artist's hand, it selects his material and determines the form of his work. Art and literature, as they now exist, are god-forsaken. At least in the field of the aesthetic, Nietzsche's prophecy has, for better or worse, been fulfilled.

A more complex picture emerges if we examine the hegemony of *philosophy* over art and literature. The situation is more complex in that philosophical hegemony as distinct from the religious to which philosophy had once also been subordinated, does not have a long history. Nor had it ever been accepted either by authors or by audiences as a 'natural' kind of domination. In whatever form philosophy claimed authority over art and literature, it has almost always been deeply resented, resisted and denounced as the intrusion of a foreign power. And yet, in several different forms, philosophy has continually shaped the fate of the arts and literature for almost two centuries. It tried to fill the god-forsaken vacuum by creating a *this-wordly moral mission* for art and literature. In Nietzsche's campaign against Schiller, the *Moraltrompeter von Säckingen*, as well as in Baudelaire's cult of the 'immoral artist', we can hear the clamour of this particular battlefield reverberating. These days, the idea of a 'moral mission', once so vehemently affirmed and rejected, only lives in the catechisms of state-sponsored pseudo-art and pseudo-literature. Furthermore, philosophy introduced the novel concepts of 'progression' and 'regression', and with them, those of a 'healthy' versus a 'decadent' art and literature in a field which, for nearly all its history, had been unfamiliar with them. The art and literature of the 'high cultures' had always lived under the sign of *perfection* (that of the masterpiece, the canonic work of art, the best possible achievement which, by definition, cannot be surpassed) and of the *immortality* of the perfect art-work. But neither of these categories needed, or for that matter comprised, the binary concepts of 'progression' and 'regression'. Similarly, art and literature had always been familiar with success and fiasco, with the 'blessing' conferred on one artist but denied to another by superior forces; with 'vulgar' and 'sublime' types of work and enjoyment, but not with 'healthy' or 'decadent' masterpieces. The categories of 'progress', 'regression', 'health' and 'decadence' were unmistakably philosophical products of the period which created 'universal history', evolutionism and science as a dominating worldview. Therefore, once the seemingly infallible but short-term authority of all these concepts was shaken, the artist who had always sensed their alienness to his own problems, quickly got rid of them, and the audience soon followed suit. For the postmodernist artists or recipients, they are hollow 'ideologies' of the 'Holy Family', or a priestly caste who tyrannize an initially unrestrained artistic activity. Finally, to conclude a very short list of examples which could be extended *ad libitum*, it was philosophy that, in consecutive waves of idolization of the past, had been erecting tradition as an infallible standard and authority before art and literature as if the latter, left to itself, were incapable of coordinated action. Since the *querelle des anciens et des modernes*, counter-tendencies have always arisen from the ranks of artists and writers. Yet Peter Bürger is perhaps right in regarding the period of twentieth-century modernism or avant-garde as the crucial interlude in this process.[4] It was crucial in a dual sense: the avant-garde rejected the *whole* of tradition comprising all its antecedents in a single global negative term of 'the art of the museums'. In addition, this time art and literature had at least parts of contemporary philosophy on their side as allies in the revolt against philosophical supremacy. When, however, even this crucial and holistic revolt petered out, nothing was left but the negation of the relevance of the very problem which appeared to be the last step in achieving art and literature's autonomy from philosophy.

The hegemony of *politics* over art and literature is basically a very recent story. In the main, its origins can be traced back not farther than the Jacobin dictatorship, the first period in which the political sphere, this newly separated but at once omnipotent master of the whole of society, appreciated art and literature highly enough to prostitute them into the propagandists of the Terror. Ever since, a pendulum-like movement has characterized the attitudes of artists and writers to political hegemony. Periods of passionate commitment have been followed by an almost total lack of interest in politics, even in the most recent post-war history of Western modernity. Since with a pendulum it is physically impossible to foretell which deflection in a certain direction will be the 'last', caution with forecasts cannot be cast to the wind. However, it seems that, here too, 'postmodernism' has closed a chapter by its eclectic 'anything goes' mentality. The most directly and propagandistically political and the subtly metaphysical blend into one in the felicity of the postmodernist era.

Autonomy from the *economic* sphere needs some conceptual clarification to be properly understood. It is to the dubious glory of Karl Marx's tenets that in the last decades the most problematic and clearly untenable part of his doctrine, that of the hierarchy of base over superstructure, has gained wide recognition even among non-Marxists, in the form of a politically non-committed but 'materialist' academic subject: the sociology of art and literature. Therefore, in discussing emancipation from the economic sphere, I do not propose to tackle this doctrinal controversy, only the much narrower problem as to what extent, if at all, the economic sphere has generated ideas, attitudes, inclinations and the like which have influenced art and literature. For the initial socialist radicalism, this was not a particularly sensitive question. Marx assumed that capitalism was hostile to art and literature by which he simply meant that a society based on generalized commodity relations and commodity fetishism is too prosaic and hedonistic to be passionately involved in activities judged 'according to the measure of beauty', which he regarded as the one commensurate with the emancipated human being. It is only much later, in the mid twentieth-century theories of the 'culture industry', that radical thought proposed the idea that the organized centres of a certain section of capitalism directly and consciously control and manipulate the art-work. From here, it was but a short step to the idea that 'the categories of the market' themselves penetrate the structure of the art-work.[5] Again, I do not propose to discuss here to what extent these categories were genuine discoveries, or to what extent they were mere polemical exaggerations. I should like, however, to make the following remark. Even if the whole theory of the 'culture industry' proved to be correct, the influences, the 'ideologies' emanating from those sinister centres of manipulation have never been 'economic ideologies' in any meaningful sense of the word. The culture industry possesses an internal dynamic which strives to impose culture as commodity on ever wider circles of solvent purchasers. Let us assume, for argument's sake, that, to that end, the masters and the hired propagandists of the culture industry could successfully influence both audience and creative artists. Even here, the ideology with which they could achieve such influence must have been 'non-economic' in nature, or else the spell would immediately have been broken. In this sense, the *spiritual* influence of the economic over the aesthetic sphere (and it is a mutual spiritual influencing of distinct spheres that we are discussing here) has always been, and has remained, *indirect*. It is precisely this circumstance that made a special struggle for autonomy on the part of art and literature against the economic sphere quite superfluous, irrespective of the sociologically extremely relevant issue as to what extent artists and art works are still dependent on the culture industry.

The most complex relationship between spheres, the one in which the claim to absolute autonomy, though often raised, seems to be almost theoretically impossible for art and literature, obtains between the aesthetic sphere and that of 'life'. Beyond the sempiternal contrast of 'life' and 'art', modernity has produced yet another pendulum-like dynamic in art and literature's relationship to 'life'. Periods of a sharp emphasis on 'proximity to life', on 'fidelity to nature' are followed, almost on schedule, by 'antirealist' waves where the real can only be grasped through what is unreal, what is the negation of the really existing. *Ethically*, the same dynamic applies. High priests of the 'aestheticization of life' follow in the footsteps of prophets who are outraged by the 'immoral' attempts at reducing 'sacred' life to a mere raw material for artistic and literary experiments. And then the movement of the pendulum starts anew. As mentioned, it is highly unlikely for theoretical reasons that postmodernism can totally eliminate the contrast between 'life' and 'art'. A complete merger of the two, by eliminating the relevance of the distinction, is almost inconceivable. Yet the much too disinterested gaze of the autonomous observer, this typically postmodernist attitude which regards both 'realist' and 'antirealist' views, the aesthete of life and the prophet preaching against aestheticization alike as members of the same ideological 'Holy Family', suggests that here too postmodernist attitudes have pushed the barriers as far as possible.

The second dimension of self-liberation is *emancipation or liberation within the aesthetic sphere*. Its gradual unfolding is not unrelated to the unfolding of external liberation: autonomy. Rather the contrary is the case. The more autonomous the aesthetic sphere becomes, the more its own, that is, the 'genuinely aesthetic' principles tend to dominate art-works and their reception. The first stage of emancipation, *the dismantling of canonic prescriptions* had already come to a close before the dawn of modernity. The final resurgence of canonic art and literature was the cult of classicism prior to, during, and subsequent to the French Revolution. But even in this period of fairly synthetic canons, the elements of the recognition of highly individualistic, even idiosyncratic ways of creating art and literature had been accumulating. And the idea of canonically regulating the rules of art and literature has never since been revived with the sole exception of so-called socialist realism whose canonic principles resemble court orders rather than aesthetic recommendations.

For a while, the idea that each and every art-work presents an *incommensurable individuality* which has to be appropriated and interpreted in its own right, instead of being explained against the more general background of *styles* and *genres*, seemed to be a further step on the road towards emancipation.[6] However, in this century, attacks by emancipators have become gradually targeted on individuality as an alleged additional obstacle to internal liberation. Walter Benjamin's assault on *aura*, as the hallmark of such fully-fledged individuality, is now well-known. It was precisely because of such anti-auratic inclinations that I have referred to him as the forerunner of postmodernism.[7] The anti-auratic efforts, and the stress on the multiplicability, repeatability and the free and idiosyncratic interpretability of art-works was an 'emancipatory' act in so far as it was part and parcel of the drive against the presence of *any rules* in the aesthetic sphere. Even the principles, varying from art-work to art-work, with the aid of which the individual artist organizes his or her individual art-work, appear to the 'proto-postmodernist' as a straitjacket for both creation and interpretation.

A further step on the road to 'internal liberation', that is, emancipation, was *the theoretical and practical dismantling of the unified concept of art*. That this concept was a latecomer and an artificially created one, is proven beyond any doubt by the simple fact that several languages, including English, do not even possess the term. The English words 'art' or 'arts' are not identical with the German *Kunst*. To be sure, there are even now temporary relapses into old habits, for example through the illegitimate extension of the term 'language' to the non-lingual arts. It was in this sense that, for example, Adorno tried to construct a consistent theory of 'musical language'. The main trend is, however, the progressive separation of domains which had in any case only been unified by a philosophical theory, and not by the needs of artists, writers and audiences. Moreover, early attempts presented themselves, almost in the immediate aftermath of the victory by the zealots of unification at the end of the nineteenth century, which questioned both the legitimacy and the fruitfulness of such a unification.[8] Emancipation from the philosophical concept of 'art' as *Kunst* meant at least as much for the 'internal liberation' as did the dismantling of canons, genre and stylistic prescriptions. There was no longer any mandatory need, either for the artist or for the recipient, to watch anxiously for 'progress' in the allegedly related and intertwined fields of the other arts. Each form of art moved in its own medium without being bothered by the artificial demands of a 'parallel progress'.

The *closed, durable and lasting* character of the art-work as *objectivation* has also come to be challenged. In an era when graffiti, drawn on the subway one day only to be removed on the next by cleaners, as well as the arabesques of a 'firework artist' which disappear in the very moment of realization, claim artistic equivalence, with an untroubled conscience, to printed books, recorded compositions, framed and permanently exhibited paintings, the bases of the art-work as a closed objectivation are clearly eroding. Of course, the central category of this new development is the 'happening'. Susan Sontag who is usually and, in my view, incorrectly, regarded as the American popularizer of modernism, and who was, perhaps unwittingly, one of the most important forerunners of postmodernism, in a period when the term had not even been coined, discerned the artistic potentials of the happening in a brilliant essay a long time ago.[9] A happening is the negation *sui generis* of the art-work as a closed and durable objectivation. To start with, a happening is not an objectivation at all, it is rather a loose conglomerate of interacting subjects without any prior choreography, prescription or blueprint. Further, it is not closed *spatially* (or at least it is very difficult to mark the limits of a happening in space) and while it is closed *temporally* (in the sense that it begins and ends), it can be repeated anew any time on the basis of the same principle which is an absence of organizing principles. Finally, it is a living refutation of the *aere perennius* art-work, of durability. The point in setting up a happening is not that it lasts forever but that it happens here and now.

A further, similarly late, development of internal liberation (or emancipation) is the breaking through of the barriers separating 'low' and 'high' types of artistic activities. This trend has been considerably enhanced by a most recent development, which is as 'progressive' in its goals as it is problematic in its outcome. This is the generally anti-authoritarian drive of the last decades resulting in the overall undermining of *any kind* of authority (including what Agnes Heller calls the 'revelatory authority' of art-works)[10] and the undermining of *any kind* of elite without which the distinction between the culturally 'high' and 'low' *historically* could never have been made and certainly *cannot now* be made. I do not propose to tackle this vexed problem here *in extenso*, I would only remark in passing that the existence of cultural elites *without social and political prerogatives* is at least conceivable and, in such a form, desirable. But once the very distinction between 'high' and 'low' appears as the stigma of 'elitism' which artist, critic, and recipient alike try to shed with equal horror, once the now fashionable ideas of an 'aesthetic productionism' declare the artist or writer an 'autonomous producer' and remove the 'myth' of aesthetic value in the same breath, the last taboo is eliminated from the path of an uninhibited drive towards the *total* external and internal liberation of art and literature. Aesthetic activity stands before us with its newly gained, complete internal and external freedom. The postmodernist era has been launched.

II

The first and most conspicuous problem with giving any working definition of postmodernism consists in *its own negative self-definition*. *Post*modernism, like many of its conceptual brethren, *post*-revolutionary or *post*-industrial society, *post* x-structuralism and the like, understand themselves not in terms of what they are but in terms of what they come after. This constellation shows a marked difference to the emergence of modernism. Modernism made its appearance with much fanfare and, sometimes, bombastic manifestos. The latter can in retrospect be refuted bit by bit; the substantiality, the truth-claim and the feasibility of each and every postulate can equally be disproven. And yet, no retrospective critical campaign will change the fact that the modernists were clearly aware of the positive contents of their intentions. They knew what they stood for and what they wanted to achieve. Once actors, or those who speak in the name of actors, sum up their message by pointing to the temporal fact that they locate themselves 'after' something, they unambiguously indicate their 'otherness', their alienness to the spirit of a previous period, and the authenticity of this message should not be questioned simply because of the absence of a positive programme. However, a self-description of this kind also reveals the actor's uncertainty about his or her own self-identity and this gives the observers a dangerously wide latitude of arbitrary interpretation.

A second problem lies in the fact that all *substantive criteria* through which the postmodernist syndrome can be approached, are *equally negative in nature*. Postmodernists do *not* intend to accept the hegemony of other spheres over the unrestrained activity of the aesthetic sphere. They are *not* prepared to put up with prefabricated theoretical requirements. They do *not* tolerate closed art-works and their inherent standards *nor* do they bear with the presence of paradigmatic personalities (either in the form of representative art-works or of representative artists). They are *against* tradition for it is an oppressive authority, they are equally *against* modernism for it 'has sold out to the arts of the museum'. And whenever interpreters venture any further and try to establish *positive* principles by which to identify the postmodernist art-work and distinguish it from what is not postmodernist, they invariably end up empty-handed. This statement is not intended as a denigration. Interpreters of an allegedly positively definable postmodernist art-work are every bit as sophisticated as their predecessors but the fundamentally negative character of the elusive phenomenon they are dealing with takes its revenge upon them. As a seminal reading of *The Crying of Lot 49* by David Bennett testifies,[11] the microscopic scrutiny of supposedly postmodernist features yields categories which could have been gained from an analysis of any art-work from the whole post Second World War period.

But what is perhaps the most spectacular aspect of our dilemma is brought to light if we ask the perplexingly simple, even outright naive question: *who are the postmodernists?* To put the dilemma in perspective, a question like this would obviously have been absurd with regard to the modernists. The modernist movements, the artists and writers who termed themselves modernist, were there audibly and visibly, with their scandals, provocations, works and manifestos, and the latter contained the organizing principles of, even the blueprints for, the works to be created. The critics, steadily increasing in number, who raised modernism to the pedestal of a new dogma, were equally conspicuously there. For half a century they even dominated almost all the influential publications on art and literature. Finally, their followers, in ever increasing numbers, were equally present and they were more than happy to distinguish themselves from what they termed the 'traditional', the 'conservative' recipients, and the 'habitual' audience. In addition, the zealots of modernism could even give (good or bad) reasons for their enthusiasm for modernism.

Nothing like this is in evidence in the case of the postmodernist syndrome. There is no distinguishable artistic or literary group or individuality which would call itself 'postmodernist' albeit many of them make vague references to postmodernism whenever they want to make use of an unrestrained *poetica licentia* in one respect or another. Artists and writers keep identifying themselves through the use of modernist terms of group cohesion such as minimalist (in music or painting), abstract expressionist, neo-naturalist, concept art and the like. Critics do use the term 'postmodernism' extensively without identifying themselves with it for the very good reason that they, perhaps better than anyone else, know how difficult it would be, if pinned down, to account in a *positive form* for what they advocate. In this atmosphere of entirely negative principles of self-identification, based on what one is not, on a non-localizable actor, would it not be the most sober solution to understand the new development in terms of a 'literary conspiracy theory'? Is it not simply the last chapter in the long story of so many fashionable fictions by the learned and the professional who concocted a new theory and coined a new label for their selfish purposes only to abandon it for the next season's fashion?

My analysis of the 'war of liberation' of art and literature suggests a more serious treatment of the phenomenon. *I conceive the present postmodernist constellation as a Pyrrhic victory in this war of liberation.* The victory was complete but one akin to Pyrrhus' legendary feat: it has brought disaster on the victor. 'Disaster' here has a dual meaning. Firstly, art and literature are now 'free' from, or rather deprived of, all bonds which link them with other spheres of social life, without those beneficial 'external determinations' which Goethe regarded as crucial for each and every fruitful epoch of aesthetic activity. But secondly, and perhaps more importantly, complete emancipation, in a strange dialectic, annihilates complete autonomy. If 'internal liberation', emancipation, is complete to the degree that all rules and norms *specific to the aesthetic sphere* are eliminated, then, one may ask, in what sense will the aesthetic sphere be different to any other? But if it is not, in what sense is it autonomous with regard to them? The postmodernists seem to be cognizant of this constellation but they seem to react to it with indifference.

The postmodernist feeling of 'being after' is therefore serious and signifies considerably more than a mere passing vogue. Those who identify with postmodernism are, indeed, after traditionalists and moderns, they place themselves after periods which had a mission beyond the *sensu stricto* aesthetic. The 'postmodernists', by which I mean all artists, authors, interpreters and recipients alike who have the feeling of 'being after', haughtily turn down all identification with any of these missions, with any requirements or influences emanating from 'alien' spheres. In my view, postmodernism is nothing but the very feeling of 'being after', the expression of the Pyrrhic victory of art and literature in their war of liberation. In this sense, it is a tangible, palpable, theoretically circumscribable entity, something that exists and is more than the figment of the critics' minds who long for a new catchword to entertain their audience. But precisely in this capacity, it is a barren feeling from which (and this is stated with an unrepentant allegiance paid to a long line of tradition) no lasting and paradigmatic works will spring, one which has to be reduced to an intermezzo if art and literature are to be revived. And it is precisely in its capacity of 'being after' that postmodernism cannot but gain a merely negative definition, it cannot but create a merely negative community of denial and rejection, and can never constitute the positive bonds of common goals and aspirations.

At this point, however, two questions inevitably arise. Firstly, how can we know, and with what degree of certainty, that the 'war of liberation' has reached this final, and Pyrrhic, stage of victory? Is this not a mere assumption of the postmodernists or of the analyst? Secondly, even if this is the case, even if the cultural constellation we are living in is indeed that of the aftermath of a Pyrrhic victory, why has it occurred right now? What kind of explanation can be offered for such an intermezzo beyond the internal dynamic of the aesthetic sphere?

My reply to the first question is perforce agnostic, at least to a degree. In fact, we cannot state with absolute certainty whether or not the 'war of liberation' has reached the stage of total victory, Pyrrhic or otherwise. It may very well be the case that we are confronting the self-delusions of present actors (including this writer). In fact, in some senses we are certainly confronting such self-delusions. For example, it is clear to me that one of the most representative 'postmodernist' composers, Philip Glass, is caught up in the same dilemma as many earlier masters included in Adorno's analysis of 'modern' music. The dilemma is how time, progression, *durée* can be rendered in 'rational' musical forms. The endless self-repetition of Glass's music, a technique which most recently has found its followers in postmodernist theatre as well (with the significant difference that the postmodernist stage couples repetition with the improvization of a happening in an 'actors' liberation movement'), is a *philosophically* motivated form of coping with the problem of time-flow and *durée*. In this sense, once again the stimulus comes from outside, from philosophy whose tutelage has allegedly been shed by a totally autonomous art. Although the example attests to an existing self-delusion, the feeling of victory counts. It can be a triumphant feeling or one full of resignation. But whichever it is, the feeling of 'being after', a *desideratum*, not necessarily an accurate description of facts, fills an increasing number of modern artists and writers. And it is this syndrome that I want to denote with the projected (Pyrrhic) conclusion of the 'war of liberation'.

If we are searching for causes, I recommend avoiding explanations in the *durée*: more often than not, they are misleading and hollow when applied to extremely recent phenomena. Naturally, the whole dynamic guiding both external and internal liberation, the drive for autonomy and emancipation alike could be deduced from the general tendencies of modernity. But an understanding like this would hardly account for an atmosphere and an attitude which has been with us for not much longer than a decade. Here, therefore, is my explanation in the 'short' *durée*: Europe, by which I mean the culturally active nucleus of Western modernity wherever its actors may be located geographically, *has become a museum in the post Second World War period*. It is not that modernism has 'sold out' to 'the museum' for mysterious, or plainly pecuniary, reasons; rather, the whole cultural dynamic has undergone a process of 'museification'. 'European culture' is still with us, it shines with the brilliance of bygone high cultures, but it is an exhibit on display, and no longer a culturally driving force. It has visitors, but it does not have followers. It can, and indeed has, become an academic subject-matter worldwide, but at least for the time being, it is a dead volcano. No list of stars, no catalogue of good, even brilliant, artists can change the feeling of this 'museification' in many of its ardent admirers.

It is not my task here to address the wider connotations of this 'museification of Europe'. Therefore, I can only briefly indicate certain reasons for it. 'Europe', including its culture, had an enormous, indeed a primary, responsibility for the catastrophe which befell humankind in the War, yet it could provide no leadership once it regained its equilibrium afterwards. Rather, it has become the permanently crippled member of the family of developed nations which needs support and assistance. Furthermore, 'Europe' could cope neither politically nor culturally with the new forms of modernity, arising from its womb, from its own culture, each of them denying with its existence the very message in whose name the so-called 'European idea', in short, the message of the Enlightenment, had been conceived. 'Europe' has lost, together with its possessions outside geographic Europe, the unassailable self-confidence which filled European hearts both on the left and the right throughout the nineteenth century. It has lost the conviction that one day, the whole of the world will be 'European' in a cultural sense. True to the spirit of declining worlds, which learn to relativize their deities in the face of imported foreign gods, 'Europe' humbly inserts itself and its culture in yet another postmodernist innovation, into a 'wider context' of all cultures which are supposedly all equivalent. Finally, 'Europe', this museum, no longer has a dynamic imaginary of the future. If it has any conception of what lies ahead, not untypically it is the dreaded image of a universal Doomsday. It is hardly surprising in this atmosphere to find that 'European' art, if it intends to be more than a museum exhibit, cannot but flaunt its empty freedom, this Pyrrhic victory, over the bonds linking the aesthetic with other spheres, over bonds which were not all fetters but, at least in the case of some of them, genuine lifelines.

In the debate about postmodernism, Andreas Huyssen has asked, with irony and warning: who wants to become the Lukács of postmodernism?[12] This paper certainly harbours no such personal ambitions. Nor does it suggest a restoration of a cultural *ancien régime* as an ideal. In all probability, certain forms of our cultural heritage have become closed stories now and cannot be continued. Let me mention one area which is particularly close to my heart: as far as music is concerned, in the form Western men and women have understood it for almost three centuries, it seems to have become extinct for the foreseeable future of any generation living now. Since we are all infected with a certain need for evolution, even the anti-evolutionists among us, we cannot help viewing this perspective with melancholy feelings. But it is not perforce a tragic perspective. Perhaps we only share a fate in common with the literary elite of the sixteenth and seventeenth centuries for whom, before the rise of the genuinely great modern poetry, this genre seemed to have reached its never surpassable peak with the Latin poets. Thus they found their pleasure and edification in constantly re-reading and re-interpreting Horace. Furthermore, there are extremely stimulating aspects of the 'war of liberation' despite its present Pyrrhic stage. Our view of art and literature has become more pluralistic by abandoning the philosophically unified concept of 'art' which was one and indivisible. However that may be, for one who has not entirely lost the sense of what art and literature have been since time immemorial, a critical attitude to postmodernism and its background, the Pyrrhic victory in the 'war of liberation', is indispensable. For aesthetic activity can become free from everything except one inherent and dynamic feature:

rendering meaning to life at least in some sense. The title that predicts a postmodernist *intermezzo* suggests a degree of optimism in this respect.

NOTES

1. The persuasive force of the example he uses, Renaissance (especially Florentine) painting, is debatable, for the thesis can be argued the other way round as well. The point Lukács makes is that the vastness, the architectonic beauty and the organized yet natural harmony of High Renaissance painting, from Giotto to Leonardo, results from the gradual secularization of the great Florentines and Venetians. However, it can be asserted with almost equally persuasive force that the internal coherence of this organized and harmonic world is the result of a firmly existing framework provided by a not particularly passionate but solid religious consensus which serves as *lingua franca* for both artist and recipient irrespective of the subjective devotion of the former. In fact, this has been argued by A. Hauser in his book on mannerism, *Mannerism: The Crisis of the Renaissance and the Origin of Modern Art* (London: Routledge, 1965). Hauser deduced the attractive eccentricity of mannerist painters from the loss of this consensus which was not to be replaced by a merely subjective piety which could eventually be more vehement (or more hysterical) than the mildly religious atmosphere exuded by High Renaissance paintings. The same problematic is explored by Adorno in his analysis of the *Missa Solemnis*.
2. An example of the continuity of the problem in Lukács's life is provided by the place Dante occupies in his narrative of the history of epic poetry in *The Theory of the Novel*. The polite admiration Lukács displays towards the *Divina Commedia* never conceals his firm conviction that Dante's unique solution may reach an inimitable peak but that it remains a sublime episode and does not offer a royal road. The vocabulary of *The Theory of the Novel*, for reasons well known to those who are acquainted with Lukács, does not include the term 'liberation'. However, the text suggests that epic poetry had to 'tear itself away' from the adoration of Dante's cathedral of words in order to return to its proper itinerary and to reach its destination.
3. Gadamer's well-known interpretation in *Truth and Method*, sees in Kant's *Critique of Judgement*, and in Schiller's aesthetic theory, the pernicious subjectivization of aesthetic experience and interpretation.
4. Peter Bürger, *Theory of the Avant-Garde* (1984). See 'Select Bibliography'.
5. This assumption has always remained to some extent mysterious and unclarified. Lucien Goldmann made a well-known attempt to deduce

the form of the novel from a 'homology' with the marketplace. But when it came to a detailed elaboration of precisely what this homology meant, the answers invariably remained ambiguous and too wide to cover completely the particular problem that was raised by the very idea of a 'homology'.
6. I cannot even attempt here to indicate the tortuous way in which the emancipation of both individual art-work and the individuality of the artist or writer from genre and stylistic postulates was achieved. It will suffice to hint at the fact that this process is, at least in one respect, the story of the emergence of what we now call 'aesthetics' from the Procrustean bed of a traditional poetics. The latter had as its point of departure the firm conviction that single works of art and literature could, and should, be deduced from the general principles of styles and from the equally general rules of genres. Aesthetics sought to balance the results of this stage of emancipation, by defending the new incommensurable individuality *and* by establishing universal philosophical principles for the interpretation of works in this new situation. Hegel's *Aesthetics* was the first major step in this direction, the efforts of Romanticism constituted the second, and Lukács's early Heidelberg philosophy of art, as well as his late *opus magnum, The Specificity of the Aesthetic*, the third, and in all probability the final, step.
7. See my 'Lukács and Benjamin: Parallels and Contrasts', *New German Critique*, 34 (1985).
8. A well-known example of such questioning is to be found in the aesthetic writings of Fiedler and Hildebrandt.
9. In her *Against Interpretation* (New York: Strauss and Farrar, 1973).
10. Agnes Heller, *The Power of Shame* (London: Routledge and Kegan Paul, 1985), p. 54 and passim.
11. 'Parody, Postmodernism and the Politics of Reading', in P. Petr, D. Roberts and P. Thomson (eds), *Comic Relations: Studies in the Comic, Satire and Parody* (Frankfurt/Main: Peter Lang, 1985).
12. Andreas Huyssen, 'The Search for Tradition: Avantgarde and Postmodernism in the 1970s', *New German Critique*, 22 (1981).

CHAPTER 6

The Cultural Contradictions of Postmodernity

Boris Frankel

Sociology has long been familiar with the contradictions associated with the transition from pre-industrial to industrial society. Its central and opposed themes, such as *Gemeinschaft* and *Gesellschaft*, religion and secularization, mechanical and organic solidarity, individual and community, security and freedom, freedom and necessity, ego and id, each, in very different ways, encapsulates these contradictions of the transition. As a discipline, sociology has sought to explain how whole new lifestyles were constructed around the factory system, the automobile and the office, and to identify the new social problems thus precipitated. The major cultural and social tensions which confront both capitalist and communist societies, in varying degrees, have been variously analysed and described, not only by what might loosely be termed 'mainstream sociology', but also, more recently, by different versions of 'post-industrial theory'. Of especial interest, for my purposes as a socialist, is the work of those left-wing interpreters of contemporary society, Rudolf Bahro, André Gorz, Alvin Toffler and, in Australia, Barry Jones, whose essentially optimistic visions of the future have come to constitute a distinctively 'post-industrial' version of utopian political thought. Capitalist societies have been conflict ridden for most of their existence, but in recent decades, the public and private disputes over education, law, gender relations, family forms, gay rights, religion, the role of the media, and so on, have resulted in new splits within traditional left and right parties. The 'cultural contradictions of capitalism' have also polarized the new social movements, such as the Moral Majority and the women's movement, as each side puts forward irreconcilable views on both public and private life. In so far as Toffler, Bahro and Gorz articulate a range of alternative views, popular since the 1960s, on sexual, religious and other cultural and political relations, their views have a political immediacy, as opponents of the New Right, which makes them more than mere speculative ravings in futurology.

Two contrasting themes seem to be evident in post-industrial utopianism. One, that best represented by Bahro and by many anarchists, environmentalists, Maoists and utopian socialists, can be succinctly described as the 'revolt against modernity'.[1] A future socialist society is conceived as a tranquil, simple, harmonious answer to the complex, conflict-ridden, bureaucratized, monolithic and alienated present. Bahro's 'basic commune' is basic in its very essence: back to nature, back to basic needs, back to face-to-face relations, back to small communal experiences and peace. Of course, none of these objectives is in itself undesirable – far from it. But what is missing from these and similar utopian longings is any awareness that life might not be able to become so uncomplicated, so happily free from cultural contradictions. The other dominant theme in post-industrial theory is the belief that virtually all the cultural contradictions of the present, with its epidemics of addiction, suicide and violence, can be resolved by even more diversity, technical innovation, demassification and destandardization. In this regard, Toffler is the paradigmatic case of unreflective optimism. Every major institution, from the national government through to churches, schools, political parties, law agencies, media, hospitals, is conceived as being on its last legs or subject to radical transformation. Yet all this dissolution of the old, and the reconstruction of new post-industrial institutions, is seen as an almost problem-free process. Certainly, Toffler and others recognize the millions of casualties created as new family relations, work processes, cultural institutions and ways of thinking disturb the security and power of the old. But these problems are regarded only as ones of *transition*, rather than as cultural and social contradictions of any conceivable fully established new order. Thus, whilst Bahro yearns for the reduction of complexity, Toffler can romanticize complexity and so minimize the dysfunctional and disagreeable effects of new technology and new lifestyles.

But how could electronic environments which 'converse with you', a mass proliferation of demassified political-economic structures, individualized media outlets, the simultaneous decentralization of life and development of a 'planetary consciousness', how could all of these radical changes which Toffler anticipates, occur without serious cultural contradictions? This is not the place to engage in an exercise in cultural futurology. But it is possible to analyse and query some of the socio-cultural changes predicted by these post-industrial utopians. Toffler's mindless pluralism is no more a guarantor of cultural solidarity and democracy than the prevailing form of bourgeois pluralism in the OECD countries is the answer to social inequality and social alienation. In *Future Shock* (1970), Toffler presented a smorgasbord of every conceivable lifestyle and technical innovation. Yet he also catalogued the physical and mental costs of endless novelty and diversity: anxiety, stress, mental illness, information overload, social disintegration and loss of direction.[2] Ten years later, Toffler still suffers from some of the symptoms of this earlier bout of pop sociology, but *The Third Wave* is nonetheless less gimmicky, and more subdued. Toffler proclaims that, for all the social diversity of post-industrial societies:

> any decent society must generate a feeling of community. . . . Community offsets loneliness. It gives people a vitally necessary sense of belonging. Yet today the institutions on which community depends are crumbling in all the techno-societies.[3]

This immediately raises a fundamental question which Toffler fails to answer: if existing institutions do not provide a sense of community, and yet the future is expected to contain even more of the pluralistic forms which are thriving at the moment, how can community and meaning rise from the ashes of Second Wave social catastrophe? The problem of community, diversity and 'decency' invariably raises the related issues of whether contemporary social movements seek to deepen and radicalize the values, institutions and promises of 'modernity' or whether they are the most visible manifestations of the 'postmodern' departure from the modern epoch.

Recent years have witnessed the emergence of at least three separate discourses involving various notions of 'modernity' and 'postmodernity': firstly, an essentially aesthetic discourse on the nature of modernism and postmodernism; secondly, a discourse constructed around the debate between conservative or neo-conservative social and political theorists and their liberal and radical opponents, over the kinds of institutions and social relations which should exist in contemporary society; and thirdly, a discourse which might more appropriately be described as a set of disputes, arising from within the Marxist tradition, between proponents of post-structuralism, neo-Weberianism and post-Marxism. All three discourses, in aesthetics, on the future of society, and in the confrontation with the Marxist tradition, have overlapped with each other and with the whole emergent discussion of post-industrialism. As Jean-François Lyotard, one of the key postmodern disputants, explains: 'Our working hypothesis is that the status of knowledge is altered as societies enter what is known as the post-industrial age and cultures enter what is known as the postmodern age'.[4] These various conceptions of the postmodern clearly have some real bearing on any discussion of the shape that might be taken by a post-industrial culture and public sphere. Bahro, Gorz, Toffler and Jones very obviously still adhere to the tradition of the European Enlightenment. Although Toffler, and to a lesser extent Gorz and Jones, flirt with various 'postmodern' aesthetic and scientific practices, their representative images of post-industrialism remain animated and informed by the Enlightenment project of bringing reason to bear on public and private life. Bahro may reject the technical rationality of industrial society, Toffler and Jones may superficially agree with Lyotard that knowledge and its legitimation is altered in post-industrial societies, and Gorz may attack the religious fundamentalism of orthodox Marxist moral absolutism; but all four theorists believe that post-industrialism will maximize democracy, freedom, tolerance, equality and the other rationalist values which constitute the legacy of the European Enlightenment. In this respect, they stand in stark contrast to the nihilism, relativism and loss of direction which characterize much post-structuralist and postmodern thought.

Doubtless, the aesthetic discourse about 'postmodern' culture has raised very important issues. But it is important to note that what is lacking in post-industrial theory is precisely what is also lacking in much of the discussion about modernity and postmodernity. There appears to be little agreement in either discourse about the periodization of modernity, about whether, for example, one society, or even one part of society is pre-modern, modern or postmodern. At times, modernity and postmodernity are periodized according to changes in only one area, for instance, changes in art or technology. Hence Perry Anderson's agnostic stance towards the concept of modernity:

> On the one hand, from Weber through to Ortega, Eliot to Tate, Leavis to Marcuse, 20th-century modernity has been

relentlessly condemned as an iron cage of conformity and mediocrity, a spiritual wilderness of populations bleached of any organic community or vital autonomy. On the other hand, against these visions of cultural despair, in another tradition stretching from Marinetti to Le Corbusier, Buckminster Fuller to Marshall McLuhan, not to speak of outright apologists of capitalist 'modernization theory' itself, modernity has been fulsomely touted as the last word in sensory excitement and universal satisfaction, in which a machine-built civilization itself guarantees aesthetic thrills and social felicities. What each side has in common here is a simple identification of modernity with technology itself – radically excluding the people who produce and are produced by it.[5]

Clearly, Bahro has more in common with Anderson's first, 'anti-modern' group, whilst Toffler remains closer to the second, 'pro-modern' group. The ease with which post-industrial theorists file diverse political economies and cultures under a single label ('industrial', 'Second Wave', etc.) is replicated in much usage of such vague categories as modern and postmodern. But to grasp the historically specific nature of uneven development, whether in the sphere of science, morality, art, particular branches of capitalist and non-capitalist industry, state administration or welfare services, is crucial to any overall understanding of the manner in which these diverse practices interconnect. The central weakness in Fredric Jameson's much vaunted essay on postmodernism[6] is surely its vague use of essentialist concepts such as 'late capitalism' and the 'world market', each deployed so as to bolster his determinedly positive view of postmodernity. Mike Davis's penetrating analysis of the connections between speculative finance and certain negative postmodern developments in recent urban American architecture is in fact much more telling precisely because it is much more discriminating.[7] A parallel weakness in Toffler is suggested by the fact that Japan, one of the most advanced sites of high technology, nonetheless exhibits socio-cultural relations which are either 'pre-modern', or at the very least far less 'Third Wave' than those evident in North America. Moreover it remains unclear whether the dramatic cultural changes heralded by Toffler's Third Wave are compatible with Japan's dominance in commodity exports, or whether they would lead to less high-tech innovation, social disintegration and possibly even revolution or authoritarian repression.

In the absence of any clear criteria, it is difficult to know whether countries as diverse as Japan, France or the USSR are modern, postmodern, pre-modern or post-industrial. Of course, the extensive disagreement over the periodization of modernity (did it begin five hundred, two hundred or less than one hundred years ago?), and over the positive and negative responses to modernity by radicals, liberals and conservatives, should not, despite the elasticity of the labels, blind us to the crucial issues. There is much to be said for the various methodological attempts to 'deconstruct' overgeneralized and essentialist concepts, especially in their effort to gain greater historical specificity and awareness of non-identical social developments. But one can distrust model-building without necessarily lapsing into a post-structuralist or postmodernist cynicism and relativism. For all the problems inherent in Habermas's communication theory of society, his project of analysing the unfulfilled elements of modernity, remains fundamentally much more serious than do the various postmodernist rejections of meta-narratives, of subjectivity, and of any overall socio-political objectives.

In 1968 Habermas noted that, in Herman Kahn's list of probable technical innovations in the next thirty years, the first fifty items included: techniques for causing behaviour and personality changes, genetic engineering, and sex changes; drugs for various moods; electronic controls for surveillance and propaganda; and so forth.[8] Many of these probabilities have already become reality. Habermas warned that genetic engineering and psychotechnic manipulation of behaviour would result in a drying-up of the reflective traditions expressed in language and culture, and in the detachment of human behaviour from all value systems.[9] Without some clear notion of the rational, without some set of priorities or hierarchies of value, how could postmodern or post-industrial individuals construct a non-alienated and democratic community? But precisely such a void results from the attempt to disconnect the moral, artistic, scientific and political traditions of earlier historical periods from the struggles and dilemmas confronting contemporary generations. One key instance here is that of determining whether particular values and practices will result in social integration or in disorientation and conflict. Andreas Huyssen addresses the issue, if only obliquely, in his post-structuralist critique of Habermas:

> The critical deconstruction of Enlightenment rationalism . . . the fight of women and gays for a legitimate social and sexual identity outside the parameters of male, heterosexual vision,

the search for alternatives in our relationship with nature, including the nature of our own bodies – all these phenomena, which are key to the culture of the 1970s, make Habermas's proposition to complete the project of modernity questionable, if not undesirable.[10]

But Huyssen avoids the hard problems which flow from a rejection of the Enlightenment tradition. It is one thing to reject technical rationality, male heterosexual definitions of what is 'good' and 'desirable', undifferentiated notions of social and moral progress, and so on; it is quite another to believe that once women, gays and environmentalists have defined their values and priorities, all questions of rationality, equality, democracy in the public, as well as interpersonal private spheres, simply disappear. There is evidence here of a naive belief that, because social movements articulate legitimate values and concerns which are not identical to those of the traditional labour movements, then all these women, gays, and Greens, are somehow not living in the same society, not encountering similar problems to each other of war, economic power, public administration, religion, education, poverty, legal rights, and so on. The answers given by the social movements may very well be different, but any postmodern or post-industrial society will necessarily both have to resolve issues of the public application of reason, and have to solve the issues of how plural identities are to be reconciled with public identities and rights. A future society will hopefully be much freer and more diverse, and yet each citizen in his or her sub-cultural identity must also *share* a sense of belonging, of citizenship, of common rights and responsibilities – unless, that is, we accept an alternative nightmare of fragmentation, particularism and separatism.

Not all post-structuralist theorists are equally cynical or resigned to a directionless future. Michael Ryan, for example, attacks the rationalist tradition, using the works of Derrida and other French deconstructionists.[11] Like Huyssen, Ryan is supportive of feminist and other alternative social movements. According to Ryan:

> Habermas's goal of restoring ego and group identity would no doubt be challenged by socialist feminists who would point out that existing models of social group identity deny validity to those who see their political interests as lying in the breaking of the coercive identity the group imposes on them, by assigning them a place defined by the rationality of the group. The breaking of group identity can

be more crucial to emancipation than the restoration of group identity. And it is the metaphysical idealists, those who find such contradictions intolerable because it denies the rational categories of identity . . . who will brand it as 'irrational' and call for its resolution in the name of rational efficiency and clear knowledge, and at the expense of those such as socialist feminists who have little to gain from the restoration of either categorical or political group identity. What is at stake, then, is a politics of multiple centers and plural strategies, less geared toward the restoration of a supposedly ideal situation held to be intact and good than to the micrological fine-tuning of questions of institutional power, work and reward distribution, sexual political dynamics, resource allocation, domination, and a broad range of problems whose solutions would be situationally and participationally defined.[12]

Ryan's critique of Habermas and the 'metaphysical idealists' should be of great importance to the advocates of a post-industrial, socialist society. Like Toffler, Ryan stresses the problems of transition. But whereas Toffler notes the many potential casualties of changes in conventional Second Wave values, family structures and work practices, Ryan positively welcomes the break up of contemporary coercive group identities. The emancipatory benefits of the dissolution of conservative group identities should not, however, be confused with the attainment of socialist institutions or with the question of how to maintain social reproduction. Ryan's attack on Habermas's socialist rationalism caricatures both his theory and his intentions. Habermas has no interest in the restoration of some ideal ego and group identity in the achievement of a technical rational efficiency based on clear knowledge. Rather, he recognizes, in contrast to the old Frankfurt School, that 'man and nature' can never be fully reconciled, that residual anatagonisms can at best be minimized, but not completely overcome, by rational discourse. Habermas's aim of constructing a new socialist public sphere, based on shared or *generalizable* interests, is one which Ryan is unwilling to accept. Ryan prefers to seek refuge in a pluralist strategy in which problems will be 'situationally and participationally defined'. But this is both a relativist fiction and a politics of the *ad hoc* which would in practice mean power to those who have the numbers. For while Ryan's pluralistically organized participants in specific situations must pose and resolve problems without constant reference to some *a priori* set of absolutes, it would be stretching the possibilities of social co-operation and mutual tolerance beyond belief to suggest that each such situation will produce an entirely new set of values and solutions. Either the various pluralistically organized groups will create and redefine their generalizable interests, based on rational criteria such as equity and the elimination of discrimination based on gender, race, etc., whilst nonetheless retaining their own cultural identities, or they will risk chaos and/or disintegration if each group should seek to deny the need to construct some larger identity of citizenship.

The postmodernist rejection of rationalism, and of the human subject, makes it peculiarly difficult for such thinkers to comprehend the role of religion in both past and present societies, and to understand how a society might cohere after such religious traditions have collapsed. Discussing the differences between religious and secular cultures, Daniel Bell argues that a religious culture

> has a greater unity than most because all the elements of the culture are directed toward some common end: to emphasize mystery, to create awe, to exalt, to transcend. This unity, emphasized in mood, runs like a thread through its architecture, its music, its painting, and its literature – in its spires, liturgies, litanies, spatial representation of figures, and sacred text. Secular cultures rarely have this conscious design.[13]

While Bell and most other neo-conservatives remain troubled by the 'cultural contradictions of capitalism', the problem of cultural unity is in fact one which transcends the specific dimensions of capitalism. Toffler has argued that the proliferation of thousands of religious cults, self-help therapies and superstitious occult practices is a clear sign of the social malaise generated by the disintegration of Second Wave societies.[14] The problem, however, is that Toffler seems to have no idea about how exactly post-industrial changes might affect the survival of religious thought, or of what would be implied by the possibility of its demise. If new concepts of time, causality, space, and new forms of decentralization, should topple centralized economic, political and religious institutions, then either religious thought will be reduced to only a minor cultural role, or the number of cults and other therapies will multiply rapidly as life becomes more home-centred and decentralized. Alternatively, if Toffler's 'planetary consciousness' is to link local people with international communities, then this in turn presupposes either new global religions, or an extension of secularization beyond the bounds of the existing residues of religious tradition. While

Toffler resists Bell's call for 'a new sense of the sacred', he appears unable, like the postmodernists, to do any more than celebrate the passing of the old. But the demise of religious traditions surely necessitates some concern about the secular values which could possibly unite people in their diversity. José Casanova poses the problem well in his discussion of Bell's yearning to save modernity from meaninglessness:

> Bell identifies the sacred with Benjamin's concept of 'aura'. But if art in the age of mechanical reproduction becomes 'post-auratic', should we not expect the same of religion? Can modern or postmodern religion, in the age of administrative and technological manipulation of symbols, rituals and meanings, be anything but post-auratic, i.e., post-sacral? The experience of the sacred presupposes a collective sacred cosmos. But can such a cosmos be reconstructed once it has been broken?[15]

If secularized post-industrial societies are to survive then we simply cannot afford the cynical, fashion conscious vandalism of a postmodernism which attacks not only the religious tradition itself, but also the basis of post-sacral secularization, that is, European rationalism. Today, even the two opposed wings of the Catholic church, the Polish theological conservatives, and the Third World liberation theologians, have become the bearers of secularization in their respective fights for democracy and equality. Unless one chooses to value rationality in public life, then there are no grounds for arguing that democratic participation is preferable to dictatorship, arbitrariness, technocratic efficiency or occult ritual.

The need for certain clearly articulated principles to govern public life can hardly be over-emphasized. But public life rests on more than a commitment to ideals, whether religious, secular, democratic or authoritarian. Historically, we have witnessed the formation of nation states out of the polar extremes of parochial fiefdoms and transnational empires. The uneven development of nationalism, in both its emancipatory and reactionary moments, has coincided chronologically both with the diverse struggles of labour movements and civil liberty groups, and with the growth of inter-imperialist rivalries. Despite the proliferation of local, regional and sub-cultural public spheres, most of their members have also continued to recognize their connections to larger national public spheres. These public spheres were by no means necessarily bastions of democracy, tolerance and equality. But, within their own respectively defined limits, they remained both public and participatory, and the fact that participation in public institutions, whether establishment or oppositional, is as low as it is in the advanced capitalist countries, with their relatively free electoral processes, presents us with very serious problems indeed. The possibility of new forms of knowledge, the alteration of commodified time-space relations,[16] the proliferation of endless therapies and 'truths', all signify the enormity of the obstacles to the attainment of a new post-industrial, socialist public sphere. If the cultural and interpersonal dynamics of apathy, and of withdrawal into the private sphere, are not accidental, then the continuation of privatizing cultural and political practices into post-industrial society will almost certainly prove disastrous.

The Frankfurt School argued that the dialectic of enlightenment consisted in the unleashing of contradictory forces: on the one hand, the belief in reason, tolerance and emancipation from enslavement, on the other, the positivistic forces of technical rationality which sought domination over external nature and internal human nature.[17] In recent years, writers such as Richard Sennett and Christopher Lasch have warned of the 'fall of public man' and the 'culture of narcissism'. Both Lasch and Sennett criticize the contemporary preoccupation with self-discovery and liberation of the inner self, the transformation of social problems into problems of personality, the inability to 'feel', and so forth. The paradoxical consequence of 'getting in touch with oneself' is the 'flight from feeling', the tyranny of intimacy and the deadening of public life. We are now unable to work with others in common struggle, they claim, because of our very personalities; there is a devaluation of interest in impersonal public issues, and a dangerous tendency to destroy all spheres of privacy in the quest for ultimate knowledge about the self.[18] Two questions are immediately posed by Sennett and Lasch's own rather simplistic 'dialectic of self-enlightenment'. Firstly, is it better that people should not attempt to discover their inner selves? And secondly, how can the concern with public issues and public life be revived if there is indeed such an increasing tendency toward fragmentation and decentralization? As to the former, consider Sennett's fears about the growing preoccupation with emotions and feelings:

> What kind of personality develops through experiences of intimacy? Such a personality will be molded in the expectation, if not the experience, of trust, of warmth, of

comfort. How can it be strong enough to move in a world founded on injustice? . . . Is it humane to form soft selves in a hard world?'[19]

Sennett's questions undoubtedly appeal to many socialists educated in the tradition of self-discipline and hard 'outer-shells', the tradition of all necessary 'means' to a more 'humane' future. The problem, however, is that this onslaught on the transmutation or conversion of many political categories into psychological categories is only too easy to accept: how can one not applaud his attack on the commercial industry of self-awareness therapies and their packaged 'panaceas'? But the difficult moral questions, and hence questions of praxis, begin to open up when we turn to consider the problem of what socialists should struggle for, in relation to social welfare services, educational policies, child/parent relations, and other vital interpersonal relations. All of these areas involve precisely an overcoming of those bureaucratic, uncaring, non-intimate 'Therapeutic State' practices to which Sennett and Lasch are also opposed. But if intimacy and feelings are denied as a moral good, then what kind of non-oppressive male/female relationships and general social relations can possibly be achieved? How can socialists possibly hope to democratize state services if state workers and ordinary state citizens retain alienated and impersonal relationships? Clearly, socialists cannot ignore the central issue of 'the personal as the political' even if the need for intimacy and caring has been manipulated by commercial charlatans, and has been used to promote apolitical forms of escapism from the pain of living under capitalism. After all, no socialist rejects the values of equality and democracy simply because bourgeois politicians cynically use these concepts to promote their own narrow interests.

Doubtless Sennett is right to point to the ways in which people identify with capitalism via public 'personalities', and doubtless too he is right to suggest that opposition is often weakened by our inability to put personal relations second to the objectives of political struggle. But there is still a very positive and radical dimension, and one substantially contributed by the women's movement, to this focus on feelings, emotions and 'the self'. An interest in public personalities may well produce 'stars', but the public depiction of their everyday routines also reduces them to ordinary human mortals, rather than abstract gods and leaders. Party or movement bureaucrats, sexists, pompous workaholics, moral blackmailers, servile toadies, in short, the typical inhabitants of traditional left and non-left parties, state apparatuses and public institutions, have often been publicly attacked in recent years partly as a result of the need to 'discover the self', and the effects have been entirely beneficial. Pre-occupation with the self always represents some threat to both individuals and social movements, but a more humane and egalitarian society cannot emerge unless those very cognitive, psycho-sexual characteristics which Sennett and Lasch indiscriminately attack, are encouraged to emerge from their historical neglect and suppression. Sennett and Lasch are forced to identify with those pre-capitalist moral and psycho-cognitive processes which pre-date the 'culture of narcissism'. They fail to see that capitalist hegemony is parasitically dependent on traditional non-intimate, authoritarian, puritanical and patriarchal social relations. Certainly, various aspects of the 'counter culture' have been incorporated into new styles of administration, management and 'public relations'. But these new modes of management are nothing like as widely utilized as Toffler, or the 'Therapeutic State' analysts, would have us believe. In most factories and offices, the older authoritarian practices, used to raise productivity and to maintain discipline, are as firmly entrenched as ever.

The excesses of the self-awareness movement provide no justification for a return to Victorian morality or to a neglect of the self. This issue, that of the balance between personal reflection and impersonal 'discipline', remains essentially 'unthinkable' in an intellectual world increasingly characterized by the relativization of truth, the commodification of therapies and philosophies, and the failure to reflect adequately on the relation between public life and the institutionalization of both participation and socialization processes. The prospect for a post-industrial, socialist public sphere must, if it is to have any chance of being realized, come to encompass more than a ritual endorsement of pluralism. For the relativization of all theories and cures necessarily undermines the possibility of any commitment to the struggles of the social movements. Socialist pluralism would have to be an explicit arrangement which sought, through the decisions of diverse groups and movements, to construct the framework within which a new form of tolerance and democratic diversity might prevail. This would entail a condemnation of those ideologies, such as racism, which violate the interests of the new public sphere. It would also involve sorting through, and condemning, the innumerable quack therapies and religious cults, which threaten the rights of women, patients, children and others. There is an understandable fear at the prospect of a new censorship and new 'community standards'.

But decisions of this type would only be democratic and tolerant to the extent that the participating social movement organizations and parties had succeeded in constructing a new pluralism which really was different from both traditional religious and absolutist communist moralities.

What post-industrial theory lacks, and what it most conspicuously requires, is a much clearer discussion about the institutionalization of new democratic forms of representation, education, media and cultural outlets, legal structures and welfare services. Decentralization can add to the democratization of public life only if there is some clear notion of the relationship of decentralized public spheres to one another and to the whole. Just as the possibility of new plural family forms and individual lifestyles depends very much on the provision of communal 'social wage' programmes, legal structures and alterations in paid working conditions, so too, decentralization would be disastrous if the decentralized communities were then left to their own devices and resources. The 'cultural contradictions of capitalism' are not some figment of the conservative imagination: neo-conservatism's failure is in its cure rather than its diagnosis. A pseudo toleration of all ideas, therapies, pedagogical principles, child-raising practices, cultural messages, work practices, legal statutes, such as much postmodern 'radicalism' seems to recommend, is both dangerous and naive. Of course, decentralization is desirable. But to leave individuals in their 'electronic cottages' or 'basic communes', with no mediating national-political institutional networks between them and the global order, is equivalent to leaving isolated individuals to fend for themselves without families or kinship structures. What has to be overthrown, or drastically changed, are those existing political institutions which monopolize power and privileges, which are insensitive to local needs and social movements, which impose discriminatory laws and regulations while destroying natural environments. But a society which has no national institutions, also has no real chance of establishing and maintaining a democratic public sphere. If one believes that the age of city states is over, that the specialized division of labour will never be completely overthrown, that some form of monetary system is indispensable, that administration and social planning would be necessary to maximize equality, to preserve environments and to support all those unable to do paid work, that some form of defensive defence system would be necessary, and that disputes between individuals and groups require for their resolution some system of rules and rights, then either one places all of humanity's hopes in world government, or else one acknowledges the necessity for national institutions.

The Frankfurt School, having depicted the commodification and reification of everyday life, remained unable to explain how the agents of human liberation could possibly break through this totally administered system. So too, with Toffler, Jones and the other post-industrialist theorists: what is clearly missing is any developed sense of political strategies, a sense of the political as it determines and is determined by social struggles. The old industries, lifestyles and institutions may be doomed, but how is a new social order to emerge from the cultural contradictions of the present? Commenting on Toffler's vision of the coming break-up of large, centralized political institutions, Gorz warns of the dangers ahead:

> If this decentralization and diversification of society – where a plurality of partial orders co-exists, adjusting to each other by means of successive trade-offs without ever becoming unified – is not thought out, desired and consciously prepared for, the consequences will be inescapable: either society will fragment into anarchy through violent confrontations, or a totalitarian dictatorship, in attempting to re-establish a unified order through the use of terror and constraint, will reproduce the system of 'waste, irresponsibility, inertia, corruption; in short, totalitarian inefficiency', exemplified in the Stalinist and National Socialist state models.[20]

But while Gorz's warning is timely, he is himself quite vague about such issues of political strategy, about the future role of unions, parties and political representation in post-industrial society, for example.

There is little doubt that dramatic new developments in communications technology are transforming the conventional forms of print and electronic media. But the proliferation of individualized and global outlets and connections does not in itself provide any guarantee that ownership and control of the new media will be any less monopolized or undemocratic than at present. However, even if we assume that future societies will be much more democratic and egalitarian, then we are still confronted by the fundamental issue of whether there should be only local, community-organized media outlets, or whether there should also exist national or supranational communication organizations. Given the crucial role of books, newspapers, electronic media, film, theatre and other communication outlets in disseminating, constructing or inhibiting particular notions of citizenship, rights, moral values and so forth, it is difficult to imagine how a democratic socialist pluralism could survive if there were no media institutions which linked local communities into larger entities. Certainly, local groups could have their own networks for communication with other local communities. But this would neither resolve the problems of political representation in larger legislatures, nor those of the cultivation of non-parochial values, unless the model to be adopted was one of unrestrained pluralism, rigorous self-sufficiency and haphazard contact with the outside world. It is not difficult to imagine a situation where far greater access to media outlets, cultural institutions and resources was made available to different groups in society. This would be one of the great benefits to be had from decentralization and from eliminating the political and economic monopolization of communication outlets. But the retention of national and regional media and cultural institutions in no way presupposes the retention of old forms of control and ownership. At the moment, there are radio and television stations and cultural institutions which operate at more than local level, and yet are based on democratic federations of participating groups. Thus, it is possible to imagine a whole range of new organizational structures which democratize the media, but it is virtually impossible to imagine a democratic national public sphere with no national media outlets.

If the post-industrial utopians are correct in their diagnosis of the impending demise of industrialism, then it becomes imperative that new values and social identities do not become even more fragmented, alienated and conflict-ridden than at present. The unplanned nature of endless new marketable technologies and products, coupled with the almost religious faith that small-scale, decentralized institutions are inherently good, threatens to produce a post-industrial 'refeudalization' of everyday life. The resources and structures needed to mediate, facilitate and strengthen those values and practices which maximize democracy and socialist pluralism, cannot spring solely from within the boundaries of local communities. Here perhaps is the central dialectic or paradox of the new post-industrial public/private spheres: the maximization of democratic decentralization is in fact dependent upon certain requisite institutions of democratic centralization. For while central institutions can survive without local democracy, it is most unlikely that decentralized institutions would last very long without the positive support of national institutions. This is the unpleasant truth which believers in stateless societies refuse to confront. If the new state institutions are to be much more democratic, and in that sense vastly different from existing state apparatuses in both capitalist and communist societies, then the very crucial issue of political transformation will have to be accorded a much higher priority and profile than that normally given it by post-industrial theorists.

It is worth noting that the conflicting visions of post-industrial society are largely determined by pessimistic or optimistic views of the new technology, rather than by any adequate consideration of private/public relations. The pessimists point to those developments in micro-electronics and genetic engineering which lead to Big Brother, to a loss of critical and reflective educational and cultural institutions, to the increased isolation and fragmentation of social life, as leisure and work become more home-centred, while public life, undermined by the new technocratic privatism, is increasingly manipulated and subject to authoritarian rule. By contrast, the optimists depict a scenario based on varying images of a revived and committed citizenry, whether in the 'electronic cottage' or the 'basic commune', running their own lives, overcoming private alienation and social malaise in a system of self-help, small-scale, decentralized public and private spheres. I have tried to show that whether one believes in Toffler's high-tech scenario or in Bahro's industrial disarmament, the issue of how to construct alternative public spheres, which presuppose new definitions of the private sphere, self-identity and socialization, can be addressed only if one is prepared to confront the question of the decisive role of state institutions. One may have particular interpretations of how governments maintain legitimacy, of the decisive role of religion, ideology, coercion, narcissism, exterminism and so forth. But these explanations of existing public/private relations tell us more about what is wrong with the present, than about the relations and institutions necessary for the construction of new public spheres. New technological and social developments may very well lead to the abolition of nine-to-five work patterns, the redefinition of the use of time and social space, the alteration of the conventional life-cycle pattern of childhood to old age. The key question, however, is this: will these new developments bring about the end of even limited democratic forms, as we know them today? Or will they provide the ground for an enhanced and vibrant social struggle to construct one of the, as yet unfulfilled, goals of the Enlightenment, the first generation of truly democratic public spheres?

NOTES

An expanded version of the argument advanced in this paper forms part of my *The Post-Industrial Utopians* (Cambridge: Polity Press, 1987).

1. For a discussion of the varying responses of social movements to modern social conditions, see A. Honneth, E. Knodler-Bunte and A. Widmann, 'The Dialectics of Rationalization: An Interview with Jürgen Habermas', *Telos*, 49 (1981), pp.5–31 and Jürgen Habermas, 'New Social Movements', ibid., pp.33–7.
2. Alvin Toffler, *Future Shock* (London: Pan Books, 1970), part 5.
3. Alvin Toffler, *The Third Wave* (London: Pan Books, 1980), p.377.
4. Jean-François Lyotard, *The Postmodern Condition* (1984), p.3. See 'Select Bibliography'.
5. Perry Anderson, 'Modernity and Revolution', *New Left Review*, 144 (1984), p.99.
6. Fredric Jameson, 'Postmodernism, or the Cultural Logic of Late Capitalism'. See 'Select Bibliography'.
7. Mike Davis, 'Urban Renaissance and the Spirit of Postmodernism', *New Left Review*, 155 (1985), pp.106–13.
8. Jürgen Habermas, *Towards a Rational Society* (Boston: Beacon Press, 1970), p.117.
9. Ibid., p.118.
10. Andreas Huyssen, 'The Search for Tradition: Avantgarde and Postmodernism in the 1970s', *New German Critique*, 22 (1981), p.38.
11. Michael Ryan, *Marxism and Deconstruction* (Baltimore: Johns Hopkins University Press, 1982).
12. Ibid., p.116.
13. Daniel Bell, *The Cultural Contradictions of Capitalism* (New York: Basic Books, 1978), p.99.
14. Toffler, *The Third Wave*, pp.376–7.
15. J. Casanova, 'The Politics of Religious Revival', *Telos*, 59 (1984), p.33.
16. See Anthony Giddens, *A Contemporary Critique of Historical Materialism* (London: Macmillan, 1981), ch.6, for a discussion of the relationship between the development of capitalist societies, and the transformation of concepts of time and urban space.
17. See Theodor Adorno and Max Horkheimer, *Dialectic of Enlightenment* (London: Verso, 1979).
18. See Christopher Lasch, *The Culture of Narcissism* (New York: Warner Books, 1979), and Richard Sennett, *The Fall of Public Man* (Cambridge: Cambridge University Press, 1977); see also Richard Sennett, 'Destructive *Gemeinschaft*' in R. Bocock et al. (eds), *An Introduction to Sociology* (Milton Keynes: Open University Press, 1980), pp.91–121.
19. Sennett, *The Fall of Public Man*, p.260.
20. André Gorz, *Paths to Paradise* (London: Pluto Press, 1985), p.84.

CHAPTER 7

Postmodernism or Post-Colonialism Today

Simon During

Construction of the concept 'postmodernity' proceeds today at a rapid pace. A welter of articles and books define, elaborate, celebrate and denounce this thing, the postmodern, whose very existence is matter for separate, energetic debate. Clearly interests are at stake, careers are being made. But this activity is finally produced by the concept itself, which, being based on paradox, generates discussion. On the one hand, 'postmodernity' names the loss of critical distance in the world today, and on the other, it names the delegitimation of those categories by which a cultural centre or a socio-economic base might be identified. So writing about postmodernity implies its absence. If there is no critical distance under postmodernity, then how can there be distance enough for analysis of it to proceed? And if it is knowable only as decentred then how can its essence be recognized at all? To be dispersed in this sense is no longer to take the form of an identifiable object. Such paradoxes, which resist closure, produce the deeply problematic object of their attention.

The most persuasive accounts of the postmodern are those – like Jameson's essay 'Postmodernism, or the Cultural Logic of Late Capitalism'[1] or Lyotard's recent work – which remain sensitive to these paralogisms. It is for this reason that I shall be concerned with Jameson and Lyotard here. But, partly in order to escape capture by the paradoxes of postmodernity, my argument will proceed from three positions which counter the conceptual underpinnings of 'postmodernity'.

First, I propose, against Jameson, that postmodernity ought not to be conceived of as 'a cultural dominant'.[2] Next, I want to urge that it is just as rewarding to construe literary postmodernism as an enemy of postmodernity as to consider it as its expression and helpmeet. Thus in ethico-political terms postmodernist texts do not differ from modernist texts which are simultaneously enemies of, and moments in, modernity. (This is to take a different line from that of either liberals like Trilling or Western Marxists like the later Adorno, who see contemporary culture as characterized by the disappearance of adversarial possibilities.) And, third, I take the position that, if there is something that may be called postmodern thought, it too works in ways that cannot be regarded as a mere expression of an underlying postmodernity.

We can, rather brutally, characterize postmodern thought (a phrase which is useful rather than happy) as that thought which refuses to turn the Other into the Same. Thus it provides a theoretical space for what postmodernity denies: otherness. Postmodern thought also recognizes, however, that the Other can never speak for itself *as* the Other. One should hesitate to call a discourse which revolves around these positions either for or against postmodernity, but it is certainly not simply consonant with it.

These propositions, none of which is either original or uncontentious, and all of which will be fleshed out below, allow me to mount my central thesis. This is that the concept postmodernity has been constructed in terms which more or less intentionally wipe out the possibility of post-colonial identity. Indeed, intention aside, the conceptual annihilation of the post-colonial condition is actually necessary to any argument which attempts to show that 'we' now live in postmodernity. For me, perhaps eccentrically, post-colonialism is the need, in nations or groups which have been victims of imperialism, to achieve an identity uncontaminated by universalist or Eurocentric concepts and images. Here the argument becomes complex, since post-colonialism constitutes one of those Others which might derive hope and legitimation from the first aspect of postmodern thought, its refusal to turn the Other into the Same. As such it is threatened by the second moment in postmodern thought.

If postmodernity is regarded as a condition which is dominant today, then the question immediately arises: what else is there? Jameson, for instance, does not cope with this question easily. He conceives of postmodernity as the culture produced by multinational capitalism: a totality which is the effect of another totality. All the cultural phenomena that Jameson refers to instantiate postmodernity. (In fact, he comes ultimately to think of it as so powerful as to be literally inconceivable, that is, as only to be thought of indirectly, as the sublime.) The only tool for analysing an emergence as immense and total as postmodernity is expressive causality. For a theorist as sophisticated as Jameson elsewhere shows himself to be, this represents a retrogressive, not to say a defeatist move.

Jameson inherits these problems. His Hegelian heritage enables him to think both of culture as a totality and of history as a succession of epochs. Indeed, current Marxist accounts of postmodernity are articulated in terms that repeat earlier accounts of modern culture by the Hegelian Marxism of the Frankfurt School. In particular, Adorno's important late essay 'Cultural Criticism and Society' lies behind Jameson's text. Adorno came to see what he too called late capitalism as a condition in which the world is totally mediated by consciousness. In it, ideology is no longer false consciousness, and high culture becomes 'neutralized'.[3] Adorno also argues that the conceptual underpinning of both transcendental critique (critique from a position outside the phenomena under analysis) and immanent critique (critique from contradictions noted within) has disappeared as society has become reified. But Adorno goes further than Jameson. He argues that the Marxist transformation of truth as correspondence into truth as praxis has been absorbed by capitalism as the hegemonic forces have turned pragmatic views of truth to their own ends. And, on the other hand, the counter-attempt to protect areas of culture from instrumental reason now fails because ideology itself has no instrumental function. It has dissolved into distraction, pleasure. Thus the world is now an 'open-air prison'; a place where, in the words of a 1937 essay by Marcuse, which feeds into Adorno's, 'men can feel themselves happy without being so at all'.[4]

Jameson's cultural pessimism, then, is already laid out by Adorno. However, Adorno refers not to postmodernity but to a formation that includes totalitarian and fascist culture. For instance, it is the totalitarian state which has aestheticized existence to the degree that poetry cannot be written after Auschwitz. That famous line does not mean, as is generally supposed, that Auschwitz is too terrible an experience to be written about; it means that writing under fascism and late capitalism has become too trivial to express real horror. The discourse in which Jameson constructs postmodernity was once used, in part, to denounce fascism. (Marcuse's essay would be another point of departure.) This matters, not because analysis of fascism is irrelevant to our culture, but because it allows us to wonder whether the categories of totality and dominance need to be rethought when we turn them to our own times.

Adorno also differs from Jameson when he imagines lines of flight from late capitalism. Jameson sees escape in a postmodern politics the vocation of which would be to map the contemporary condition, which he believes to be, under current categories, unmappable. Clearly his own essay believes itself to be engaging in such a politics. Adorno sees escape in a kind of thought 'which strives solely to help the things themselves to that articulation from which they are otherwise cut off by prevailing language'.[5] In almost a liberal spirit, Adorno wishes to provide room for self-determination. True, he cannot offer self-articulation a programme, though the fierce insistence of 'no poetry after Auschwitz' does, rhetorically, free a space in the unfreedom which is our freedom. Jameson's weak call for new forms of mapping, with its emphasis on cognitive knowledge, like his return to expressive causality, shows how trapped he is compared to Adorno. Perhaps this is so *because* Adorno has a stronger grasp of the contemporary distintegration of cognition, expression and reflection. For he calls not just for knowledge but for action.

Yet – and here we approach the crux of the matter – the weakest moment in Jameson's essay comes when, despite everything, he tries to think postmodernity dialectically. He asks himself how a positive view of its emergence can be taken, and how it permits the forward march of history. He turns to the 'internationalism' of postmodernity. Its progressive task is to realize the end of nationalism so desired by some socialisms. He adds: 'the disastrous realignment of socialist revolution with the older nationalisms (not only in South East Asia), whose results have necessarily aroused such serious recent left reflection, can be adduced in support of this position'.[6] The strongest enemies of postmodernity appear at this weak point: the new post-colonial nationalisms. Indeed, one can be forgiven for thinking that Jameson is harnessing all the power inherent in images of totalitarianism to eradicate cultural difference in the old spirit of enlightened modernity. The reason why one cannot view postmodernity dialectically becomes apparent. As soon as one allows the notion of the 'positive' or 'progressive' to reappear in analysis, the object one has in view is not postmodernity but a stage on the historical journey to the light. And progress, as ever, must be defined by determinate negation – as not the retrogressive, not the residual, not the primitive, not the irrationalism of other cultures. One can say in general, then, that in order to name postmodernity as a cultural dominant expressing itself in postmodern artefacts Jameson has to assume the coming to power of neo-imperialism, and to inflect postmodernity positively he has, for a moment, to become complicit with it.[7]

How to think postmodernity otherwise? How not to read it as the sublime, a totality so powerful as to resist our older knowledge? It seems to me that one must proceed at once on two registers: one archaeological, the other genealogical. (These words are used here at some distance from Foucault.) Postmodernity must be seen as an effect of discrete cultural systems and not as a spirit or epoch, the advance guard of history. The features of postmodernity, which no one has described better than Jameson, are produced within a finite field of what might be called cultural machines: those texts, images, discourses, each formed within particular technologies or media, each with its own way of organizing the intervention on the real, and each with its mode of subject formation.

But postmodernity is known as postmodernity within a discourse which, as we have begun to see, has its own past. Thus to think postmodernity outside the totalizing categories of Western Marxism is to interpret the ideological effects of discrete cultural systems without assuming that these effects take the form of a whole. It is also to reflect on the sources and history of the concepts one uses to describe such effects. There is always a liberating moment when one examines the genealogy of one's discourse. That discourse becomes itself not natural and inevitable but historical, provisional and open to change. In addition to these dual projects of archaeology and genealogy one must also think postmodernity diacritically. Given that 'post-' which rules its usage, it remains a notion which needs to be defined against modernity.

I cannot offer a full reading of what I have called a cultural system here, but let me show what I mean by looking briefly at Coppola's film *Apocalypse Now*. It is an especially good example because it reworks Conrad's modernist classic *Heart of Darkness*, and so allows an entry for diacritical analysis. In turn, *Heart of Darkness* is canonical just because it offers a critique of modernity by breaking down the terms in which European thought distinguished itself from the primitive. Thus if one supposes that postmodernity differs from modernity in the way it legitimates or delegitimates imperialism, or, more radically, if one suspects that the discourse of postmodernity is once again grounded on a denial of otherness, then one would expect *Apocalpyse Now* to bear these hypotheses out.

Heart of Darkness shows that the otherness of the primitive is precisely 'our' otherness – where that 'our' indicates, however tentatively, a civilized Eurocentric community. As the title suggests, it is a direct inversion of Enlightenment universalism, which assumes all human beings to be equal in so far as they are led by the light of reason, and no further. The valorization of Western reason and civilization becomes for Conrad a cloak for greed, destruction and, paradoxically, the return of irrationality because it allows men to suppose themselves gods. The story makes its point, however, in terms of an old mythic narrative: the voyage to the underground and back, with its known stages and climax. There is therefore a confidence that the culture can narrativize its reneging on enlightenment. The text also has its own positive ideological project. Marlow's voice grafts the discourse of 'the common man' on to that of the sensitive, alienated intellectual. In this way, negative universalism still works towards a consensus. Marlow also attempts, though vainly, to autonomize instrumental reason – vainly, because his work finally fulfils imperialist ends. Finally, the text presents one place in society that is protected from its own truths. Marlow, who knows that enlightenment is a form of barbarism, that the West's Other is the West itself, protects Western women from that truth by lying to them. 'The horror, the horror', Kurtz's last words, are never reported to his fiancée. She continues to believe that he dies with her name on his lips. But there is a twist here. Her values that require protection from the truth *are* the horror too, making Marlow's lie a truth.

Given this summary reading of Conrad's story, one could simply go on to read the film to mark the division between the modern and the postmodern. But the primary shift is one of media and technology, not of meaning. Conrad's tale is *written*: how to catch the voice in writing and which voice to catch are questions it is overtly anxious about. *Apocalpyse Now* consists of sounds and images. (This obvious point has a somewhat less obvious corollary. The privileging of the play in writing in current thought is in itself an act of resistance to postmodern technology.) Furthermore, Conrad's novel is the product of a man writing alone at home, autonomously; it requires no investment, no collective enterprise, and thus no high circulation. Although it was written for *Blackwood's Magazine* – no journal being less a vehicle for elitist modernism – the sense that it has no real audience is constantly foregrounded in the story. It is as if the text's implied reader belongs to Kurtz's fiancée's social space, where the truth may not be borne. But Coppola's film, which requires an audience for material reasons, cannot draw any bounds to its audience at all; its implied reader is the abstract consumer, anyone at all.

Because the film is a product of advanced technology, it has quite a different place in the world from that of the novella. In particular, it dissolves the division between truth and lie from quite another direction. Take the scene where Willard – the Marlow figure – first encounters the air cavalry. He jumps out of a helicopter into a blur of violence, noise and danger, in a scene whose production values are so strong that the film seems less the representation of a representation of battle than a recording of actual fighting itself. Suddenly a voice shouts: 'Look like you're fighting!' This is not the entry of postmodern self-referentiality. We soon realize that what we are seeing is, in part, the representation of a representation of a representation: the troops are fighting on and for the television cameras which are gradually panned into sight. Is all this totally fake, then – a mock battle for the folks back home watching the news? No: neither fake nor genuine – or fake *and* genuine. 'Real' bodies litter the ground. The fusion of theatre and war, war as theatre, is a product of modern communications technology and quite foreign to Conrad's moral sense that a lie may tell the truth.

In fact, not only is war theatre, but film is war. If we read (as good consumers) Eleanor Coppola's bestselling account of life on location, we realize that these stunningly realistic battle scenes were made possible by Coppola's hiring arms and equipment from the Filipino army.[8] During shooting these were periodically borrowed back by the army to fight real insurgents in the mountains. And the film set itself was under guard because of fears that it would be attacked for its supplies. The film is enabled by acts of neo-imperialist war: it cannot disengage itself from what it represents. The collapse of distinctions here between making films and making war is not primarily a cultural fact or a theme, but an outcome of specific material conditions. Its effects remain ideological, however: this particular system induces theories of the loss of distance between the image and the imaged.

The derealizing of the world is also an implicit theme of the film. Willard's eyes are constantly shown registering disbelief that the events he witnesses make up reality. But the naive response to this – 'Better than Disneyland', as one of the soldiers puts it – is inadequate. What the film makes clear is that Vietnam is 'irreal' because principles of intelligibility by which to experience it are missing. In Conrad these principles were narrativity on the one hand, and the unity of the subjective consciousness on the other. Marlow's story and the unity of his reponse make experiences of imperialist Africa, which he also knows to be unreal and unbelievable, ultimately meaningful. These categories do not work in the film, partly for technical reasons. Shots of Willard's eyes have to do much of the work of presenting subjective response. Yet they can never of themselves show how he interprets what he sees. Even sequences which move metonymically from an expression of disbelief to scenes of horror can only foreground the gap between each shot. The interaction between subjective conciousness and the outer world fails when subjects become visual objects: eyes, mouths, bodies. One might argue that the voice-over could do the work instead, bringing the events into the unity of a sovereign subject's response to them. The disjunction between image and sound in the film prevents that. Willard's voice-over, unlike Marlow's, is not in itself the means *both* of representing events *and* of interpreting them subjectively. In the film the representing function is given over to the camera, blocking control of representation by subjectivity. Thus the autonomy of the bourgeois subject, which depends not only on a clear division of self and world but on a means by which the self can absorb the world, comes apart in film. Here we encounter a moment in the system whose effect is the postmodern sense of the death of the psychological subject and the end of expression.

The film begins with a Doors song entitled 'The End' on the soundtrack as Willard undergoes a nervous breakdown. This breakdown is expressive, but of nothing. After all, nothing has happened to him as yet. The scene seems to be an initial exorcizing of the possibility of expression: after this his only emotion – if emotion it is – is disbelief. But the first scene works against narrative: at the beginning is the end. At the beginning is a horror signifying nothing – or everything – just as at the end. The grounds for the dismantling of narrative progress can, however, be located more precisely. Conrad's narrative is a journey away from light to darkness and back to light as darkness. It requires a world with a boundary between civilization and savagery, even if those distinctions ultimately vanish. Such a difference exists in the film only as quotation. Willard, like Marlow, travels up a river by boat, but messages to him are always in front of him. Helicopters and jets fly above him towards his destination. The form of his journey is unmotivated; it seems a Conradian echo. Because there is no outside to the technology of war, a teleological narrative exists as no more than nostalgia.

Second, the Conradian climaxes which do occur – Kurtz saying 'The horror, the horror' – do so as citation. Just as technology is there before the individual (even Kurtz's compound has radio), Conrad's text is always there before the film itself. This symmetry is much less than an equivalence, however. Coppola is using Conrad's narrative to tell the truth about Vietnam, but in the attempt we are left with historical incongruity and a mere monumentalization of modernism. Kurtz quotes Eliot; he is reading Frazer and Weston; he delivers a Nietzschean tirade on greatness as the capacity to bear the suffering of others. Though he is described as a genius, all this can never add up to charisma. It is the standard matter of a liberal arts education. His true distinction in the film's own terms is his efficiency, his refusal to play the hypocritical game of army bureaucrats. But in having him killed they do not play their own game either – so there is no final difference here. Ultimately, efficiency rules everywhere. The values of honour, truth and work for work's sake, which Conrad upholds as he reveals their limits, have disappeared along with the autonomous subject and work of art.

Finally, there is the question of cultural reproduction. In Conrad's text the story is told to a shadowy 'us' and not the fiancée. Coppola's Kurtz is obsessed with getting his truth told to his son; he entrusts that task to Willard before committing suicide. He and Willard think his truth is unrepresentable, sublime. 'I worry that you might not understand what I have had to be', he tells Willard. Yet the impossibility of representing Kurtz is not the sublime impossibility of making the boundless conceivable; it is the trivial impossibility of making the secondhand firsthand. Kurtz's greatness is a requirement of narrative climax and intelligibility; it is not in him. A strange consequence emerges: if there is nothing great to tell, if the categories of intelligibility collapse, then it looks as if the culture might not reproduce itself historically. The age of history may disappear into history. Here we catch sight of the way in which postmodernity consumes history, in the sense of nullifying it. It remains an effect rather than an expression or theme.

Yet the failure to reproduce will not happen in silence. After all, Kurtz is on the screen for us all to see. Conrad believed his message to be so dangerous that it might really not have hearers. Coppola's film, which tells us that it bears an image so dangerous as to resist comprehension, requires that the unreproducible be shown everywhere. The true message is that nothing now is unreproducible; it is just that cultural reproduction has divorced itself from cultural values.

These remarks do not make up a full reading of the film, but they offer enough for us to see that it functions as a system creating *effects* of postmodernity within a quite specifical technological, economic and ideological frame, rather than an *instance* of that octopus 'postmodernity' or even 'multinational capitalism'. What seems most deeply entrenched in these effects is the encroachment of Western power and technology upon the Third World. The destruction of narrativity is an effect of that power's being able to reach anywhere. The film itself becomes war within the frame of neo-imperialism.

At this point it is worth recalling a final difference between Conrad and Coppola. The original inhabitants of Africa are represented in Conrad's text. It is true that they are falsely presented as cannibals, but they play a role that allows the West to know itself as Other to itself. The Vietnamese enemy are nowhere in Coppola's movie. The film achieves its sense of total irreality by wiping them out of the screen. If the discourse of postmodernity characterizes the postmodern as that which knows no Other, then in this film that Other is eliminated by fiat. If there were an enemy available for representation, perhaps then there would be narrative rather than just citation. In the failure to concede Third World nationalism a right to existence, what is revealed is that will to totality and failure of imagination we have already found in Jameson. This seems more than coincidence. Is there, after all, a secret key with which to unlock postmodernity? If so, can it be found in those who come not to denounce the postmodern like Jameson, nor in that which produces effects of postmodernity, but in that very postmodern thought which is totality's enemy?

II

For Lyotard, postmodernity is a condition of knowledge at least as much as an epoch. It is a moment within and behind modernity, conceived of again much in the spirit of Marcuse and Adorno. Instead of proposing a history centred on the development of the capitalist mode of production, he thinks of modernity as a process of social rationalization. In his first account of the topic, *The Postmodern Condition*, this process is conceived of negatively: the modern is marked by the emergence of instrumental reason. In modernity, criteria of what he calls 'performaticity' overcome appeals to tradition or metaphysical truth. What counts is not why an act is done or why a thought is thought, but how efficiently and to what immediate end. Applied science is the home of instrumental reason, which (as research) gradually comes to be the standard against which all knowledge is measured.

This development has discursive consequences: cognitive utterances which can be verified and permit control over nature are privileged over those which cannot. But ultimately science cannot validate itself; only its services to power, its instrumentality, permit it to cast a spell of 'self-legitimacy'. The recognition of the failure of science's claim to self-legitimation spells the end for the grand narratives of human emancipation and philosophical speculation. Their collapse reveals a fragmented set of discursive formations and practices. The postmodern just accepts that science itself must act in terms of prescriptives, and cannot validate itself. It must be tolerant of paralogism, seeking no solace from the fragmentation and incommensurability of discourses. And in *The Postmodern Condition*, though not in Lyotard's later work, narrative knowledge takes the place of science as the preferred order.

Lyotard's *Le Différend*, though not directly concerned with postmodernism, examines both the moral consequences and the philosophical grounds of discursive heterogeneity.[9] The paradigm for a *différend* is a case in which two parties in dispute cannot articulate their cause in the same idiom. He distinguishes an injury (*un dommage*) from an injustice (*un tort*). In an injustice, the injury is not judged according to the litigant's own criteria of validity, so that the litigant (who then becomes a victim) is in effect silenced. This juridical paradigm is not limited to the courts. The privileging of descriptive statements over prescriptive ones is a *différend* which occurs within end-means rationality; the West places the colonized peoples in a *différend*; capitalism, with its ties to universality, creates a *différend* for the specific, the unexchangeable, and so on.

For Lyotard, in a Cartesian spirit, what exists beyond doubt is the phrase or phrase event. But each phrase occurs as a *différend*: to link one phrase to another is to commit an injustice to possible genres which the first phrase might obligate. Once the nothingness between phrase events is bridged in the interest of a use, as it must be, a *différend* already exists. Thus Lyotard is able to say, 'politics is a matter of linkage between phrases' and is constituted within the 'civil war of language with itself'.[10] Here the Wittgensteinian sense that the limits of language are the limits of the world grasps hands with Derrida's proposition, in his remarks on Lévi-Strauss, that 'violence is writing'.[11] The groundlessness of language, its edging out on to nothing, its character as mere *event*, the fact that it does not exist as a unity declaring its own linkages to itself, all enable the possibility of disagreement, of cultural difference, of violence, as well as the mirage of self-identity.

Unlike Wittgenstein and Derrida, Lyotard returns from these transcendental claims to history. The result disappoints at least as much as it promises. Because language is not a unity, because it necessarily sets *différends* into play, those meta-genres of discourse which claimed to cover all other genres of discourse (speculation) or which promised an end to injustice (narratives of human emancipation) are ungroundable. Philosophy alone is not responsible for their devalidation, however; they die in history. In modern history it becomes impossible to ignore certain cultural *différends*. These *différends* are recognized in the feelings signalled by the silences around certain proper names: Auschwitz is the example he uses most often. No genre of discourse presents itself which would permit a litigant to appeal for justice against the wrong Auschwitz connotes. This silence spells the end of the *grand récits* of Occidental emancipation and speculation which were the secular cover of Western cultural imperialism. Beyond it, no hope of a bridge between heterogeneous discourses survives. One must accept the *différend*. From the other side, capitalism itself works to undo the force of the order of discourse. In capitalism, money, rather than language, installs exchangeability as the dominant relation between objects in the world. But money is also stored time and security – one might add, stored pleasure. Thus capitalism disburdens itself from notions such as humanity and progress which underpin high-cultural imperialism. But it also discounts the formations which resist these ideas: in particular, nationalism and philosophic deliberation. Ultimately, for Lyotard, capitalism even implies the end of effective political institutions. The play of exchange, the production of money as security, will delegitimate the discursive presuppositions of institutions too. In fact Lyotard's derationalized capitalism is close to Jameson's multinational capitalism, and, like Jameson, Lyotard sees post-colonial nationalism as not just archaic but dangerous. Post-colonial nationalism articulates itself in the 'narrative-mythic'[12] which constructs an immutable cultural origin; it neutralizes the phrase as event, and it projects a 'home' in which difference is suspended; its greatest modern exemplar is Nazism. Thus it too is countered in those names surrounded by silence, pain and, finally, deliberation. Deliberation as doubt leads back to the phrase event, and, if one is not to conspire in the concealment of a *différend*, one must punctuate the ebb and flow of phrases only by '*Arrive-t-il?*'

There is here the hope that the breakdown of legitimations for cultural imperialism will free the world both from the spell of instrumental reason and from the nostalgia for mythic origins. It is as if postmodernity would today be the play of post-colonialisms set free not only from the requirement of universality embedded in emancipation, but also from the hunger for identity implicit in narrative as myth. Lyotard aims to clear a space for maximizing the potential of articulation within all idioms. The problem is not just the universalism of Lyotard's own Cartesian approach. Nothing very much in the book softens the shock of the transition from 'Auschwitz' to '*Arrive-t-il?*' This last seems a slight result for the promise implicit in his vision of discursive heterogeneity.

For Lyotard, Auschwitz is not only a name with a halo of silence; it produces a particular emotion, signalling a *différend*. Within what context does the binding of this emotion to the name occur? The events at Auschwitz do not come into the world with feelings attached to them as if by nature. Let us think of another name, one which has as little feeling attached to it as any for Western philosophy: New Zealand. This is the country that the Maoris call Aotearoa. When one recalls this, one recalls the massacres, the deaths by introduced diseases, the destruction of a culture and a society which the name New Zealand silences. It is Lyotard's virtue to recognize that mere cognition of these matters can never be enough. How can we account for the difference between the respective silences around the names New Zealand and Auschwitz? One might say, of course, that Auschwitz happened to *us*, whereas New Zealand did not. That, however, would be to assume that we know who we are extra-discursively – by blood; and it is another of Lyotard's virtues that he does not want to concede that either. One might point to a qualitative difference – but how can we measure the loss of a culture against the loss of lives?

Auschwitz resonates for us, not because we are who we are genetically, but because memories of it are constantly circulated orally and in writing. New Zealand's history, on the other hand, is told within a different rhetoric and is barely circulated even inside the country itself. The emotions attached to Auschwitz are attached to language; they remain analytically inseparable from the discourse that produces them. The difference between affect and language begins only when one asks 'Does one have a right to a feeling?' It seems clear that one has a right to articulate the injuries one feels. It is less clear that one has a right to feel feelings as injuries in the first place. In philosophy this question rarely arises because it is generally assumed that an injury is simply felt as an injury, in a way that a bird is not simply seen as a bird. Lyotard does not address himself to the question of the transmission of either language or emotion. If the phrase event is the beginning and end of deliberation, it does not follow that it comes into the world merely bordered by nothingness. It comes transmitted, always already in the history that it makes possible. If philosophy cannot confront the phrase as transmitted, then again that marks a philosophical limit.

What one misses from Lyotard is any sense that a phrase occurs in, or in the gaps of, a particular language. Indeed, on one breathtaking occasion he declares succinctly: 'all *langue* is translatable'.[13] If he were to accept that the question of what is and what is not translatable across languages is interminably debatable, then he would have to accept once again that the limits of specificity within his own frame are not found in the phrase itself. To observe that phrases happen within a particular language is to note something other than the phrase: the language the phrase is in. And for philosophical deliberation to confront a particular language at the point where presuppositions end would also and again be to confront a socio-cultural order inseparable from linguistic diversity. This order cannot be covered by the phrase and its linkages. In its flight from categories of totality, Lyotard's linguistic turn evades the one totality – so-called 'natural' language – which it cannot reduce or ignore *on its own terms*. It is precisely to this totality that post-colonialism today appeals.

III

The post-colonial desire is the desire of decolonized communities for an identity. It belongs to that programme of self-determination which Adorno, unlike Jameson, could envisage. Obviously it is closely connected to nationalism, for those communities are often, though not always, nations. In both literature and politics the post-colonial drive towards identity centres around language, partly because in postmodernity identity is barely available elsewhere. For the post-colonial to speak or write in the imperial tongues is to call forth a problem of identity, to be thrown into mimicry and ambivalence. The question of language for post-colonialism is political, cultural and literary, not in the transcendental sense that the phrase as *différend* enables politics, but in the material sense that a choice of language is a choice of identity.

The link between post-colonialism and language has a history. In his recent book, *Imagined Communities*, Benedict Anderson has argued that nationalism has always been grounded in Babel. That is to say, nationalism is a product of what he calls 'print-capitalism'. He writes: 'the convergence of capitalism and print technology on the fatal diversity of human languages created the possibility of a new form of imagined community which in its basic morphology set the stage for the modern nation'.[14] One does not have to accept the faulty psychology hidden in the phrase 'imagined community' to take the point. Nationalism emerges when some languages get into print and are transmitted through books, allowing subjects to identify themselves as members of the community of readers implied by these books.

Let us take Anderson's history further. Of all the works that created the new print languages, none had more authority than the sacred books. A whiff of heresy attaches itself to the story at this point. The sacred books, as vehicles of God's word, cannot be translated. No doubt, when God reveals himself in natural language, transposition of a kind has already taken place, but the human language becomes divine through the breath of God's voice, the trace of his hand. To deliver the Bible (or the Koran) to *any* demotic language is not just to allow nationalism to overpower the old church, but for meaning to precede form, for communication to precede revelation – it is to admit, in fact, the arbitrariness of the sign.

Anderson does not make a further argument which seems to me inescapable. Once the sign becomes arbitrary, once divine self-revelation becomes transferable across secular languages, then not only may national identities attach to the print language, but language itself no longer permits of any proper identity. If one language can be translated into another, if there is no such thing as a dead language, what untranslatable residue remains to be the property solely of those who speak it? Its form, which cannot be communicated in – as one says – any other form? Yet an identity granted in terms of the signifier (which I use, as it is often used, as a figure for form as such) is an identity that necessarily cannot be communicated. It would seem to be written into the fate of nationalism as print-capitalism that national identity is conferred in the form of its own death warrant. Indeed, there are moments in our culture where an unquenchable nationalist pathos confronts its own mortality: one thinks of Hölderlin's poetry.

The appeal to what is unexchangeable in language is especially tempting under capitalism, which deals with things and words for their exchange value. In the classic formulations of nationalism – Fichte's *Addresses to the German Nation*, for instance – national identity is based on both language (the home of culture) and soil. When a post-colonial nationalist like the Kenyan novelist Ngugi, living under multinational capitalism, looks at the soil, he sees it as a means of production, and means of production do not articulate identities; indeed, where they can be owned, they are often owned by foreigners. This leaves him language and, within language, culture. (One might note that for decolonized nations the other great ground for nationalist pathos – war – has little place. Most post-colonial nations and tribes have a history of defeat by imperialist powers. Freedom is often the enemy's gift.)

Pre-colonial language shelters all the particularity elided over by colonial stereotyping, by modernist valorization of the primitive and by anthropology. In return, as identical to itself, national language excludes the web of contacts, the play of sameness and difference which weave one society into another. It does so in having the advantage that it is not unique. The number of languages available to be spoken is infinite; the economy of Babel is not restricted. And yet language is not identical to itself, and in translation a residue is always left behind.

Ngugi, who places language at the heart of his post-colonialism, was arrested for co-writing plays in Gikuyu, although no doubt his crime was also to aid Gikuyu's transformation into a print language. It is clear that he is not troubled by the sense that an identity given in print language is given as a death warrant. Thus, when he, or someone like him, enters a novel by a post-colonial writer who is disturbed by such questions, the mode of encounter is predictable. Near the beginning of Salman Rushdie's novel *Shame*, the narrator is interrupted by such a speaker, disputing his authority to tell the tale.

> *Outsider! Trespasser! You have no right to this subject!*. . . I know: nobody ever arrested me. Nor are they ever likely to. *Poacher! Pirate! We reject your authority. We know you, with your foreign language wrapped around you like a flag: speaking about us in your forked tongue, what can you tell but lies?* I reply with more questions: Is history to be considered the property of the participants solely? In what courts are such claims staked, what boundary commissions map out the territories? Can only the dead speak?[15]

This is a dialogue across the bar which internally divides the post-colonial. The divide separates what one can call the post-colonized from the post-colonizers. The post-colonized identify with the culture destroyed by imperialism and its tongue; the post-colonizers, if they do not identify with imperialism, at least cannot jettison the culture and tongues of the imperialist nations. Of course there is not always a choice here. For many ex-colonies the native tongue is the world tongue – English. This is not just true for Australia and Canada, say, as it was once for the United States. It is also true for West Indians as well as for many Maoris and Aboriginals. Indeed, there exists a largely unrecognized but crucial difference in the various post-colonial nations. A country like Australia has almost no possibility of entry into the post-colonized condition, though its neighbour, New Zealand, where Maoris constitute a large minority, does. New Zealand retains a language, a store of proper names, memories of a pre-colonial culture, which seductively figure identity. I have no doubt that the very name New Zealand, and its *différend*, will pass one day, the nation coming to call itself Aotearoa. What one encounters here is a politics of language which rests not on the power within language, the power of rhetoric, but on the power behind language. From the side of the post-colonizer, a return to difference is projected. But, from the side of postmodernity, English (multinational capitalism's tongue) will museify those pre-colonial languages which have attached themselves to print and the image so belatedly.

Rushdie's dialogue between the post-colonized and the post-colonizer takes place in a language which is not quite transatlantic English. For instance, the position of the adverb in the phrase 'Is history to be considered the property of the participants solely?' marks a tone at the slightest of removes from that English. But its difference may not be invested with nationalist pathos. It remains too close to what is not different but the norm, the language of world power. The sense that Indian, New Zealand, Australian or Irish English is not as different from transatlantic English as French is from English, let alone as different as Maori or Gikuyu, figures the post-colonizer's emptiness. 'Can only the dead speak?' Rushdie elliptically asks, hinting, among other things, at the powerlessness of the pre-colonial tongues and at the death warrant involved in finding an identity through fallen languages, of which his own has fallen furthest.

Rushdie answers the post-colonized challenge in terms of the *différend*. The narrator enquires: 'In what courts are such claims staked?' Now it is he, whose side is not quite that of the oppressed, who appears as victim. He cannot find a place for justice, nor plainly articulate his case, partly because he speaks neither the language of the international market nor a post-colonized language. What he is charged with is what he inherited. If Rushdie, as a post-colonizer, speaks from a place in contemporary history where a *différend* is dramatically foregrounded, then Lyotard's retreat into transcendental philosophy, his mysticism of selected proper names, his preference for experiment, have a strong competitor. If Jameson cannot fully distance himself from the sublimity and internationalism of what we can call image-capitalism, then that is perhaps because he has not listened carefully enough to those voices which talk of the *différend* on its borders.

To consider the *Apocalypse Now* system alongside *Shame* is chastening. The problem is not one of varieties of postmodernism. Rushdie's work is sometimes called postmodern, but it certainly does not reflect postmodernity. *Shame*'s purpose is to reconnect shame – that epic, indeed pre-capitalist, emotion the Greeks called *aidos* – to the recent history of Pakistan. In redirecting shame, the novel calls upon a violence, both feminine and monstrous, which does not, like that of *Apocalypse Now*, reach a climax from the very beginning. *Shame* imagines an unlocalizable, inexpressive, ethically proper violence we never see in *Apocalpyse Now*. Indeed, the novel as a whole works in precisely the opposite direction to Coppola's movie. History is not derealized, affect is not atomized into intensity, narrative triumphs, other cultures are not confined within Occidental myth, nor outside the Western screen. So we can say that, when confronted by his post-colonized accuser, Rushdie is startled into an articulation of the problematic of the *différend*, but, when faced with modern Pakistan, he acts as accuser in turn. Here his novel remains connected to those concepts of justice and reason that totalizing denouncers of our postmodernity assure us are in their safekeeping.

NOTES

1. Fredric Jameson, 'Postmodernism, or the Cultural Logic of Late Capitalism'. See 'Select Bibliography'.
2. Ibid., p.27.
3. Theodor Adorno, 'Cultural Criticism and Society', in *Prisms* (London: Neville Spearman, 1967), p.34.
4. Herbert Marcuse, 'The Affirmative Character of Culture', in *Negations: Essays in Critical Theory* (London: Allen Lane, 1968), p.122.
5. Adorno, op.cit., p.29.
6. Jameson, op.cit., p.88.
7. This article was written before Jameson's essay 'On Magic Realism in Film' (*Critical Inquiry*, 12 (1986), pp.301–25) appeared. This represents a departure from the 'cultural logic' piece because it does allow that post-colonial films differ from postmodern artefacts in ways that offer promise. But from my point of view the essay remains based on doubtful assumptions, i.e.:
    1 Certain 'First World' films (nostalgia films) still *instantiate* postmodernity.

2 Post-colonial films are more realist than 'First World' films because they are produced in conditions not totally dominated by late capitalism.
3 Post-colonial films are also postmodern in that they exemplify 'denarrativization' and a 'reduction to the body', both of which 'libidinize' cultural residues.

However suggestive an account which moves from these theses may be, it continues to rely on expressive causality and reflection theory; it still assumes that the 'postmodern' and 'realism' are textual features, not effects, or constituted by discourse on texts; and finally it does not allow for the particular mode of ethico-political debate and intervention which takes place only and precisely in post-colonial nations. There is a danger that the post-colonial here becomes both something like Europe before 1848 for Lukács and a site saturated by the progressive materialism of postmodernity, rather than a field of forces which postmodern thought must analyse without idealization or condescension.

8. See Eleanor Coppola, *Notes* (New York: Pocket Books, 1979), p.9.
9. For what follows, see Jean-François Lyotard, *Le Différend* (Paris: Minuit, 1983).
10. Ibid., p.204.
11. Jacques Derrida, *Of Grammatology* (Baltimore: Johns Hopkins University Press, 1976), p.135.
12. Lyotard, op.cit., p.219.
13. Ibid., p.226.
14. Benedict Anderson, *Imagined Communities: Reflections on the Origin and Spread of Nationalism* (London: Verso, 1983), p.49. For further material on this topic, see John Edwards, 'Language and Nationalism', in his *Language, Society and Identity* (Oxford: Basil Blackwell, 1985).
15. Salman Rushdie, *Shame* (New York: Vintage Books, 1984), p.23.

CHAPTER 8

The Issue of Bataille

Julian Pefanis

The publication, in 1985, of a collection of Georges Bataille's writings from the thirties, has given new impetus to the reception of his work in the English-speaking West. For some time now there has been a quite intense interest in Bataille's texts, but one confined to specialist journals of cultural theory.[1] The publication of *Visions of Excess*[2] marks Bataille's posthumous irruption into the wider discourse of French theory. For the moment I will refuse specification of that theory as either post-structuralist or postmodernist in order to avoid the easy retrospective projection of Bataille into a seminal pre-history of these two categories; not from an aversion to the tautologically true, but rather as a result of a certain caution about the rush to canonize writers and thinkers in the name of postmodernity. The rush to canonization could easily repeat the mistakes of modernism in the construction of a revised pantheon of universal culture.

Biographical and historiographical research into Bataille has already attempted to situate him in the context of his immediate theoretical world, all the better to understand the general orientation of his writing, and all the better to limit the destructive movement of his text. In this context two works should be mentioned: *Georges Bataille politique* by Francis Marmande, and *Reading Georges Bataille* by Michèle Richman.[3] These studies have attempted to specify Bataille's relationship to several discursive fields: anthropology, philosophy, psychoanalysis, Marxism, literature and art. This immediate theoretical world refers also to details of a biographical and bibliographical nature, details that relate to the charged inter-war years and to the whiff of cordite and death that permeated the thought of the era. To examine Bataille in relation to this world is not simply an exercise in historicism, designed to forestall his apotheosis in postmodernity, which is the fate that Habermas has reserved for him.[4] Nor is it a defiance of those who might dismiss Bataille from the forum of theory before the questions that might arise from a study of his texts have even been properly formulated. No, to examine Bataille in this context is to witness his critical engagement with, and his ultimate rejection of, the major currents of modernist thought – neo-Hegelianism, French sociology, Surrealism, etc. – from the standpoint of a prophetic return to Nietzsche.

That it is possible simultaneously to call Bataille a modernist, pre-modernist and postmodernist says as much about our own heoretical tendency towards closure as it does about Bataille. The first observation to make about the discourse on Bataille is that it exhibits a certain tendentiousness, no less evident in Habermas's claim that French postmodernism embarked on the path of self-destruction when it followed Bataille,[5] than in Foucault's claim that Bataille's thought is a guiding light in the darkness of a new era of the *unthought*.[6] The second observation to make about the discourse on Bataille is that it never properly succeeds in appropriating his thought. In the psychoanalytic model of appropriation employed by Bataille, 'appropriation' destroys the distinction between subject and object. In the 'oral' phase the 'different' (food) becomes the 'same' (the 'me'), but equally, excretion re-establishes the 'different' in its expulsion from the body of that which cannot be assimilated.[7] If the bodies change, the process remains the same. Bataille consistently demands, and we cannot escape this demand, that we confront whatever is expelled, not because he is a philosopher locked in an anal phase of development, although he has been accused of this,[8] but because the theme of exclusion refers not to the myth of the origin of humanity, but to its end. The texts of Bataille are a theatre of the excremental in whose scenes one may glimpse golden threads: of textuality before the letter of Barthes; of deconstruction before the letter of Derrida; of transgression before the letter of Baudrillard, or Foucault and his 'return' to Nietzsche. And so the cat leaves the bag and tendentious thought demands speech: it is simply impossible *not* to imagine the centrality of Bataille to an intellectual history of Parisian thought, impossible *not* to formulate questions that coalesce around this proposition. Quite properly, the rules of rational discourse discourage such exaggerated claims by their demands for evidence and qualification, in the face of which such a claim might appear bizarre, if not certifiable. What, then, is going on here?

How do we explain the delay of Bataille? Why is it that, after successive waves of French theory, beginning with Sartrean existentialism, which have periodically been diffused through the English-speaking West, it is *now*, rather than twenty years ago, as it was in France, that we finally get a taste of Bataille? I think we can discount a conspiracy theory on the part of publishers desperately dredging the field to bring us ever more obscure figures from French literature: the enormous energy required for translation for little return would argue to the contrary. The problems of translation would come much closer to the mark. Since translation is the interpretation of a text across the conventional frames of language, one could well imagine the translation of Bataille's texts as a formidable task indeed. But this cannot be the whole story. Fashion is probably a factor here, and probably not an inconsiderable one. Yet who is afraid of fashion? Those for whom fashion, like fetishism, is something that other people are afflicted with. How do you attack fashion without appearing a vulgar moralist? As Lyotard reminds us, the couplet fashion/fetishism is well known to a 'critical' discourse that has always theorized it in pejorative terms.[9] False consciousness likewise is what other people have, for to admit that we are all afflicted, and equally, before its mystery would mean that 'criticism' is itself a function of a fashion for critical thought, and that its object of analysis is itself fetishized in relation to criticism. Yet fashion in itself, the play of an arbitrary code within the field of discourse, is insufficient to explain the delay of Bataille, because it fails to account for a movement in discourse which *is* governed by an internal logic. For some time now, we have experienced the effect of Bataille's thought in secondary literature without being able to specify its precise origins. It has been like the movement of a large dark body, maybe a black hole, whose presence in the heavens has been discernible in the erratic orbits of the visible plants: Foucault, Barthes, Derrida, Baudrillard and the rest. To be sure, these thinkers have made no secret of their interest in Bataille, nor indeed of the special place in discourse occupied by him. One need only refer to the *colloques* (organised in the first instance by the *Tel Quel* group)[10] and to the reviews (*Critique, L'Arc*, etc.)[11] dedicated to the analysis of Bataille's text, to understand the intense interest inspired by the French rediscovery, at the heart of the modernist project, of a heterogeneous element, which placed the entire tradition into a vertiginous relationship with its real and imaginary ends.

The 'issue' of Bataille can be understood in three senses: as what has emerged from the theoretical and contextual background in the name of Bataille; as what issues from his text in the form of the impious, transgressive and impossible; and as a metaphor for a fundamental philosophic exclusion. To put it another way, and in order to satisfy a desire for closure and continuity in a discontinuous realm, the issue of Bataille is that of the third term which he sets into play. Neither the result of a dialectical synthesis, nor the reference of a semiotic practice, the third term (or third order, since this is the project) has neither a Hegelian nor a structuralist origin but a Nietzschean, Sadean one, the 'beyond' of good and evil. Thus also it sustains a powerful ethic of the pagan.[12]

To speak of Bataille's work, or works, is to refer to a very substantial body of writing, collected in nine volumes, and written over approximately forty-five years until his death in 1962.[13] Largely ignored in the pre-war years, Bataille's reception was given impetus by the group connected with *Tel Quel*, which included Phillippe Sollers, Julia Kristeva and Roland Barthes. For Barthes, Bataille was particularly valued as a precursor of that general 'mutation' in the status of literary and critical writing, which challenged the traditional classifications and the claims to primacy of the original work of literature over its secondary criticism.[14] Bataille's texts transgress the boundaries of the old disciplines and in so doing produce a violent juxtaposition of the discursive and the discontinuous. They are thus difficult and refractory texts, and this is especially evident in the matter of the 'voice' in the text, an incessant shift of the designation of the *je* and the *moi*, that is, in short, in the locus of subjectivity. It could be said that there are always at least two voices in the text. The one, the voice of the outlawed and prohibited Bataille, crosses the path of Bataille the continuous and discursive thinker, erupting, as it crosses, into an intense display of the sacrifice of meaning at the altar of a crucified, authorial, sovereignty. The act of writing is itself transgressive, perhaps ultimately the model of transgression for Bataille, in that the epistemological and linguistic foundations upon which the discrete disciplines are based are here constantly 'put into question'. This is as true for the putatively 'scientific' discourses of linguistics, anthropology, Marxism or psychoanalysis, as for the meditative and speculative discourses of philosophy or literature and criticism. For Barthes, Bataille's writing is the 'exemplar of textuality':

> What constitutes the Text is, on the contrary (or precisely), its subversive force in respect of the old classifications. How

do you classify a writer like Georges Bataille? The answer is so difficult that the literary manuals prefer to forget about Bataille who, in fact, wrote texts, perhaps continuously one single text.[15]

Here too we see another reason for the delay. To classify Bataille is the same problem as that of 'situating' him. That this is so difficult helps to illuminate, by example, in the very act of writing itself, the process of the *heterogeneous*, understood as both category and activity.[16]

Let us therefore describe the issue of the text as, firstly, this category of the heterogeneous, for this is what is expelled from the *homogeneous* body, be it political, textual or corporeal. The figure of the sovereign leader, a narcissistic being-for-himself, borrowed from Freud,[17] forms, along with dangerous base elements, the mad, the criminal and the revolutionary, the sphere of the heterogeneous in relation to the homogeneous social body. But for Bataille the pre-eminent category of social exclusion is the 'sacrifice'. What is expelled from the organic body is the excremental and the sexual, bits and partial objects of the eroticized and fetishized body. These elements, like the entire realm of the heterogeneous, are governed by ritual prohibitions that link, at an unconscious level, the religious and profane practices subject to the rules of the Symbolic. Above all, what must be kept apart is the body in death, in putrefaction, and this heterogeneous element is subject, like the other elements of the body, to the strictest of taboos. These taboos give rise to those universal practices that seek to purify the contamination provoked by this profanation of the body. For Bataille these practices mediate the relationship between the living and the dead, between the profane and the sacred. For him they are the ultimate reference for literature and art: practices that seek to return to the homogeneous social body, in a purified form, *in the form of bleached bones*, that which nature and catastrophe have torn from human society. From the textual issues the censored and the unspeakable in a perverse relation that associates the restricted discourse of divinity with the abject texts of pornography. Here I think we should recall Bataille the pornographer, tirelessly and 'heroically' carrying on the 'sovereign labours' of de Sade. Bataille's pornographic works have been referred to as among the finest examples of the genre produced in the twentieth century.[18] We might note that Bataille's reputation as a pornographer, producing texts that never failed to provoke scandal, preceded his reception as a social theorist, and that this reputation might indeed be related to what we are calling his delay. The heterogeneous elements, and I give here but the barest account of them, are thus theorized as the realm of the unconscious, representing for Bataille the concrete and social expression of its structure and function. The analysis of the heterogeneous, which Bataille refers to as 'heterology', thus combines psychoanalytic categories (desire, transgression) with critical and philosophic concepts, in a particular anthropological vision. This ironic 'science' proceeds in its analysis according to a dream-like movement that associates the heterogeneous elements on the *plan* of the unconscious; a movement exemplified, for Barthes, by the declension and shift of the signifier, the eye, in *The Story of the Eye*:[19] *œil, œuf, soleil, couille*. The movement is (over-)determined by mimesis (sphericity) and by the linguistic *glissement* (slide) that associates the word-shapes of the signifiers. In terms of a 'science', this process is clearly exotic, and this is precisely the point. For Bataille, the appropriating function of scientific analysis is a procedure of the homogeneous mind that is constitutionally incapable of theorizing the heterogeneous. Science itself represents a limit to the experience of the impossible.

But Bataille is not content to remain in the analytic stage of the heterogeneous, within limits that restrict access to its mysteries. On the contrary, in postulating an identity of sexuality and death, certainly demonstrable in psychoanalysis, Bataille takes a decidedly Nietzschean turn, by linking the experience of the loss of subjectivity in ecstasy and sexual rapture with the philosophic loss of sovereignty in the death of God. With this death there disappears the transcendental guarantee of individual sovereignty. What also disappears is the limited condition of thought that God represented: there is no exteriority of being. This lack of an existential guarantee, though hardly to be regretted, is associated with the demise of the 'sacred', a theme of the Durkheimian school. It leads, in Bataille, to a strategy and a method, as opposed to a project, of going to the limits – of thought, belief and morality – and then transgressing those very limits in order to de-limit both their operation and that of the sovereign authority needed to exceed them by transgression.[20] This Nietzschean turn also places Bataille within the problematic of writing and death, as addressed by the 'philosophers of death', Maurice Blanchot and Pierre Klossowski.[21] It also brings us to the issue of transgression.

Foucault's essay on transgression furnishes us with an example of a text which challenges the privilege of the original (joyfully ceded by Bataille), in that one day (perhaps already), it will be impossible to consider transgression without first conceiving it

The Issue of Bataille 139

in Foucauldian terms. Referring to the death of God, Foucault writes:

> Bataille was perfectly conscious of the possibilities of thought that could be released by this death . . . but what does it mean to kill God if he does not exist, to kill God *who has never existed*? Perhaps it means to kill God both because he does not exist and to guarantee he will not exist – certainly a cause for laughter: to kill God to liberate life from this existence that limits it . . . – as a sacrifice; to kill God to return him to this nothingness he is and to manifest his existence at the centre of a light that blazes like a presence – for the ecstasy; to kill God in order to lose language in a deafening night . . . – and this is communication. The death of God does not restore us to a limited and positivistic world, but to a world exposed by the experience of its limits, made and unmade by that excess which transgresses it.[22]

In this fragment of Foucault's text on transgression, we are led to re-duplicate the movement of thought in Bataille's text: from the Dionysian laugh to the profligate loss in the sacrifice, a movement from the blinding light that was God to the dusk of a false consciousness that opens onto the night of transgression, the night of *l'expérience intérieure*. This latter was the title of Bataille's work written during the darkest night of the Nazi occupation, a work that celebrates abject despair and the acephality[23] of *non-sens*, of the subject deprived of thought and discourse, of reason and even of subjectivity itself. It is this that is at the basis of Bataille's mysticism: this will to self-loss in the transgression of sovereignty, as Bataille expresses it, 'the practice of joy before death'.[24] Of course, the reference to Nietzsche has more than a thematic significance, since it defines an entire orientation at a political-epistemological level. To specify this level, we must refer once again to the 'philosophy of death', as it were, and ask what was the origin of the Surrealist disdain for bourgeois culture? Was it not of the same origin as Nietzsche's vehement contempt for bourgeois mentality and forms, his contempt for religion and for a feeble bourgeois art, which had betrayed its true supra-historical character by becoming confounded with a utilitarian and mercantilist morality? Thus when Foucault claims, in the 'Orders of Discourse', that whether it is through logic or epistemology, *whether through Marx or Nietzsche*, our entire epoch struggles to disengage itself from Hegel,[25] we must consider this placement of Marx and Nietzsche 'on the same map' as a commentary on the political-epistemological orientation of this earlier generation of Bataille, Klossowski and Blanchot. Foucault specifies this relation, in the 'Preface to Transgression', when he claims that the category of transgression will one day 'seem as decisive for our culture, as much a part of its soil, as the experience of contradiction was at an earlier time for dialectical thought'.[26] For Foucault, Bataille was a key figure in the escape from the Absolute Spirit. It is arguable whether modern philosophic thought has succeeded in this struggle, or whether we have entered into the era of transgression, the Batailleian millennium. The question we might pose is this: is what Foucault says true for us as it is for him? We should recall the circumstances of the appearance of the 'Preface to Transgression', in the double issue of *Critique* honouring the passing of the founder and editor of a review that had held a privileged position in the world of French letters.[27] The list of contributors in this memorial issue is formidable: Foucault, Maurice Blanchot, Pierre Klossowski, Raymond Queneau, Michel Leiris, André Masson. When Foucault writes that transgression will occupy this decisive role *for our culture* it is thus pertinent to enquire *who* is this collective subject? Is he referring to the intellectual culture of Paris, or is he speaking of ours? Is the distinction valid any longer? Is there, for that matter, any strong tradition of dialectical thought, which we must surpass, in the English-speaking world?

There is a missing factor in Foucault's equation: contradiction is to dialectical thought as transgression is to x, x here representing modern thought. Does Foucault mean his own experience? For if he does, then this experience is precisely his experience of Bataille and his transgression; and the former age to which he refers is not a dim past but a recent, still-present past, in which the dominant mode of philosophic thought, and of writing, would have been and would still be dialectical. Bataille therefore marks a moment, a milestone, on the road from Hegel to Nietzsche, from dialectical (Kojève, Merleau-Ponty, Hyppolite) to genealogical thought.

In a universe stripped of all the means of transcendence, whether religious or scientific, the destiny of the subject is forever immanent in experience. *Expérience*, in Bataille's text, is another of those terms furnished with a specific and exclusive sense: it is the experience of transgression, and thus has nothing to do with experience in general, except in opposition to the continuity and discursivity of its homogeneous existence. A word here on transgression: it is difficult to speak of transgression in terms of a definition, for the reality is that transgression in Bataille is a disposition, a 'method of obstinacy', as Klossowski puts it,[28] rather than a more or less precise practice. As experience is the experience of transgression, transgression is the transgression of sovereignty, and sovereignty is related to pure loss, or *dépense*.

Sovereignty is subject to a double usage in Bataille. On the one hand, it is read in its philosophic context as a 'personal' sovereignty, inherited from the Cartesian ego in Kant's transcendental and Hegel's trans-historical subjects; on the other, it can be derived from a socio-anthropological origin, as a feudal concept which grounded the privilege of a social group, the aristocracy, in the dilapidation of wealth and the obligatory nature of conspicuous consumption. Moreover, this is for Bataille an obligation that the bourgeoisie has historically avoided, preferring to conceal its expenditure, and using it instead to 'consolidate a symbolic code of distinctions between itself and the workers'.[29] Thus Bataille struggles to strip sovereignty of its ideological associations with the bygone aristocracy, without delivering it to a heroic bourgeois individual. For it is precisely this sovereign subject and its authorial forms which Bataille aims to annihilate, by reserving it for a type of mystical experience of limits – of the poetic, the erotic.

The will to self-loss in sovereignty as the transgression of limits is thus related, in a general way, to the entire problematic of death that is inherited in French Hegelianism. In Hegel, the crowning moment of sovereignty is victory or death in the wake of a risk of death, in the struggle with the consciousness of the Other. But in a world purged of the battle of the masters, in which death returns as representation and spectacle and simulacrum, the negativity of the master is deprived of all historical meaning and is bequeathed to the slave as destiny through work. It is here that Bataille takes issue with the Hegelian *anthropos* and, by extension, with Marx's reworking and inversion of the dialectic of history. For Bataille there is an alternative to the negativity that positivizes work: the operation of the process of the sacred and sacrifice.

The theme of the sacred, and its supreme category of the sacrifice, rejoins the science of heterology as a definition of the socially heterogeneous: of those things and practices which are subject to prohibition and censorship, excluded from contact and interest in quotidian existence. It is possible to locate this interest in the sacred and in sacrifice within the tradition of French sociology, to which Bataille paid repeated tribute. But where Durkheim, in *The Elementary Forms of the Religious Life*, draws an irreducible discontinuity between the sacred and profane, Bataille finds a possible reconciliation at the level of the heterogeneous. Durkheim had written:

> In all the history of human thought there exists no other example of two categories of things so profoundly differentiated or so radically opposed to one another. The traditional opposition of good and bad is nothing beside this; for the good and the bad are only two opposed species of the same class, namely morals, just as sickness and health are two different aspects of the same order of facts, life, while the sacred and profane have always and everywhere been conceived by the human mind as two distinct classes, as two worlds between which there is nothing in common ... howsoever much the forms of the contrast may vary, the fact of the contrast is universal.[30]

Bataille rejects both this absolute division and Durkheim's impulse to read the sacred as heterogeneous in relation to the profane. For Bataille, the sacred and profane have to be read together as the excluded in relation to the world of homogeneity, linked at a psychic and philological level.[31] Nonetheless, the two thinkers both tend to view the sacred, and its expression in the sacrifice, as a now lost principle of social cohesion. For Durkheim, it is the collective consciousness, strengthened and quickened in the presence of the sacred, which forms the social bond; for Bataille it is 'in the festivity of sacrifice and in its sacred violence that man attains that community in sovereignty which is lost in the social order founded on the primacy of production and acquisition'.[32]

Therefore, whilst it is true that sacrifice must ultimately be theorized in the discourse of anthropology, its very absence from our contemporary social formations must also be accounted for in our anthopology of ourselves. This was the project of the College of Sociology,[33] the result of a collaboration of Bataille, Roger Caillois and Michel Leiris between 1937 and 1939. In addition to a dedication to the exploration of the realm of the sacred, the substantive aim of the college was the analysis of the structure and function of secret societies, in which no discrimination was to be made between secret groups in so-called archaic or primitive societies and those of the advanced societies. Fraternities of warriors, initiatory groups, heretical and orgiastic sects were considered alongside fascist and revolutionary organizations, terrorist groups and crime syndicates. In the ways to which we have alluded, Bataille's project was antithetical to that of the French sociological school of Durkheim and Mauss. True to the spirit of the college, a secret group was formed associated with the review *Acéphale*,[34] a 'secret society', Nietzschean in outlook, dedicated, *inter alia*, to the experience of human sacrifice. (It is reported that the problem with the scheme was that, while there was no shortage of volunteers for the role of victim, no one was willing to perform the act of execution. At a secret rendez-vous in the forest, the cult sacrificed a goat instead.) The college folded in 1939 under the pressure of the impending chaos, but not before it had organized several conferences, some of which attracted the exiled Adorno, Horkheimer and Benjamin. At this juncture, it becomes possible to specify some common ground between Bataille and Critical Theory, in particular on the question of the sacred and its disappearance from modern social formations, and on the relationship between this disappearance and the growth of instrumental reason and universal *mathemesis*, the world of homogeneity.[35]

We can note the parallel paths followed by the Frankfurt School, in the *Dialectic of Englightenment*, and by Bataille, who stands here as a representative instance of a radical moment in French socio-anthropology. Their common direction may be expressed in terms of Horkheimer's and Adorno's 'dialectical anthropology', in its critique of 'equivalence', of abstraction, and of the ideological construction of a 'necessity' that is afforded a privileged status, as the basis for life, in both bourgeois and socialist societies.[36] 'Dialectical anthropology' maintains a fidelity to Marx's critical model, while at the same time surpassing the sub-Hegelian limitations of its understanding of liberation and domination. This parallel critique of homogeneity and production becomes even clearer in the later exponents of the French anthropological critique, particularly in the thought of Pierre Clastres and Jean Baudrillard. To this critique – which, I argue, holds a key to the understanding of post-structuralist theory and which is deeply indebted to the thought of Bataille – we must now turn.

When Marx luxuriates, in *The German Ideology*, in his vision of life under communism as hunting in the morning, fishing in the afternoon, herding cattle in the evening and criticizing late into the night, he expresses an unconscious anthropology that is at odds with his own more explicit anthropology of the progressive development of modes of production.[37] For what this unconscious anthropology entails is a vision, admittedly slightly productivized,[38] of paleolithic society, of society prior to the great neolithic revolution, which, by establishing permanent human settlement based on the practices of farming and the ownership of land, confined and marginalized the nomadic paleolith. Thus, Marx the champion of technique and industry opts, not without irony, for the decidedly unproductivist practices of the hunter-gatherer.

Not for Marx digging coal in the morning and working the lathe in the afternoon; no, Marx in communism lives in a world of natural abundance. Now in a world of natural abundance nothing, properly speaking, is produced, and game and fish are there for the taking, 'dispensed', as it were, by a generous mythological moment of grace.[39] Of course, too much could be made of this apparent lapse in Marx's concentration, and it must be remembered that it occurred in the context of a discussion on the division of labour (a discussion that derides the German understanding of historical and pre-historical categories). But as Freud has taught us, loose talk has the capacity to reveal a repressed content of thought. What is set loose in Marx's dream is the (Baudrillardian) ghost of anti-production, a ghost that haunted Marx the productivist, and all productivist thought, *as its true end*. Could Marx really have believed that the world of natural abundance, which would be communism, could be achieved by steam and steel, wheat and harvesters plus the re-united organs of the original division of labour, the hand and the mind? It would be a tall order indeed, a simulacrum of the very first order. It is, possibly, what he had in mind: at some point, production in its capitalist and socialist modes would have to be surpassed; at some point, it would cease to be the central category of human activity; at some point, humanity would stop producing its life so as better to live it.

Did Marx in fact 'glimpse' an anthropological truth, which has only recently been demonstrated, on the basis of a re-examination of the evidence, and a revaluation of the perspectives, of a particular field of anthropology? This truth is that paleolithic society, far from being the site of a wretched struggle for existence, was, while knowing only few types of personal possessions and no ownership of land, nonetheless a society of abundance. This, of course, is Marshall Sahlins's thesis in *Stone Age Economics* and in *Culture and Practical Reason*.[40] What Sahlins suggests is that, even were we to accept that paleolithic society 'produced' its material existence, and this is precisely what is in question, then the time strictly necessary for production and reproduction remained remarkably short. Not only was this labour-time brief, but the actual tempo and intensity of the 'labour' also varied enormously. The process of the hunt involved many non-productive activities including, one may imagine, criticizing. If one considers the concrete struggles of the contemporary working classes for wage and time conditions, then Marx's glimpse could only be disturbing in the extreme, and certainly a case for some type of sublimation. In truth, Marx's anthropology is an anthropology of scarcity, where starvation 'stalks the stalker' who is condemned, in the economic debate, to play the role of the bad example: the so-called subsistence economy.[41] (And playing the role of the bad example is the centrepiece of anthropological ethnocentrism, the most serious character disorder of all philosophies of totality.)

An anthropology based on an evolutionist vision condemns anterior society, beyond the idiocy of rural life, to a grim ordeal of living within a blind nature, a nature indifferent to the cares of people who are themselves blind to the ordeal of their own nature. The *telos* of growth, the progressive development of social institutions, kinship structures, technology, belief systems and the form and content of 'material conditions', is animated by that same spirit which allows the Darwinian to express surprise that he (invariably a 'he') is in the privileged presence of the 'perfectly accomplished' form of the species, be it a tiger or a tree or even a Hegel. Somehow across the galactic wastes of evolutionary time the species have evolved, in the process of adaption for survival, for the sublime benefit of the scientific observer. It does not occur to the evolutionist that the tiger and the tree were always perfected forms, and of course their very existence attests to this: perfection in survivability is simply survival, and this was dealt with in the first fifteen minutes. So too with human survival: it simply never was indexed to the survival of individuals (what Marx refers to as the first 'moment').[42] Human survival was always in terms of the group, and the collectivity was always the perfected form of the human; without it humans would die, or cease to be social, and this amounts to the same thing. If a discourse of anthropology imagines a so-called primitive communism as the repressed of capital and the order of production, then in its counter discourse, in a schema in which time is reversible, production itself is the repressed, and 'primitive' society is society against production.[43]

I would argue that the critical schema outlined above is representative of a 'political anthropology' that characterizes certain species of post-structuralist thought. That structuralism is a discourse on anthropology, which takes its most developed form in Lévi-Strauss, permits us to specify certain conditions of the 'posterity' of structuralism. To do so we might refer to an example of structuralism's anti-thetical moment which appeared in its conceptual firmament at the very beginning. This moment is to be found (by no means exclusively) in the double reading to which Mauss's *The Gift*[44] is subject, setting in motion two related, but ultimately conflictual, anthropological and epistemological models. Mauss's work is 'split' on the question of 'production'. Failing to theorize this realm, Mauss created the *aporia* within which these divergent theories took shape. On one side, the structuralist 'inherits' the gift in the form of the Melanesian *kula*, a single and total form which circulates as a vehicle for messages of categorically different types, symbolic, political, economic, strategic, etc. In Lévi-Strauss the *kula* exemplifies the exchangist character of human society: for him 'primitive' society is society-for-exchange, as it is through the exchange of gifts, words and women (his categories) that the social bond is sealed, and the symbolic discourse of the interrelated structures nourished and maintained. It is a homeostatic principle *par excellence*. But there is, claims Pierre Clastres, a silence in Lévi-Strauss's text on the question of war. From its origins, anthropology has divided over the definition of the character of 'primitive' society. And here Clastres parts company with his former mentor. Against the model of the primitive society as society-for-exchange, Clastres opposes primitive society as society *against* war. This is an inversion of the classical view of primitive society as society-for-war, but one which nonetheless maintains the centrality and ethnological reality of a level of fundamental violence constitutive of the social. Exchange as potential war averted, or war as the issue of a bad exchange, 'is contrary to the sociological reality' of primitive society, since war is *prior* to exchange: 'war implies alliance and alliance implies exchange. War is not failed exchange, but exchange is a tactic of war'.[45]

If the *kula* is the metaphor for exchange in Mauss, then the potlatch is the metaphor for war, and it is here that Bataille's reading of Mauss has proved crucial for the development of structuralism's counter-tradition. The potlatch is the gift of excess, the *prestation* that is accompanied, on occasions, by a display so antagonistic that it is indistinguishable from an act of war. The significance of the potlatch for Bataille, however, is not as a pure celebration of destruction, but rather in its normative function. The potlatch society prevents accumulation by the immediate sacrifice of the surplus, *la part maudite*, through an active principle of consumption which ensures an undivided social body and forbids the development of class society. This is, I believe, the central message of *La Part maudite*,[46] and its value to social theory is that it sets into motion an analysis of society based on modes of *dépense*. This latter term must be understood in a restricted sense, in that it refers to all expenditure that is dedicated to unproductive practices: war, sex, death, art and literature. In this analysis it is precisely the means of disposing of the surplus, which even the most reputedly subsistence economies will produce, that characterizes the nature of different social formations. Thus, societies of production, capitalist or socialist, distinguish themselves from the rest by their reinvestment of the surplus into the machinery of production. Contrary to appearances, industrial society is society which defers consumption, preferring, in the terms of the Situationists, to substitute the spectacle for the festival.[47] To draw the thread tighter, we could say that Baudrillard's critique of the systems and modes of productivist thought are filiated, via the agency of the Situationists and the critique of the spectacle, to Bataille's analysis of modes of *dépense*.

A period of sixteen years separates Bataille's major works on the 'Notion of Expenditure', which appeared in the review *La Critique sociale* in 1933,[48] from *La Part maudite* (the 'cursed portion' or the 'damned part') of 1949. This latter work Bataille considered to be his major theoretical contribution, a systematic exposition of his vision of the world, his philosophy of man, nature and history.[49] Here Bataille returns to many of the themes previously addressed in the 'Notion of Expenditure': to the critique of the 'classical principle' of utility; to the social function of sacrifice in the potlatch (the victim as the quintessential *part maudite*); and to a general theory of the potlatch that inverts the terms of classical and critical political economy by giving priority to the 'dilapidation', rather than to the accumulation, of wealth. In theorizing the restricted economy of use-values (political economy) *together* with the sacred economy of sacrifice, Bataille arrives at a theory of the *general economy*.[50] This theory sets out to go beyond the limits that bound 'economic man' and economic reason. The general economy is an expression of Bataille's cosmology, which assigns a pre-eminent place, as did the Aztecs with whom he felt so much affinity, to the figure of the Sun. For the Sun is the source of a boundless and generous superabundance of growth and energy. It is the gift without return that makes us the 'sum of its energy'.[51] Just as Bataille claimed that Mauss misread his own evidence, so Baudrillard claims that Bataille 'has read Mauss badly', since the 'unilateral gift does not exist':

> He who had so well explored the human sacrifice of the Aztecs should have known, like them, that the Sun gives nothing, and it is necessary to nourish it continually with human blood to keep it shining. It is necessary to defy the gods with sacrifice so that they will respond with profusion. Put another way, the root of sacrifice and the general economy is never *dépense* or who knows what drive of excess brought to us by nature, but an incessant process of defiance.[52]

(One might note in passing a basis for Baudrillard's symbolic exchange, as the counter-gift, within the Batailleian problematic.) For Baudrillard it is not, therefore, in the notion of *dépense* that Bataille's response to his 'true question' must be sought. That question was: 'Why is it that people have always proved the need and felt the obligation to kill living beings ritually? By fault of not knowing how to respond, all people have remained in ignorance of what they are'.[53] It is, rather, at a level below that of the text, at its interstices, that Baudrillard locates the answer: in the mythic assertion of the existence of the sacred. Bataille's mythic force is constituted, for Baudrillard, as for what seems to be an entire generation, by 'a subject of knowledge' always 'at the boiling point' which is retrieved 'at the height of death': the sacrificial force of writing.[54] Knowledge confronted 'at the height of death' returns us to the Preface to Hegel's *Phenomenology of Mind*, and to Alexandre Kojève's Marxist construction of the philosopher, in his famous initiatory readings to the rising generation at the Sorbonne, in the 1930s. Kojève's *Introduction to the Reading of Hegel* produces a thoroughly Marxist conception of the philosopher on the eve of the Battle of Jena, and conversely, a thoroughly Hegelian Marx. It is from Kojève that Bataille inherits each of these two conceptions.[55] Without going into the peripatetics of the Hegelian schema of history we can say simply that what appealed to Bataille, and for that matter to Lacan, in this account, was the primordial basis of history in the master/slave dialectic, a dialectic that is translated, in the psychoanalytic discourse, into the father/son relationship, and in Marxism, into the conflict between the bourgeoisie and proletariat. Hegelian negativity is given a specific value in both cases, that is, the value of the proletariat and the value of the son, as the negation of the negating action of the bourgeoisie and the father. In addition, the master/slave dialectic reserves a pre-eminent role for the irrational principle of violence in the formation or constitution of consciousness. Historical consciousness in the case of Marx, and individual consciousness in the case of Freud, is finally taken or prised (in a *prise de conscience*) in the violent action of revolution and the symbolic violence of Œdipus.[56]

The conflict between Bataille and the project of history, outlined in Hegel and Marx, can be understood as one further episode in a conflict that has shadowed all philosophic thought when it claims to speak in the name of some higher authority, be this Reason, the State or History. Jacques Derrida tells the story of Kant's disapproval of those he described as mystagogues, the imitators of the 'true' philosophic overlords. These people are given to the display of poetics and prophecy, they ironize and subvert the original significations of philosophy as a rational *savoir-vivre*, by announcing, in a particular tone, 'something like the end of philosophy'.[57] In the parliament of philosophy the voice of reason is ridiculed by the mystagogue who opposes the gift to work; the intuition to the concept; the genius to the scholar; and the aristocracy to the democracy. By replacing evidence with 'analogies and verisimilitudes', they 'resort to poetic schemas'. One supposes that this is neither more nor less than what Derrida himself achieves, in drawing the analogy between Kant's struggle with the mystagogues and Derrida's own struggle against the contemporary mystagogue. Derrida might indeed be his own *bête-noire* when he remarks that there is something of the mystagogue in each of us, and that all discourse is likewise ambiguous to some degree. Naturally Derrida refuses, in his characteristic double dealing, to take sides, by arguing that there is a collusion between foes, and that to play Aristotle against Plato, as Kant is happy to do, simply puts another head beneath the crown of the sovereign. But before Derrida returns the crown to the prop-box of philosophy, he lingers a moment and gives it a little buff, in order to conjure up its power before its fall from grace, before its transformation from an authentic auratic symbol, commanding in its own right, into a simulacrum of the once sovereign character of the philosophic overlords. But before philosophy is definitively screwed by its perverse *Doppelgänger*, before the parliament of the overlords is converted or should I say reconverted, into the theatre of the who knows what – The Theatre of the Apocalyse – there must be staged the scenes of the discourses of the end, featuring Hegel, Marx and Nietzsche, combined and recombined in a bewildering profusion. Derrida:

> I tell you this in truth; this is not only the end of this here, but also and first of that there, the end of history, the end of class struggle, the end of philosophy, the end of God, the end of religion, the end of christianity and morals (this [*ça*] was the most serious naïveté), the end of the subject, the end of man, the end of the West, the end of Œdipus, the end of the earth, *Apocalypse Now*, I tell you, in the cataclysm, the fire, the flood, the fundamental earthquake, the napalm descending from the sky by helicopter, like prostitutes, and also the end of literature, the end of painting, art as a thing of the past, the end of psychoanalysis, the end of the university,

the end of phallocentrism and phallogocentrism, and I don't know what else.[58]

Even to declare the end of the end is to 'participate in the concert', as it is the 'end of the meta-language on the subject of eschatological language'.

To put an end to the apocalyptic babble Kant, in his exasperation, calls for a 'scientific police', which would rout the chapel of 'arrogant philosophy', and return the debate to a rational discourse on *practical* reason.[59] The first motion of practical reason, in the philosophy of modernism (for we may as well start with Kant as anywhere else), is this expulsion of the poetic and prophetic discourse on ends. This scene, rehearsed at the philosophic level with Kant, is played out in the cultural formations called modernist, including, let it be said, in the discourse on capital.

We will call this philosophic expulsion the final issue of Bataille's text. In writing a pornography that is philosophy, and *vice versa*, the text is rendered beyond use-value, except as a negative reference for the human sciences. Yet the fact that Bataille's thought resonates in a particular field of French (and not so French) theory, whose scope I have tried here to indicate in a limited way, must cause us to reflect on the conditions of our own appropriation and exclusion of species of thought and knowledge, some of which are indeed forms of this French theory. Thus we must ask the question: how do we deal with Bataille's fictional philosophic metanarrative? Would it be good or bad to take Bataille seriously? What would it mean to take Bataille seriously?

To subject the text to a pious critique or a rational *détournement* would surely be a case for laughter to one, I suppose Nietzschean, way of thinking; yet to ignore the text would be a refusal to drink at the waters of Lethe that Bataille so generously offers to those in pursuit of history and society. This water is writing, but writing without time or memory, writing that returns from its source to an oceanic tradition that affirms itself as thinking the impossible, of 'opening notions beyond themselves'.[60] It is writing that affirms, as Foucault has written, that before anything else, thought is 'a perilous act'. He goes on to say that:

> Sade, Nietzsche, Artaud and Bataille have understood this on behalf of all those who tried to ignore it; it is also certain that Hegel, Marx and Freud knew it. Can we say that it is not known by those who, in their profound stupidity, assert that there is no philosophy without political choice, that all

thought is either 'progressive' or 'reactionary'? Their foolishness is to believe that all thought 'expresses' the ideology of a class; their involuntary profundity is that they point directly at the modern mode of being of thought . . . [which advances] towards that region where man's Other must become the Same as himself.[61]

On the issue of Bataille, one is compelled to conclude paradoxically, since the burden of his argument and criticism is never to foreclose discourse, but, on the contrary, to expose thought by opening it up to the condition of its own impossibility. Bataille's method and practice – heterology – ineluctably concern a metadiscourse on writing. This, as I have tried to show, is recognized by those thinkers called post-structuralist: Foucault, Derrida, Barthes, Baudrillard, Lyotard, etc. The project of writing claims Bataille as an exemplar who, in setting into play a third term beyond the habitual dualisms, of good and evil, left and right, material and ideal, literature and pornography, thus also sets into motion a project of the critique of criticism. Hence the paradox.

NOTES

1. See, for example, *Semiotext(e)*, 2:2 (1976) or October, 36 (1986).
2. Georges Bataille, *Visions of Excess: Selected Writings, 1927–1939* (Manchester: Manchester University Press, 1985).
3. Francis Marmande, *Georges Bataille politique* (Lyon: Presses Universitaires de Lyon, 1985) and Michèle Richman, *Reading Georges Bataille: Beyond the Gift* (Baltimore: Johns Hopkins University Press, 1982).
4. Jürgen Habermas in 'The French Path to Postmodernity: Bataille Between Eroticism and General Economics', *New German Critique*, 33 (1981).
5. Ibid.
6. Michel Foucault, 'Man and His Doubles', *The Order of Things* (New York: Vintage Books, 1973) and 'Preface to Transgression', in *Language, Counter-Memory, Practice* (Ithaca: Cornell University Press, 1977).
7. See Sigmund Freud, 'Identification', *Group Psychology and the Analysis of the Ego* (New York: Bantam Books,1960).
8. See Denis Hollier, *Le Collège de sociologie* (Paris: Gallimard, 1979), especially Georges Sadoul, 'Sociologie sacrée', p.569.
9. Jean-François Lyotard in *Instructions païennes* (Paris: Galilée, 1977). He writes: 'Some very good things have arrived in the name of commodities since the industrial revolution, why not ideas? Some are certainly

feeble, but do you believe that those of Merleau-Ponty or Lévi-Strauss, which are certainly not, are exempt from all marketing?' (p.13). 'One may certainly judge our thinkers as lamentable, but let us not invoke from that the fact that they are famous' (p.15). Great thoughts do not have to be produced in obscurity: 'The principle that the more it is obscure the more it is just, is false . . . .' (p.16).

10. See *Bataille*, a publication of *Tel Quel* at Cerisy-la-Salle in 1972 (Paris: 10/18 U.G.E., 1973).
11. *L'Arc*, 32 and 44.
12. This ethic is at work in the writings of Robert Jaulin, *La Paix blanche* (Paris: Seuil, 1970), who argues that 'primitive' societies are not 'survivals', but diverse models of human society, some of which belong to the future. Likewise Lyotard makes reference to Clastres's analysis of primitive society in terms of an 'ethic' of the pagan in *Instructions païennes* and in *Rudiments païens* (Paris: 10/18 U.G.E., 1977).
13. See Georges Bataille, *Œuvres complètes*, 9 vols (Paris: Gallimard, 1970–9). For excellent bibliographies, see Richman; Marmande; Alain Arnaud and Gisèle Excoffon-Lefarge, *Bataille* (Paris: Seuil, 1978); or *Semiotext(e)*, 2:2 (1976).
14. For Barthes, mutation rather than rupture characterizes the 'relativization' of the relations between the writer, reader and critic. In the wake of the demands of Marxism, Freudianism and structuralism, the relativity of the frames of reference is of an Einsteinian rather than a Newtonian order. There is also thus the requirement for a new object to oppose the discipline-bound 'work', and this is the Text. See Roland Barthes, 'From Work to Text' in *Image-Music-Text* (Glasgow: Collins, 1977), pp.153–64.
15. Ibid., p.157. Barthes goes on to say: 'If the Text poses problems of classification (which is furthermore one of its 'social' functions), this is because it always involves a certain experience of limits . . . the Text is that which goes to the limit of the rules of enunciation (rationality, readability, etc.). Nor is this a rhetorical idea, resorted to for some 'heroic' effect: the Text tries to place itself very exactly *behind* the limit of the *doxa* (is not general opinion – constitutive of our democratic societies and powerfully aided by mass communications – defined by its limits, the energy with which it excludes, its *censorship*?). Taking the word literally, it may be said that the Text is always *paradoxical*' (pp.157–8).
16. The category of the 'heterogeneous' is introduced in the essay 'La structure psychologique du fascisme' in *La Critique sociale*, the review co-edited by Bataille and Boris Souvarine. The latter's split with the Communist Party over the trial of Trotsky marked the beginning of a non-PCF Marxism in France. The essay is translated in *Visions of Excess*.
17. See Freud, op. cit. According to Franz Alexander, Freud took a dim view of the viability of democracies and was 'thoroughly impressed by the indestructibility of the profound emotional need of humanity for strong leadership, which is the cornerstone of all his sociological speculations ...' (ibid., p.ix).

18. Susan Sontag, 'The Pornographic Imagination', in Georges Bataille, *The Story of the Eye* (Harmondsworth: Penguin, 1982), p.111. She writes that: 'Pornography that is serious literature aims to "excite" in the same way that books which render an extreme form of religious experience aim to "convert" ' (p.95). Pornography is ultimately more about death than sex, and in it Thanatos surpasses Eros in an 'erotics of agony'.
19. Roland Barthes, 'The Metaphor of the Eye', in Bataille, *The Story of the Eye*, pp.119–27.
20. For Bataille, the taboo and prohibition is the essential condition of transgression. Taboos exist in the profane world, and it is only through limited acts of transgression that a sacred and ecstatic state can come about. In the case of the death of a sovereign, the 'door to unlimited transgression is opened'. It was this mythic force and energy which exercised Bataille in his 'revolutionary' writings of the thirties, connected to the movement of *Contre-Attaque*.
21. There is a continent of thought just beyond the horizon: the matrix formed by Blanchot, Bataille and Klossowski. This continent is the territory of an aesthetic of anti- or post-Surrealism, its critique and its critical moment. The discourse on the relationship between death, sexuality and writing is another means of describing the triad. We might place the discourse in the space of Blanchot's 'literary', as inherited from the Surrealists in the form of *écriture automatique*. In effect, it is a Nietzschean aesthetic. See Pierre Klossowski, *Un si funeste désir* (Paris: Gallimard, 1963), and his *Nietzsche et le cercle vicieux* (Paris: Mercure de France, 1969), and Maurice Blanchot, *L'Espace littéraire* (Paris: Gallimard, 1955) and *L'Entretien infini* (Paris: Gallimard, 1969).
22. Michel Foucault, 'Preface to Transgression', in *Language, Counter-Memory, Practice*, p.32.
23. Georges Bataille, *L'Expérience intérieure* (Paris: Gallimard, 1954). Acephality or 'headlessness' is the term Bataille coined to describe this lack of existential guarantee and loss of sovereignty produced by the death of God. *Acéphale* is the name of the review co-produced by Bataille, Klossowski and Masson between 1936 and 1939.
24. Georges Bataille, 'La Practique de la joie devant la mort' in *Acéphale*, 5 (1939). The June date of this issue of *Acéphale* provides an unmistakable context for Bataille's meditations. In the sixth issue, Bataille declares, playing on the sense of his own name, that: 'I AM MYSELF WAR. I represent a human movement and excitation whose possibilities are limitless: this movement and this excitation can only be *pacified* in *war*' ('Méditation héracliteénne', p.22).
25. Michel Foucault, 'Orders of Discourse', in *Social Science Information*, 10 (1971), p.28.
26. Michel Foucault, 'Preface to Transgression', p.33.
27. *Critique*, 195/196 (1963).
28. In Marmande, op. cit., p.89.
29. See Richman, op. cit., p.88.
30. Emile Durkheim in *The Elementary Forms of the Religious Life* (London: George Allen and Unwin, 1976), pp.38–9.

31. Annette Michelson refers to the 'philological ambiguity' of the sacred, what for Freud was an example of the 'antithetical meaning of primal words' by simultaneously referring to the 'holy and the accursed' – see 'Heterology and the Critique of Instrumental Reason' in *October*, 36 (1986), p.115.
32. Ibid., p.116.
33. See Hollier, op. cit.
34. A reproduction of the five issues of *Acéphale* is available: *Acéphale* (Paris: Jean-Michel Place, 1980).
35. See Michelson, op. cit., pp.125–6.
36. Theodor Adorno and Max Horkheimer, *Dialectic of Enlightenment* (London: Verso, 1979), pp.38–41.
37. Karl Marx and Friedrich Engels, *The German Ideology* (London: Lawrence and Wishart, 1970), p.53. On the idea of a progression, Marx and Engels write: 'Empirically, communism is only possible as the act of the dominant peoples "all at once" and simultaneously, which presupposes the universal development of productive forces and the world intercourse bound up with communism' (p.56).
38. Michelson reports that Horkheimer 'was heard to observe toward the end of his life that even Marx appeared to envisage life as a vast workhouse' (op. cit., p.127).
39. See Jean Baudrillard, *L'Échange symbolique et la mort* (Paris: Gallimard, 1976), Ch. 2. In 'Un-knowing: Laughter and Tears', Bataille relates fishing to the concept of sovereignty: 'Fishing is not quite work. It is, if we like, the work of primitive man, but it is work which does not create that alienation which characterizes the slave's work. In our time still, anyone who considers himself a master can fish. Fishing is the property of the master' (*October*, 36 (1986), p.101).
40. Marshall Sahlins, *Stone Age Economics* (Chicago: Aldine and Atherton, 1972) and *Culture and Practical Reason* (Chicago: University of Chicago Press, 1976).
41. *Stone Age Economics*, p.1.
42. Marx and Engels, op. cit., p.50.
43. This argument is essentially the same one argued by Pierre Clastres in *La Société contre l'état* (Paris: Minuit, 1974).
44. Marcel Mauss, *The Gift, Forms and Functions of Exchange in Archaic Society* (London: Routledge and Kegan Paul, 1970).
45. Pierre Clastres, *Recherches de l'anthropologie politique* (Paris: Seuil, 1980), p.184.
46. Georges Bataille, *La Part maudite, précédée de 'La Notion de dépense'* (Paris: Minuit, 1967).
47. See Guy Debord, *The Society of the Spectacle* (Detroit: Black and Red, 1983).
48. *La Critique sociale*, 7 (1933), trans. in *Visions of Excess*.
49. Jean Piel, 'Introduction' to *La Part maudite*, p.17.
50. *La Part maudite*, Parts I and II.
51. Jean Baudrillard, 'Quand Bataille attaquait le principe metaphysique de l'économie', *Le Quinzaine littéraire*, juillet 1–15 1976, p.5.
52. Ibid., p.6.

53. Ibid., p.6.
54. Ibid., p.7.
55. Alexandre Kojève, *Introduction to the Reading of Hegel*, assembled by Raymond Queneau (New York: Basic Books, 1969).
56. Raymond Queneau in 'Premières confrontations avec Hegel' wrote that he and Bataille had hoped to come to the aid of a 'sclerotic dialectical materialism' by enriching it with the best ideas of bourgeois thought, Freud, Durkheim and Mauss. There is no dialectic of nature, but a dialectic rooted in the human condition and lived experience. This is the specific value of negativity in psychoanalysis and Marxism (*Critique*, 195/196 (1963)). Jean-Joseph Goux in *Freud, Marx économie et symbolique* (Paris: Minuit, 1973), claims that Marxism and Freudianism reveal a profound unity on the question of the constitution of the subject as an 'ensemble' of relationships, either the subject of ideology or neurosis (pp.31–9).
57. Jacques Derrida, 'Of an apocalyptic tone recently adopted in philosophy', *Oxford Literary Review*, 6:2 (1984).
58. Ibid., pp.20–1.
59. Cf. Jean-François Lyotard and Jacob Rogozinski, 'The Thought Police', *L'Autre journal*, 10 (1985).
60. Bataille, *L'Expérience intérieure*.
61. Foucault, *The Order of Things*, p.328.

CHAPTER 9

Marx and the 'Postmodern' Image of Society

John Rundell

There is an internal tension between Lyotard's *The Postmodern Condition: A Report on Knowledge* and the piece that appears as an appendix to its English edition, his parody of Kant, 'Answering the Question: What is Postmodernism?'.[1] Perhaps this tension reflects the fact that the former was first published in 1979, the latter in 1982. But there is more to it than an inconsistency created by a mere temporal distance between two texts. The tension runs between alternative images of the temporality and the contextuality of modernity and postmodernity. These, in turn, bring into relief two of the key issues in the modernity/postmodernity debate, the issue of the 'criticality' and robustness of conventional Marxism as a general theory of society, and the nature and dynamics of modernity itself. As these are inextricably entwined they will provide both the starting point and the underlying focus of this paper. In this context, a few further preparatory remarks are required.

I have an unusual thesis to present: that postmodernity is both internal to and inimical to modernity. By this I mean that there is both a change *and* a continuity – and hence a series of tensions – between the modern and the postmodern. I put forward this thesis not only on 'substantive' grounds, but also on the metatheoretical ground of an anthropo-philosophical theory of culture as a conflict of imaginary significations. Located within this enterprise is an idiosyncratic reading of Marx which explores and is constituted by this tension between modernity and postmodernity. My reading is intended to establish an interpretative dialogue with Marx by drawing each of the issues mentioned above together and placing them in relation to what I will argue are suppressed and paralysed moments in Marx's theorizing. What I present of Marx is therefore an over-interpretation that sits outside the basic conceptual framework of historical materialism.[2] Moreover, implicit in these two issues is the problematic of interpretation as it pertains to the nature of human contextuality, that is, the problematic of social theory and its possible philosophical anthropologies.

Lyotard's own answer to the question 'What is Postmodernism?', attained by way of Kant's *Critique of Judgement*, is that 'it is undoubtedly part of the modern' (79). In reaching this conclusion he establishes a heterogeneous and pluralized image of contemporary social life as peculiarly free of the need for a possible socio-cultural unity such as is posited by Habermas. Rather, Lyotard's general theoretical understanding of contemporary societies is derived from the ideal of 'slackening', of an experimentation that de-totalizes an assumed totality. This de-totalization is born out of conflict in any number of pluralized locales. These provide both a site of struggle and the formation of a 'public', which in turn articulate various particular demands about power (73). Moreover, these demands are more than simply the articulation of particularity. For Lyotard the emergence of modernity, which he identifies with industrial capitalism, dissolves 'realities', constituting itself against the background of the 'lack of [traditional] reality' by inventing other realities which themselves attain a consensus of some sort (77). What is meant by all of this? According to Lyotard the important aspect of modernity is not so much that it invents rules which construe the relations between objects and concepts, but rather that this is achieved only by the imposition of a falsely conceived unity constructed in either transcendental (Kant) or ontological (Hegel) terms, which offers not only consistency but also solace and pleasure. These rules become what he terms 'metanarratives'.

Despite such comforting metanarratives motivated by the logic of regret, there is also another key in which the aesthetics of modernity can be played out in a specifically *postmodern* fashion. Lyotard draws our attention to 'the invention of new rules of the game' (80), rules which do not fissure the pre-established metanarrative but rather are located 'outside' it. As Lyotard says:

> The postmodern would be that which, in the modern, puts forward the unpresentable in presentation itself; that which denies itself the solace of good forms, the consensus of a taste which would make it possible to share collectively the

nostalgia for the unattainable; that which searches for new presentations, not in order to enjoy them but in order to impart a stronger sense of the unpresentable. . . . [The works the postmodernist produces] *are not in principle governed by preestablished rules, and they cannot be judged according to a determining judgement, by applying familiar categories to the text or to the work.* Those rules and categories are what the work of art itself is looking for. The artist and the writer, then, are working without rules in order to formulate the rules of *what will have been done.* Hence the fact that work and text have the characters of an event. . . . (81 – the emphasis is mine.)

Significantly, Lyotard does not conceptualize this difference, this paradox, in temporal or historicist terms. The postmodern does not typify a new epoch here. Rather, the exteriority of the postmodern is a constant feature of the modern: 'Postmodernism thus understood is not modernism at its end but in the nascent state, and this state is constant' (79).

It is this image of constancy which becomes the *immediate* issue once one turns back to *The Postmodern Condition*. Here the relation between modernity and postmodernity is temporalized: modernity is the age of metanarratives *per se*, of Enlightenment discourses which appeal for self-legitimation to 'the dialectics of the Spirit, the hermeneutics of meaning, the emancipation of the rational or working subject, or the creation of wealth' (xxiii). These discourses run aground, exhausted and without credibility, in the late twentieth century. *Post*modernity means precisely this: a form of society typified by an incredulity about metanarratives, located in the so-called post-industrial centres of the world where technical and cybernetic knowledge is the assumed basis of the reproducibility of socio-systemic impulses (even if these are highly diffentiated and diffused). Diffuseness is itself another essential ingredient; whereas earlier metanarratives were totalizing in their image of society, postmodern informational relations presuppose a heterogeneity of contexts, notwithstanding the new forms of totalization and control by the state which may or may not centre around the Party or around the consumerist demands of a vociferous and eclectic multinational capitalism. Such a view entails a different (and competing) image of society, one which empties of critical force the open-ended idea of invention argued in the 'What is Postmodernism?' essay. In implicit recognition of Luhmann's systems theory, and as a response to Habermas's communication theory, postmodern society is presented firstly as functional, yet highly differentiated; secondly, as bounded by functionality in its patterns of action, which proceed according to the criteria of technical production, expertise and performativity constitutive of information-based societies; and thirdly, and importantly, in spite of this functionalization each differentiated sphere is constituted as a site of struggle where the 'rules of the game' are tested, reimposed or reinvented by the participants (9–17).

Lyotard grapples with this third feature, that is, with the constitution of social relations. He presents us with a dual core to the image of society which propels his analyses of modernity and postmodernity. On the one hand, intersubjective relations are necessarily agonistic or contestatory, although not always bound to the criterion of success (invention is a case in point). On the other hand, and following Wittgenstein, 'language moves' compose 'the observable social bond' (11) through pragmatic rules that determine the boundaries of the game, 'the properties and uses to which it can be put' (11). Every utterance is a 'move' in a game, and any alteration to the rule is an alteration to the nature of the game. Lyotard makes a categorical distinction between traditional, modern and postmodern societies based on the composition of their respective agonistic language games.

Leaving aside Lyotard's analyses of the pragmatics of narrative knowledge that typify traditional societies, which are arguably the most interesting part of the book, I will concentrate briefly on his analysis of modernity and postmodernity. According to Lyotard modernity is a fusion of horizons between *science* on the one hand and *universalizing unifying narratives* on the other. The 'rules of the game of science are immanent in that game, [so] that they can only be established within the bonds of a debate that is already scientific in nature' (29). Universalizing unifying narratives, by contrast, function as legitimators for social prescriptions, the referents for which are external to those narratives. These referents are either: knowledge derived from science; or the people as the hero of liberty; or the rational bureaucratic state staffed by professional officials. It is this externality (whatever its source), and the status of normativity given to these referents, that in the main transforms a narrative into a legitimating metanarrative. There are two paradigmatic versions. One, which first appears in the Humboldt report, consists 'not only in the acquisition of learning by individuals, but also in the training of a fully legitimated subject of knowledge and society' (33). This legitimate subject is a synthesis of three things: an original principle (corresponding to scientific activity), an ethos and a political ethic (a *Sittlichkeit* in the Hegelian sense), and homologous with this, the coincidence of the search for scientific truth with the pursuit of just ends in moral and political life (33). Here the subject is not a state, but rather a philosophical system, a totality which establishes the grounds for knowledge and criticism. The other emerges from the Napoleonic reorganization of the French state under the legitimating auspices of nationhood (the people), stability (the state) and progress (science), in which the state and its technicians intervene in ever widening areas of social life. This latter narrative construes 'a relation of knowledge to society and the state which is in principle a relation of means to the end' (36), that is, a relation which is utilitarian (and positivistic).

According to Lyotard these metanarrative paradigms lose their credibility in the decades after the Second World War. This loss of credibility is not to be explained, however, either by the explosion of techniques and technologies, or by the redeployment of market strategies and the atrophy of the welfare state which typify advanced liberal capitalism. Rather, its source lies *within* the first of modernity's metanarratives. The speculative current, which is part of its constituting logic, erodes the very basis of the legitimating principles of knowledge. Once speculation is re-forged it can be wielded as a critico-destructive weapon, for example, in the shape of Nietzsche's hammer.[3] No longer subsumed under and absorbed into a totalizing system, each field of knowledge begins to stand on its own, incapable of legitimation except on its own terms. This has similar consequences for utilitarian and positivistic knowledge. There is simply a plurality of language games. According to Lyotard's reconstruction of the historicity of modernity there is no longer any legitimacy, but rather only incredulity.

It is not merely, however, an incredulity towards metanarratives that leads to postmodernity and becomes its hallmark. Even more importantly postmodernity also results from the different constitution of the legitimacy of its social relations. In Lyotard's view, postmodern social relations are *paralogical*, that is, they are pragmatic, 'discontinuous, catastrophic, nonrectifiable and paradoxical' (60). This is what sets postmodernity apart from modernity. He argues, against Luhmann,[4] that it is not performativity, which he sees as ultimately the retotalizing myth of a positivistic determinism internal to the new systems theory, that establishes the nature of postmodern institutional forms, interactions and social relations (46–53). It is, rather, paralogy, the main focus for which is power relations. It is here that agonistics enters, with both a critical *and* occluding force.

On one level Lyotard argues that the heteromorphology of language games and the specificity of their (meta)prescriptive utterances – *meta* because 'they prescribe what the moves of language games must be in order to be admissible' (65) – have been matched by a recognition of the centrality of paradox and instability, which emphasizes dissension. This paralogical activity, which is a field of action located within the parameters of a system, is then able to challenge the rules and so transform them. Hence, the limits are not systemic as such; they are 'the stakes and provisional results of language strategies within the institutions and without' (17).

This, however, brings us to more troublesome features of the analysis of postmodernity in *The Postmodern Condition*. I will introduce each briefly and then introduce (again briefly) an alternative image of modernity, as a permanently incomplete 'mosaic'.

When Lyotard argues that the 'stake' of any postmodern language game is the capacity of any of the social actors to transform the rules of the game, he leaves out of his analysis the *nature* of the stake. To be sure, at the end of *The Postmodern Condition* he posits as large a participation as possible in the access to and control over information and its techniques. However, this remains an empty gesture, for in his haste to demolish any transcendentalism he retains only traces of the actors' dispositions as the points of orientation for social action. As Wellmer points out:

> Once we discover in the idea of a pluralism of language games the problem of democratic institutions, which would make possible the mediation of individual and collective self-determination, then . . . we cannot think of this democratic universalism under the conditions of 'postmodernity' without fundamental agreements; agreements which concern this democratic universalism itself . . . as an ensemble of common practices, basic orientations and meanings.[5]

It is this problem of the cultural imbeddedness of meanings (democratic or otherwise) that is occluded in Lyotard's analysis, and which will be examined below through a Castoriadian reading of Marx.

Secondly, 'a reflection on the political dimension of a "pluralistic" reason'[6] necessitates a reflection on Lyotard's own image of modernity and postmodernity. This returns us to my point concerning the relation between his two such images. There is an implicit, yet essential, one-dimensionality and flatness in

Lyotard's analysis, in spite of his commitment to paralogy. The 'flatness' is represented in particular by his construction of modernity. In the hiatus between *The Postmodern Condition* and 'What is Postmodernism?' one is reminded of the *'querelle des anciens et des modernes'*: the sense of an interstice or break between epochs is the same.[7] Of course, in the first *querelle* the question of authority, of authenticity was crucial: one epoch was posed in terms of tradition (antiquity), the other in terms of a uniqueness and self-definition which became represented by the idea of progress. This is the image that Lyotard essentially accepts and projects co-extensively with modernity; all else is ultimately subsumed under its umbrella. This projection is sustained by the two ghosts that provide the background assumptions for his postmodernist critique. The first is modernity's contestatory movements which masquerade as emancipation, but which embody domination and totalitarianism under the guise of a universal reconciling Subject. The ontological status of this Subject is such that it is the site where the dialectics of freedom/unfreedom, rationality/irrationality are fought out, to be resolved not in more freedom and more rationality, but in less and less and less.... The victory of the Subject entails the annihilation of subjectivities. This constitutes modernity's negative utopia. The first ghost mirrors a second that elucidates the nature of the constitution of modernity itself: on the one hand, a functionalization of all social relations and activities; on the other an increasing instrumental rationalization typified by the bureaucratization and scientization of social life (the Napoleonic model). In the sociological tradition, Durkheim and Weber are the main heirs to analyses which plot these processes: 'the destruction of traditions, then the destruction of the ecological environment, finally the destruction of "meaning", as well as the unitary self, which was once both the product and motor of the process of enlightenment'.[8]

Apart from an essential flatness, which leaves aside other constituent features of modernity, there is also in Lyotard a one-dimensionality which not only undermines the sense of exploration and uniqueness located in paralogy (for he concedes that systems logic may be right), but also occludes the possibility that uniqueness might be a constituent feature of modernity itself. This image, which is explored somewhat tendentiously in 'What is Postmodernism?', provides the organizing principle behind the account of modernity (which *includes* the period Lyotard posits as postmodern) developed in Berman's *All That is Solid*

Melts into Air. Berman's basic argument is that modernity is principally characterized not by its construction of metanarratives but by its paradoxical inventiveness, its constant movement and search for 'the now' which not only dissolves traditions but presents an endless array of possibilities. Against what he argues is the 'blank context' of the postmodern image of the eclipse of modernity, Berman wishes to 'bring the dynamic and dialectical modernism of the nineteenth century to life again'.[9] In so doing he shows the ironic face of modernity – a modernity, moreover, identified not only with Progress and States, but also with cities and publics. Underlying Berman's thesis is a theoretical discourse which constructs modernity as heterogeneous and open-ended, though, to be sure, this discourse remains *theoretically* unthematized throughout. But it does invite us to conceptualize, at the meta-theoretical level, a quite different image of the self-development of modernity. It is to this that we now turn.

Modernity is not merely the historical and geographical backdrop to a historicist history of ideas. Rather, it is constitutive of social relations in a double sense. On the one hand, the category of modernity refers to the historically specific series of complex social forms and institutions that social actors themselves create and inhabit; on the other, it is simultaneously a practico-interpretative nexus through which these social forms are themselves constituted.

The socio-historical form of modernity can be conceptualized as a process of societal and cultural differentiation propelled by a series of developmental logics located within each of the differentiating spheres. These developmental logics or dynamics include the general capitalization of social life; industrialization; the autonomization of art where it becomes, among other things, a twofold field for the destruction of tradition (religious aesthetics), as well as a critique of the other logics of modernization; and democratization (i.e., the debates and conflicts concerning the sovereignty of civil society and persons as autonomous beings). This last logic, associated with the emergence of the public sphere, interacts and clashes with the developmental logic of the state and its tendency to absorb society. Either together or separately these logics create crises and tensions between societal differentiation and societal integration. This results not only in pluralization, but also in a privileging of one logic over others and a tendency towards systemic or societal reunification and totalization. In other words, modernity can be viewed as a field of multiple tensions between combinations of these logics rather than as being constituted by any one logic.¹⁰

This first conceptualization of modernity is linked to the more general but no less important problem of philosophical anthropology, that is, of the way in which humankind is interpreted and conceptualized. Often embedded only implicitly in formal theoretical structures, philosophical anthropology can either problematize these formal structures, or can be absorbed and paralysed by them. In the context of the broad intellectual and cultural current that encompasses the Renaissance, the Reformation and the Enlightenment, philosophical anthropology is recast to mean the modern individual's relation to his or her own world. It establishes humankind, understood as both genus and composite of social actors, as fundamentally autonomous. As Taylor notes, this constitutes a fundamental shift in the core problematic of human self-definition: 'The modern subject is self-defining, where on previous views the subject is defined in relation to the cosmic order'.¹¹ This problematic develops through the Enlightenment's specific reformulations of rationality and freedom around a pattern of differentiation according to three images of humankind: *homo cogitans*, *homo politicus* and *homo economicus*, i.e., knowledge, politics and work. Under the auspices of the self-defining subject the epistemological and cognitive re-orientation of humankind as *homo cogitans* is tied to scientificity and technological innovation and competence. *Homo economicus* is orientated through the strategies and the language of interest. *Homo politicus* is expressed though the norms and ethics of participation and sovereignty. Thus each anthropological image is apparently confined to its own object domain. Moreover, these images, or, in Castoriadis's terms, imaginary significations,¹² themselves became the contested core of the developmental logics of modernity.

These images, or at least their internal constitution, lead to the construction of what Lyotard calls the metanarratives of the Enlightenment: the three worlds of reason which are 'cast in terms of the possible unanimity between rational minds' (xxiii–xxiv), those of truth, universal peace (freedom) and happiness in human actions. But how unanimous and consensually constituted are the modern images of humankind? Was there unanimity over the *immanent* form of any particular mode of rationality? Was there unanimity in terms of the *relationship* between each of these forms of rationality?

To pose such questions is to relocate our interpretation around the key notion of self-definition. This notion establishes a field of tensions and competing interpretations within modern thought. It is in this context that we can locate Marx who radically transforms the more or less explicit, yet systematically minimized, anthropology of his predecessors, in particular Kant and Hegel. He not only recentres the self-defining subject, but does so in a manner that (purportedly) gives to it a full capacity for self-formation and self-activity, through the *theoretical formulation* of an intersubjectivity constituted by conflict. The notion of labour is the ground upon which Marx radicalizes the Enlightenment's notion of self-activity and self-definition, and into which is absorbed the Enlightenment's differentiated formulations of rationality and freedom. Through labour Marx raises self-definition as an explicit and generalizable claim: humankind makes its own history and society. It is this claim, developed into a series of theses, that lies at the heart of Marx's theoretical formulation and critique of the modern world. Through it he reinterprets and transforms the problem of freedom from one dealing with civil sovereignty to one concerning the free autonomy of the (labouring) subject. This in turn leads to the construction of the specifically Marxian metanarrative of production. Marx's attempts to come to terms with the processes of social transformation and the dynamics of class conflict result in a series of conceptual residues and overloads. Thus an identification of Marx with the paradigm of production and a philosophy of history (and the justifiable criticisms levelled against these) does not exhaust an interpretation of his *œuvre*. This is the important point. What I term Marx's 'hidden imaginary' points towards and explores a possible residual philosophical anthropology neither derived from nor reliant upon the notions of labour and production for critical force or conceptual robustness. This 'hidden imaginary' indicates that textual interpretation and criticism are never wholly bound to the formal parameters and structures of an author-imputed meaning.

Moreover, this marxological approach is not a desire to 'save' or 'return to' Marx through idiosyncratic twists and turns of 'the text'. Rather, our interpretation and reconstruction of Marx recentres his work in the light of the nascent self-conscious anthropological turn in the early modern epoch. This points towards an incomplete, yet extensive and heterogeneous, cultural modernity which configures itself as a 'socially embodied argument . . . an argument precisely about the goods which constitute that tradition'.[13] Modernity is a living tradition which embodies the continuities of conflict. As such it opens not only onto the reality of competing interpretations of Marx's work, and but also onto the reality of competing interpretations as a general paradigmatic principle in social theory.

II

In the 'Economic and Philosophical Manuscripts' (1844) a tension appears within Marx's as yet untheorized anthropology. While the notion of labour is central to these works, it is counterpointed by the notion of self-creation, from which Marx generates a critique of capitalist development. Capitalism, from this standpoint, merely replicates, but in a more antagonistic way, the arduous task of labour which besets humankind. On the one hand, it develops industry, 'the *open* book of the essential powers of man';[14] but on the other, it reduces the human properties of a person to that of worker, and in so doing, not only *dis*recognizes, *dis*enfranchizes from the community the person who is without work ('1844 Manuscripts', 355), but also universalizes this 'worst possible state of privation' ('1844 Manuscripts', 360) through the 'science of asceticism' ('1844 Manuscripts', 361). In Marx's view, this replication leads in both cases to a one-sided development that either occludes or denies the worker's existence as a person with sense and sensibilities. For Marx these should embody the full range of not only practical, but also emotional, aesthetic, spiritual and reasoning capacities that affirm his or her existence as a *real* subject in an objective world ('1844 Manuscripts', 353–4). In this context, Marx's image of post-capitalist society goes beyond utilitarianism; it is portrayed as a society of cultural development that 'produces man in all the richness of his being, the *rich* man who is *profoundly and abundantly endowed with all the senses*' ('1844 Manuscripts', 354).

This suggests that another image of emancipation is brought forward by Marx. It resides outside his restrictive notion of labour; although it contains the elements that inform his later model of 'communal and autotelic totality', it need not rely on the notion of industry (as an early synonym of the productive forces) ultimately to ground it. It implies a multidimensional (rather than either a homologously structured or explicitly reductive) anthropology, which at the very least *includes* the problematic of consciousness, not only as an essential human characteristic but as one that objectifies itself historically.

For Marx, consciousness embodies the self-understanding of the species at any one time. In other words, it denotes its historically contextualized historicity. History, according to this interpretation, is the conscious realization of, and reflection upon, the forms that self-creativity takes. This other problematic of the anthropological status of historicity is, I suggest, translated or transposed into the notion of the 'forms of intercourse', and as such is actually given the formal status as a co-constituting moment within Marx's anthropological precepts. Marx does not restate social intercourse (or its constituting moments) in terms of the pure subjectivity of the Hegelian *Geist*-philosophy. Language, the practical form of consciousness ('1844 Manuscripts', 354), is no longer the vehicle of a self-reflecting and self-positing spirit, but is itself the way through which the practical and socially configured activities of people are co-determined.

This means that society is also the context for cognition, the production of knowledge that is simultaneously both technically orientative and interpretative. The notion of human practice implies not only humankind's production of material goods that satisfy its needs, but also of interpretations (which contain the imaginary significations) that guide and contextualize this production as a feature of humankind's historicity. In this context, consciousness embraces a continuum from myth to critique. By this time Marx's notion of species-being is a *background* notion that includes consciousness because, for him, the species becomes conscious of itself, or attains an image of itself through the cognitive forms it creates, whether they be generated through myth or reason. Historicity, then, is not merely a social product conccerning the immediate sensuous environment of other human beings; it is more importantly the realm of norms and rules that embody humankind's cognitive capacity to create either mythologically or rationally constituted knowledge that denotes the subject's relation to both nature and society. This knowledge is, for Marx, mythological if it portrays nature and society as objective, alien and unassailable forces ('1844 Manuscripts', 51).[15] It is rational if, through it, humankind 'consciously treats all natural premises as the creations of hitherto existing men, strips them of their natural character and subjugates them to the power of the united individuals'.[16]

The introduction of the problematic of cognitive forms implicitly problematizes the categorical distinction that Marx makes between the material content which pertains to the rules of use of human-made objects or use-values and the social form which pertains not only to the types of social organization that contextualize them, but also to their restrictive norms of employment. Each side of the 'equation' is problematized. There exists in every society, on the side of the material content, constituting ways of human activity that refer to persons and not only to the use of objects. The forms of intercourse, as relations between persons, are the most obvious and important of such activities. They are constitutive through the acquisition of the rules and techniques of language. Language is the means of achieving aims *external* to the acting subjects, and as such can be referred to as what have been later termed the pragmatics of communication.[17] Alternatively, as Markus argues, there are objects the proper use of which belongs *constitutively* to the social form, and not to the technical rules.

Although this expansion of the anthropological terrain to include language remains problematic and constrained by the basic separation between form and content, there is in Marx's work at least one important pointer towards the coincidence and interpenetration of these two categories in a way that basically dissolves them. As Markus points out, the

> coincidence of 'material content' and 'economic form' means that in the objects of this type [that is, money] it is impossible to separate the questions: 'How has it to be used?' and 'who may employ it, at what social occasions etc.?': these products are *objectivations* of human needs and abilities *relating to the various historical forms and modes of social communication and intercourse as such* and therefore the 'how' of their use *eo ipso* defines a given type of human contact in a definite social situation.[18]

In this formulation, then, it is not a *particular* type of rule-forming, (for example, purposive-technical rule-forming), that establishes humankind as a unique species, but rather that generalized rule-forming activity takes place as such, which *necessarily* includes, as a co-constituting determinant, norm-employing interpretations. Marx anthropologically reinterprets Hegel's problematic of consciousness in a way that is suggestive of a broad notion of interpretative praxis that refers to the constitutive dimensions of meaning, of which rules and norms are part. In other words, the norms and rules do not themselves exhaust the interpretative framework, rather they are located within it. It is this complex that both co-determines and mediates the heterogeneously structured and assembled social forms of intercourse. Moreover, it also generates, in the body of Marx's work, another strategy for his critique of capitalism.

III

This implicit and never theorized or thematized ambivalence in Marx's background anthropological assumptions is also necessarily accompanied by a similar ambivalence in his approach to the critique of capitalism. Emerging from the gaps and unfinished pages of his work as a whole, the critique oscillates between an immanent analysis of the functional reproduction of capitalism found in *Capital*, and one concerning the historical universalization of capitalist relations, or what we prefer to term the 'capitalization of social relations'. This latter aspect characterizes Marx's model of the subsumption of labour under capital.[19]

Marx generates the subsumption model through, and in conjunction with, the forms of intercourse, cultural patterns, which necessarily include social relations and their historical formation. In this way, the subsumption model is suggestive for the analysis of other forms of domination (and not only the one that it mostly refers to – the subsumption of labour under capital). What becomes important for the internal composition of this model, then, is neither capitalism's function nor the developmental and teleologically imputed impulse of the productive forces, but rather the clashes and interpenetrations between four phenomena: firstly, the essentially different, and for Marx unique, pre-capitalist forms of social intercourse; secondly, the constantly tension-ridden nature of the stabilization of capitalism itself through extensive expansion and renewal; thirdly, the class conflicts that are constitutive of capitalism's stabilization as a societal type; and lastly, other configurations of the modern epoch that are not constituted through capital.

To be sure the subsumption model begins, like Marx's other critical theories, with his central question: what is capitalism? Marx's definition of it in 'The Results' is, to be sure, similar to that in *Capital*. For him 'it is a process which absorbs unpaid labour, which makes the means of production into the means for extorting unpaid labour'.[20] This definition can be read in terms of an economic problem or a problem of social organization. Read as a problem of social organization, capitalism refers not only to the functional mechanisms that enable the production of surplus-value but also to the problematic of the struggles that initiate, constitute and reproduce the *organizational regime* of capital. In other words it is suggestive of a discourse concerning power and control.[21] This oscillation in Marx between a discourse concerning functional reproduction and a problematic concerning power also involves an oscillation within the anthropological terrain itself. The problematic of power that becomes central to the subsumption model necessarily includes the processes of societal self-understanding located in the forms of intercourse, as co-constituting moments. It is through his analysis of the historical transformation of the processes of social organization that Marx momentarily undermines the theoretical principles of the paradigm of production. It is here also that he confronts the limitations of one of his most central, yet least reflected, notions – that of use-value – and the way in which it imposes a restriction on his analysis.

Marx's implicit reliance on the forms of intercourse within the model of subsumption guides his historical analysis of capitalism from the vantage point of its own evolution and subsumption of other historically contextualized value-forms and relations. The dual processes of valorization and rationalization signify, for Marx, the fundamental shaking loose of traditional values and the creation of a fundamentally new value – an assumed valuelessness of the modern value-form, the transposition of interest into indifference, of quality into quantity ('The Results', 1012–14). This constitutes its own value. The new, dependent, social relationships do not then evolve purely from the realm of production, they are conditioned and structured co-determinately by the relations of exchange. The value-ladenness of the valorization process, in shattering traditional forms of integration, asserts its domination and ethical vacuity by being constituted through production *and* intercourse. This is what enables the processes of first formal and then real subsumption to achieve such far-reaching effects.

To conceptualize this, though, Marx cannot but rely implicitly on the notion of an imaginary signification for explanatory force.[22] It is here, if one likes, that society constructs and confronts its own concrete historical self-definition, though which it organizes itself and from which it cannot escape. It is (drawing on a different theoretical tradition) society's hermeneutical circle. Marx in some ways realizes this. His opening to (and our reading of) *The Eighteenth Brumaire of Louis Bonaparte* is suggestive of this. He states:

> Men make their own history, but not of their free will; not under circumstances they themselves have chosen but under the given and inherited circumstance, with which they are

directly confronted. The tradition of the dead generations weighs like a nightmare on the minds of the living.²³

Analogously, Marx's argument concerning the history (historicity) of capitalism is sensitive to this problem.²⁴ Capitalism develops its own self-understanding that does more than merely *describe* (as a necessary appearance) the type of class relations. This self-understanding is a co-constitutive process, a process which Marx implicitly analyses through labour, production and wages, not merely as forms of material organizations, but rather as constructed notions for a form of life, each variously defined in relation to value (*Grundrisse*, 196). Capitalism, as Castoriadis has argued a century later, has its own central imaginary which becomes a distinct constitutive component of the multidimensionality of the modern epoch. Under the regime of capital exchange-value, or price, is co-constituted through its own value structure – the value-ladenness of value.²⁵ This ensures 'that production is not an end in itself for me, but a means'.²⁶ In other words, the period of formal subsumption creates and systematizes the culturally activated presuppositions that become the ground for the complex and multidimensional development of the period for real subsumption – advanced modernity. Its decisive features also include an increase in the continuity and intensity of labour, as well as the development of the personality structure of inner-directed, autonomous independence dictated by 'the consciousness (or better: the idea[s]) of freedom, responsibility and frugality' (*Grundrisse*, 1031).²⁷

Marx's analysis of money plays a far more significant role in the context of this model than it does in the model of the primacy of the productive forces. It does this in two interrelated ways: by pointing to the *nature* of the historical transformation that capitalization takes and by conceptualizing this so that it problematicizes the foundations of historical materialism and its anthropology. Money's *value* of commensurability becomes the 'front' between pre-capitalist and capitalist social forms. The money relation between (at least) the wage-labourer and the capitalist replaces the nature-like relations of patriarchy which, for Marx, characterize the relation between master and journeyman that exists prior to, and simultaneously in, the period of formal subsumption (*Grundrisse*, 191).²⁸ In this context, *money* can be seen to undermine or subsume and transform the pre-capitalist forms of intercourse and personality; it becomes a form of intercourse *per se*. As such, and if Marx's analysis of money in the *Grundrisse* is presented in conjunction with the subsumption model contained in 'The Results', something of note occurs. The notion of money is transformed from a phenomenal expression of value (price), which in turn is the expression of abstract labour (capital), to a social process of symbolic encoding that co-constitutes a new relation of power and domination. It is to this analysis that we now turn.

In the *Grundrisse*, money in the modern epoch is portrayed as a social symbol that co-determines, expresses and cyphers a social relation of universalized yet isolated reciprocal dependence that is distinct from prior historical fixed forms of personal dependence. However this entails that money becomes a form of intercourse, which itself is constituted anthropologically. The key formulation is 'money as the autonomous representative of value' (*Grundrisse*, 236).[29] Marx's description of the developed autonomy of money as a symbolic objectivation in the capitalist phase of world history can be read to suggest that this later form reveals, in a completed although antinomially structured fashion, the structures and configurations of symbolic/linguistic forms in general. Just as 'the human anatomy . . . contains a key to the anatomy of the ape' (*Grundrisse*, 105), the modern category of money can be seen to contain not only the insights into the structures and relations of pre-capitalist as well as capitalist social forms, but also insights into the determining capacities of humankind.

Money could be seen to have an existence *analogous* to that of language. Although Marx rejects comparisons between language and money on the grounds of the doubling effect (*Grundrisse*, 162–3), their function as forms of intercourse is similar. For Marx, language/symbolism is the 'practical form of consciousness'. Language/symbolism can only be so conceptualized if it is also conceived as an objectivating human universal in the same way that labour is. Hence, exchange as a form of intercourse can be conceptualized though the notion of symbolic objectivation. Marx, in his remarks on barter among certain Negroes on the West African coast, puts it thus: 'The commodities are first transformed into bars in the head and in speech before they are exchanged for one another' (*Grundrisse*, 142). This is not conceptualized, by him, as an act of pure subjectivity. Rather, the functioning of the social system through forms of intercourse requires socially recognized symbols. His comments on the world market make this clear: it is conceptualized as a *'material and mental metabolism* which is independent of the knowing and willing of individuals' (*Grundrisse*, 161 – my emphasis). The co-determining objectivation of symbolization and language is not separated from its socio-historical context. It not only underpins the nature of the processes of societal intercourse, but also, by being an historically bound objectivation, indicates the nature of society.[30] In other words the value-complex of the objectivation, that is, the form of consciousness or imaginary signification which gives the objectivation meaning which is socially understood, is neither separated from its socio-historical domain, nor from the constituting moment of human life in which it is ultimately embedded (*Grundrisse*, 222–4).

Under capitalism, money as a symbol signifies the *value* of quantification and the organizational strategies that are encased within it. Following Castoriadis in 'The Imaginary Institution of Society' rather than Marx in this instance, money is a symbol of a symbol – a symbol of an imaginary that contains, co-determines and articulates the norms, values and rules of the social form of intercourse through which the societal identity of capitalism is forged. To be sure, Marx cannot analyse money in the *Grundrisse* if money's value (or imaginary) content is not assumed. Money is thus an essence of capitalism and not a 'necessary appearance'. It is an objectivation that is understood, that is, it has meaning. Marx puts it thus:

> Exchange value as such can exist only symbolically although in order for it to be employed as a thing and not merely as a formal notion, this symbol must possess an objective existence; it is not merely an ideal notion, but is actually presented in the mind in an objective model. (*Grundrisse*, 154)

In this context, the pre-capitalist processes of identity-formation become, for Marx, both the essential precondition of capitalist development, as well as the counterpoint against which the modern world is evaluated. Marx uses money as an 'analytical tool' (albeit symbol) by which he contrasts the pre-capitalist (unconscious) autotelic community with the capitalist one of mutual independence and generalized impersonality. The critique, though, obtains critical power, not merely because of Marx's *use* of 'money' as a tool, but because he realizes and presents it as a constituting feature of modern society. Money in its 'third function' smashes the ancient community to become the community itself. It is worth quoting Marx at some length on this point:

> This reciprocal dependence is expressed in the constant necessity for exchange, and in exchange value as the all-sided

mediation. . . . [This] reciprocal and all- sided dependence of individuals who are indifferent to one another forms their social connection. This social bond is expressed in *exchange value*, by means of which alone each individual's own activity or his product becomes an activity and a product for him; he must produce a general product – *exchange value*, or, the latter isolated for itself and individualised, *money*. On the other side, the power which each individual exercises over the activity of others or over social wealth exists in him as the owner of exchange values, of money. *The individual carries his social power, as well as his bond with society, in his pocket*. . . . This . . . is a condition very different from that in which the individual or the individual member of a family or clan (later community) directly and naturally reproduces himself, or in which his productive activity and his share in production are bound to a specific form of labour and of product which determine his relations to others in just that specific way. (*Grundrisse*, 156–7; see also 225–6)

These processes quicken during the period of real subsumption. The identity structure of the community, which Marx deconstructs through an analysis of the money nexus, stabilizes into an identifiable mode of life. There is a general and universal capitalization of not only social life, but also the technical/material requirements that, for Marx, underlie it.

This reading of the money process then, is suggestive of a change, or at least an ambivalence in Marx's work: should primacy be attributed to the social relations, social form, or the productive forces, or material content?

Marx's analysis of the movement from pre-capitalist societies to capitalism within the subsumption model suggests an ambivalent 'slide' towards causal primacy of the social form, which displaces not only Marx's teleologically imputed contradiction between the material content and the social form, but also his conceptualization of the social form in terms of the relations of production. The functionalization of life for capital cuts across the divide between base and superstructure. Functionalization does not require the universalization of the money-form merely as a necessary appearance, nor the processes of redefinition and cultural reorientation towards work as a derivative ideological component. They belong as co-determining factors that stabilize a new epoch.

What we have been hinting at can now be put plainly: the

subsumption model can be combined with the thesis that society generates its own understanding as a cultural objectivation. This objectivation, which is located in his notion of the forms of intercourse which themselves embody the forms of consciousness, is posited as a co-determining feature of any society. Under capitalism, 'the autonomously functioning mechanisms of realization of value and surplus-value through [the market]'[31] can be understood as a culturally situated law. The law of value is not only expressed through exchange-value but also as the catch-cry 'production for production's sake' and functions as a co-determining form of intercourse which establishes the dynamic for capitalism's own expansion into, and colonization of, other '*spheres* of [life] and their sub-spheres' ('The Results', 1037–8).

Furthermore these culturally constituted and located processes of functionalization and reification are not conceptualized by Marx purely in terms of the evolution, expansion and reproduction of a society without subjects. These processes are social relations based on typologies of power that contain the dynamics of self-interpretation. To be sure, an argument by Marx that attempts to address and include the problem-complex power, can lead either to a circumscription of conflict within the parameters of economy and function, or to a complete submersion of conflict and the development of the one-dimensional theory that occurs in *Capital*. Each current belongs to Marx's 1844 critiques of Hegel and political economy. Each obscures the problematic of contestatory action. Based on an anthropological critique of Hegel that gives the totality of human powers over to the objectivating capacity of labour, Marx's critique of political economy sees this labour as alienated during work under capital. The outcome of Marx's analysis in *Capital* is either a theory of exploitation based on the buying and selling of labour-power (and evident in conflicts over wages) or a thesis that posits the complete commodification of labour. In each case, Marx's notion of labour-time and its corollary, the increasing rate of exploitation, begins, as Castoriadis has shown, 'from a postulate: that the worker is completely "reified" . . . by capitalism. Marx's theory of crises starts from a basically analogous postulate: that men and classes . . . can do nothing about the functioning of the economy'.[32]

In the context of *our* reading of the subsumption model, the disjunction that Marx sees between the increases in social wealth that are obvious under capitalism and the relative pauperization of the worker, need not be addressed by him from the standpoint of an absolutized anthropology of labour, nor from that of a one-dimensional analysis that subsequently slides into a philosophy of history. The real reason why the processes of subsumption and reification remain incomplete is that they are necessarily contested on the basis of an imposed power relation. Under capitalism, both the criteria and practices of functionality are challenged by the bearers of labour-power – the working class. And, for Marx, the battleground is the money-form – the tension-ridden repository of the modern epoch's identity, even if it is forged through a specific logic of domination.

Marx argues that 'what money circulates is not commodities but their titles of ownership' (*Grundrisse*, 194). It is on this basis that capitalism is contested by the working class. Marx's analysis of wages, as it unfolds in 'The Results' (incompletely and not without the other restrictive features present), has implications for the anthropological determinations of an open-ended notion of society in which conflict is a necessary feature. The pay-packet is, for Marx, a sign-form that both determines and mediates the worker's subjugation to capital. It continually renews the 'illusion' that the contract between buyers and sellers of labour-power is both established by equals and only concerns the production of commodities. In Marx's view, it simultaneously assures and transfigures the reproduction of social relations established between unequals which is based in an organization (and imaginary) of despotic control by capital over the work-force. As he states:

> The constant renewal of the relationship of *sale and purchase* merely ensures the perpetuation of the specific relationship of dependency, endowing it with the deceptive *illusion* of a transaction, of a contract between equally free and equally matched *commodity owners*. ('The Results', 1064; see also 1063)

This power-relation, though (like any other) *functionally located*, draws on other dimensions of social life for its meaning and reproduction, dimensions that are not reducible to its location. The logic of Marx's 'critical sociology of class' indicates that the conflicts which are immanent to capitalism and to modernity in general are informed and structured by normative complexes that belong to the total life-processes and self-understanding of the conflicting parties. The actions that take place refer not only to the practical patterns of modern life, but also to often competing and tension-ridden normative-interpretative complexes that form patterns of cultural identity. It is from these value-complexes that the claims, which either enhance or challenge dominating power-relations (in this context, capital), are generated.

The essential point of difference, for Marx, between the pre-modern and modern movements and classes that contest the processes of modernization and capitalization, is established implicitly through the specific nature of their value-complexes. These are, for him, located in the specific identity of the community. In using the model of subsumption, Marx could be read as suggesting that the periods of formal and real subsumption are open to contestation from those who experienced alienation as a loss of communality because of either the strictures placed on the process of work itself, or the relation of impersonal dependence between wage-labourer and capitalist. During the period of formal subsumption the precapitalist forms of intercourse, thematized by Marx as forms of property, become the primary point of reference for conflict. However, in Marx's view the communitarian unity can be of a more or less despotic character, and more or less dependent on other-worldly references.[33] In a reconstruction that problematically minimizes and historicizes the role of tradition, Marx views the working class in the period of established capitalism as marshalling under the banner of autonomy and freedom, interpreted by him as an opposition to all forms of authority. Once the money-form is seen as embodying an organizational imaginary of despotism by those embroiled in it during their daily working lives, it can be challenged by another imaginary, that of freedom which Marx posits (at his most Kantian) as a participatory democracy.[34] It is from this perspective that he enthusiastically supports the Paris Commune.

In this way, the subsumption model could have been enlarged to encompass other aspects of domination and conflict. The *social* forms of intercourse, with which the subsumption model is concerned, provide Marx with an opening through which he could have analysed other configurations of domination and conflict that are both older and broader than the class-form. These are, for example, conquest, the relation between town and country, patriarchy, medieval corporatism (guilds and estates) and the state.[35] In this context Marx never explicitly refers to struggles concerning either the emancipation of civil society from, or its subsumption under, the state.

In *The German Ideology* Marx argues that he locates the process of societal stabilization and conflict in the contradiction between the productive forces and the forms of intercourse.[36] But as we have argued, the message of the hidden imaginary is that the forms of intercourse also have their own internal logic and dynamic that is not reducible to their interaction with the productive forces. This suggests a shift towards the primacy of the social form over the material content.

The shift, though, alters both sides of the conceptual 'equation' that constitutes Marx's materialist conception of history. The alteration occurs not only by Marx outlining implicitly another anthropological determinant apart from labour, that is, consciousness, but also by analysing it both historiographically and sociologically, that is, by contextualizing it. In other words, Marx's anthropology of the hidden imaginary works implicitly with a conception of cognitive structures that denote a general and universal human capacity for self-interpretation and self-representation. Moreover, the organization of all social activity, including the metabolism with nature, cannot but be referred to as an interpretative complex. It is this interpretative complex, and not only human practices, that also determines and stabilizes the socio-historical organization of society; and yet it can only exist within a socio-historical context.

My reading of *The German Ideology*, the *Grundrisse* and 'The Results' brings Marx to a specific point where his problematic of the anthropological self-constitution of the species meets later problematics that are concerned with the dimension of norms and values. It can be argued that contemporary social theory shares a common ground that in part draws some insights from both the unfinished and latent aspects of Marx's theorizing, notwithstanding an often intensely critical relation to his work, and from the same underlying problematic with which he was concerned – the anthropological determinants of the self-defining subject, particularly in the context of analyses and formulations of the modern world. The communication theory of Jürgen Habermas, Cornelius Castoriadis's notion of imaginary significations, Alain Touraine's theory of social movements, the paradigm of objectivation which stems from the Budapest School, especially the work of Agnes Heller, and Foucault's genealogical studies on the micro-technics of power, each in its own way denotes a turn in contemporary social theory towards viewing culture as a primary constituent of social relality, thus accepting, momentarily, both the interpretative constraints of the hermeneutical circle and the placing of theories of politics and power within this problem-complex. These projects constitute the implicit reference points for this paper and the horizon beyond its immediate path.

In the light of what I argue are the suppressed insights in Marx's theorizing, the respective images and theories of society that emanate from these contemporary theoretical enterprises can be transposed into three theses (thus also transposing the problematic of self definition into contemporary socio-theoretic terms):

1. Society is not only a totality, but also a series of autopoietic power centres composed through idiosyncratic identifying logics which may or may not intersect and interconnect.
2. Classes, groups and social actors constitute them-selves through an identity-forming process typified by a culture, that is, norms, values and a mode of life. These can be either contrasted to or imposed upon other classes, groups or social actors.
3. Society is also constituted as a series of objectivations that are simultaneously institutional and cultural. The cultural component is cognitively structured and embedded in linguistic and symbolic forms, and mediated and limited by practical relations with nature and other socially constructed societal reproductive (institutional) mechanisms. This culture carries the socio-historical function of a society's intepretation (or social imaginary) of the world, as well as its historical function of communicative self-understanding.

Each thesis develops the modern paradigm of the human condition in specific ways – through either the socially configured paradigm of system and action, the normatively constituted notion of intersubjectivity, or the notion of the culturally located processes of the interpretation of humankind, society and nature – that return to and problematize the anthropological constituents of the self-defining subject in Marx's work. In the light of my construction of 'the hidden imaginary' we can see that Marx joins hands (so to speak) with the hermeneutically conscious theorists of the late twentieth century, and gives the constructed social world back to society and social actors, thus side-stepping his own tendency to break out of the hermeneutical circle. Together they suggest that the key processes of societal structuration or institutionalization take place through interpretative value-relations that can now be defined provisionally as normatively constituted cultural objectivations or interpretative spheres that carry the historico-social function of communicative self-understanding. These are, in modernity, both ideological, self-reflective and structurally differentiated (although of course, there are tendencies and strategies of retotalization). In other words, we can interpret Marx's 'hidden imaginary' as implying that the transitions between historical epochs, the relations between systems of material production and their natural environment, social actors and classes, are constituted and mediated by the development of interpretative complexes, at the heart of which lie imaginary significations.

But here we have reached the absolute limitations (the 'outer limits') of our (over)-interpretation of Marx.

NOTES

1. See the 'Select Bibliography'. Numbers in brackets in the body of this essay refer to page numbers in the Manchester University Press edition of *The Postmodern Condition*.
2. See John Rundell, *Origins of Modernity. The Origins of Modern Social Theory from Kant to Hegel to Marx* (Cambridge: Polity Press, 1987). This paper is an edited and partly refocused part of my book.
3. See Friedrich Nietzsche, *Twilight of the Idols* (Harmondsworth: Penguin, 1986). Lyotard cites a line stretching from Nietzsche to Wittgenstein to Heidegger. One of the points in my argument is that the line should also include Marx.
4. See Niklaus Luhmann, *The Differentiation of Society* (New York: Colombia University Press, 1982); *Love as Passion* (Oxford: Polity Press, 1986); 'The World of Art and the Self-Reproduction of Art', *Thesis Eleven*, 12 (1985), pp.4–27. Systems theory analyses power relations in terms of the self-learning capacities of social systems as they take stock of the relation to their environments. In this context, knowledge and power are both pragmatic and self-referential (in a way similar to that of traditional narratives) rather than normative and metadiscursive (61–3). A hyperpragmatism, that is, a complete identification of the technocrats with the requirements of the system via performativity, leads to the system becoming terroristic, that is, the criterion of efficiency is raised by eliminating, or threatening to eliminate, a player from the language game one shares with him. 'He is silenced or consents. . . .' (63)
5. A. Wellmer, 'On the Dialectic of Modernism and Postmodernism', *Praxis International*, 4:4 (1985), p.359.
6. Ibid.
7. See T. Schabert, 'Modernity and History I: What Is Modernity?', in A.Moulakis (ed.), *The Promise of History, Essays in Political Philosophy* (Berlin: Walter de Gruyter, 1986); Hans Baron, '*Querelle* of Ancients and Moderns', in P.O.Kisteller and P.P.Wiener (eds), *Renaissance Essays* (New York: Harper Torchbooks, 1968).
8. Wellmer, op. cit., p.356.

9. Marshall Berman, *All That is Solid Melts into Air* (New York: Simon and Schuster, 1982), p.35.
10. Cornelius Castoriadis argues that the modern world revolves around two competing imaginaries (rather than logics): that of the market and that of the autonomous society. He posits a third which, for him, typifies and constitutes another 'version of modernity and is the central imaginary of Soviet-type societies – the strato-bureaucratic imaginary'. See his 'On the History of the Workers' Movement', *Telos*, 30 (1976–7), pp.3–42; 'Socialism and Autonomous Society', *Telos*, 43 (1980), pp.91–105; 'Facing the War', *Telos*, 46 ((1980–1), pp.43–61; and 'Reflections on "Rationality" and "Development" ' *Thesis Eleven*, 10/11 (1984–5), pp.18–36. For the Budapest School the modern world is conceptualized as a series of separate developmental logics that appear simultaneously in modernity, thus none is coextensive with it. These logics are democracy, capitalism and industrialization. More specifically the logics refer to constantly competing patterns of institutional complexes which form relational patterns in conjunction with the other logics that are themselves guided by 'value-ideas', the main two in modernity being freedom and life. See Ferenc Fehér and Agnes Heller, 'Class, Modernity, Democracy', *Theory and Society*, 12:2 (1983), pp.211–44; Fehér, Heller and Gyorgy Markus, *Dictatorship over Needs* (Oxford: Basil Blackwell, 1983). Jürgen Habermas's approach is somewhat different. According to him, whilst modernity is an historical complex, it represents the outcome of a specific evolutionary trajectory as a rationalization of two quasi-transcendental cognitive resources or competences. These, undergoing a massive expansion and reorientation during the Enlightenment, give rise to a systemic reorganization or a cultural differentiation pertaining either to cognitive-instrumental (scientific), moral-practical or aesthetic-expressive (artistic) types of rationality. (See his 'Modernity versus Postmodernity', *New German Critique*, 22 (1981), pp.3–14 and 'The Entwinement of Myth and Modernity', *New German Critique*, 26 (1982), pp.13–30.)
11. Charles Taylor, *Hegel* (Cambridge: Cambridge University Press, 1975), p.6; see also pp.3–11. Up to and including Hegel the notion of the self-defining subject is developed through the category of reason which orientates the investigation and reconstruction of the world according to the principles or processes of subjectification and objectification. The former refers to humankind's self-declared patterns and structures of meaning, whilst the latter refers to the humankind's finite processes of observation and measurement through which the natural and empirical worlds are studied and objectified.
12. See Castoriadis, 'The Imaginary Institution of Society', in John Fekete (ed.), *The Structural Allegory* (Minneapolis: University of Minnesota Press, 1984); 'Value, Equality, Justice, Politics: From Marx to Aristotle and from Aristotle to Ourselves', in *Crossroads in the Labyrinth* (Brighton: Harvester Press, 1984), pp.260–337.
13. Alasdair Macintyre, *After Virtue: A Study in Moral Theory*, second edition (London: Duckworth, 1985), p.222.

14. Karl Marx, 'Economic and Philosophical Manuscripts' (1844), in *Early Writings* (Harmondsworth: Penguin, 1981) p. 354. All further page references to the '1844 Manuscripts' will be to this edition and will appear in the body of the essay.
15. Marx's attitude towards mythological knowledge is presented a little more cautiously in the 1957 'Introduction' to *Grundrisse* (Harmondsworth: Penguin, 1973), pp.110–11. In that work it is seen as evidence of an unfettered ability of humankind for imagination. Marx argues that the mythologically construed patterns of artistic and cultural creation count as norms and models of beauty to a modern world encased in technological consciousness. As technological consciousness advances it demolishes the creative nature of mythology which becomes only the memory of a world to which humankind cannot return. All of this does not diminish Marx's own tendency to positively attribute a maturation process to technological consciousness itself, and by so doing, view the world of antiquity as the precocious childhood of humanity. All further page references to the *Grundrisse* will be to the Penguin edition and will appear in the body of the essay.
16. Karl Marx and Friedrich Engels, *The German Ideology* (New York: International Publishers, 1974), p.86.
17. Habermas represents one current that develops this in his quasi-transcendentally constituted paradigm of communication. See his 'What is Universal Pragmatics?' and 'Historical Materialism and the Development of Normative Structures', in *Communication and the Evolution of Society* (Boston: Beacon Press, 1979), pp.1–68 and 95–129 respectively.
18. Gyorgy Markus, 'The Human Use of Man-made Objects: Marxian Materialism and the Problem of Constitution' (unpublished MS), p.35. (Now published as 'Practical-social Rationality in Marx – A Dialectical Critique', *Dialectical Anthropology*, 4 (1979), pp.255–88, and 5 (1980), pp.1–31.)
19. Although the subsumption model, too, stems from the paradigm of production, there are indications that Marx conceptualizes it as a model for an otherwise bypassed and undeveloped critical theory of capitalism, in terms that transcend the totalizing sphere of production with its reductive anthropological determinants. The subsumption model is found in the fragmentary text of 'The Results of the Immediate Process of Production', although it has a place in the *Grundrisse*, particularly in the chapter on money, where, I will argue, the 'hidden imaginary' breaks through more explicitly. Moreover, this reading back, so to speak, enables us to disconnect our interpretation from Marx's construction of the *Grundrisse* as a whole. This interpretation of Marx's chapter on money problematicizes the core anthropological precept from which the *Grundrisse* and *Capital* spring – the contradiction between the material content and social form – and occurs through Marx's own reflections on money as a symbol. In Volume I, Marx subsequently put it aside for reasons that are still unknown. We can only surmise that he recognized the aforementioned difference between it and the *project* of *Capital*, Volume I (as a critique of

capitalism presented as a functional totality). For a theoretically stilted interpretation of this piece see E. Mandel's 'Introduction' to *Capital* (Harmondsworth: Penguin, 1979), I, 943–7.

20. Marx, 'The Results of the Immediate Process of Production', appendix to Volume I of *Capital*, op. cit., I, 1044. All further references to 'The Results' will be to this edition and will appear in the body of the essay.

21. The social configuration of functions and the reduction of labour to time, which denotes 'the very necessity of first transforming individual products or activities into exchange-values, into *money*', confronts the producers, so Marx argues in 'The Results', 'as a *capitalist* arrangement that is *imposed* on them' (1052). See also *Grundrisse*, p.158.

22. The notion of imaginary signification is taken from the later work of Castoriadis. According to him, socio-economic formations organize themselves through an imaginary signification which is a complex of terms and referents for which there is no sufficient real or rational basis, yet is socially constraining for all societal members. See notes 10 and 12, above.

23. Marx, *The Eighteenth Brumaire of Louis Napoleon*, in David Fernbach (ed.), *Surveys from Exile* (Harmondsworth: Penguin, 1973), p.146.

24. This is recognized in the '1844 Manuscripts', particularly the first, and is developed as late as the *The Theories of Surplus Value*.

25. See for example 'The Results', particularly Marx's analysis of the relation between productive and unproductive labour (1039, 1046–9) and wages (1062–4).

26. This problematic of the socially created hermeneutical circle is the aspect that Castoriadis later transforms, via Aristotle, into the notion of the proto-value, and traces back as the core problem in Marx's critique of capitalism. He argues that:

> we find ourselves trapped in the same circle: what is the worth of this worth, the value of this value? What is the merit of this merit, and the dignity of this dignity? Or, to put it another way: why is *this* value value? This circle is the circle of Proto-value, which is to say of the institution of a nuclear imaginary social signification; and it is impossible to account for it, or give reasons for it. ('Value, Equality, Justice, Politics', pp.296–7)

Weberian sociology also confronts this problem and addresses it through the notion of the meaning of social action. For other contemporary approaches see Agnes Heller, *A Theory of History* (London: Routledge and Kegan Paul, 1982), and Habermas's formulation of the paradigm of communicative action in 'What is Universal Pragmatics?'.

27. See *Grundrisse*, pp.1028–34, 106 and 232. Here, once again, Marx notices the phenomenon of Protestantism and its 'alliance' with capitalism. However, he fails to take it seriously. Following Max Weber, *The Protestant Ethic and the Spirit of Capitalism* (London: Unwin, 1971), and N. Elias, *The Civilising Process*, 2 vols (Oxford:

Basil Blackwell, 1978, 1983), especially the second volume, the emergence of Protestantism in the Occident is a major point of reference for the analysis of the transition to the period of real subsumption.

28. See also 'The Results', where he states:

> [The master] now confronts his journeyman only as the owner of capital, while the journeyman is reduced to being a vendor of labour. Before the process of production they all confront each other as commodity owners and their relations involve nothing but *money*; *within* the process of production they meet as its components personified; the capitalist as 'capital', the immediate producer as 'labour', and their relations are determined by labour as a mere constituent of capital which is valorising itself. (1020)

The inverted commas surrounding capital and labour are significant; they indicate that Marx has not yet subsumed the actors to their functional location.

29. Marx's comments on barter in *Grundrisse* are suggestive of this interpretation. On the level of exchanges he notes that:

> In the crudest barter when two commodities are ex-changed for one another, each is first equated with a symbol which expresses their exchange value, e.g. among certain Negroes on the West African coast, = *x* bars . . . (The bar has a merely imaginary existence, just as in general, a relation can obtain a particular embodiment and become individualised only by means of abstraction). (142)

This partial and incomplete form of exchange indicates, for Marx, that exchange does not

> yet dominate production as a whole, but concerns only its superfluity and is hence more or less *superfluous* (like exchange itself); an accidental enlargement of the sphere of satisfactions, enjoyments (relations to new objects). It therefore takes place at only a few points (originally at the borders of the natural communities, in their contact with strangers), is restricted to a narrow sphere, and forms something which passes production by, is auxiliary to it; dies out just as much by chance as it arises. The form of barter in which the overflow of one's own production is exchanged by chance for that of others' is only the *first* occurrence of the product as exchange value in general, and is determined by accidental needs, whims etc. (204–5)

30. Markus, 'Alienation and Reification in Marx and Lukács', *Thesis Eleven*, 5/6 (1982), p.152.
31. Paul Cardin (i.e., C. Castoriadis), *Modern Capitalism and Rendition* (London: Solidarity Pamphlet, 1974), p.74.
32. See Karl Marx, *The Eastern Question: A Reprint of Letters Written 1853–1856 Dealing with the Events of the Crimean War* (London: Frank Cass, 1969), especially pp.277–8, 315–23, 453, 483–8. See also *Grundrisse*, pp.409–10.
33. See, for example, *The Eastern Question*, p.189.

34. Despite the sketchy and brief remarks addressed to them in *The German Ideology* where these non-class forms are found in the main (although some are developed more fully in later works), each is mediated by a notion of property, which, to be sure, foreshadows its critical centrality in 'Communal and Autotelic Totality', but in a way that moves it in an opposite direction from that model derived from the paradigm of production.
35. *The German Ideology*, p.89.
36. See Markus, ' "Ideology" and Its Ideologies: Lukács and Goldmann on Kant', *Philosophy and Social Criticism*, 8:2 (1981), pp.125–47. For a history and analysis of this current see Taylor, *Hegel*, pp.3–50; 'Interpretation and the Sciences of Man', *Review of Metaphysics*, 25:1 (1971), pp.3–51; 'Theories of Meaning', *Man and World*, 13 (1980), pp.281–302. For a slightly more epistemological vantage point, see his 'Understanding in Social Science', the reply by Richard Rorty, and the discussion between Taylor, Rorty and Dreyfus in *Review of Metaphysics*, 34:1 (1980), pp.3–55. See also Paul Ricoeur, *Hermeneutics and the Human Sciences* (Cambridge: Cambridge University Press, 1981); H.G. Gadamer, *Philosophical Hermeneutics*, (Berkeley: University of California Press, 1976); Richard Rorty, *Philosophy and the Mirror of Nature* (Princeton: Princeton University Press, 1980). In many ways Castoriadis, Habermas and Heller formulate their metatheories around this problematic.

CHAPTER 10

Blu-Tack and Temples: Artistic Practice in the Eighties, a Postmodernist View

Memory Holloway

> How are we to imagine the replacement of this old familiar cosmos of dread and elegy and Left Bank bistros with intense people blowing smoke in each other's faces and gratuitously stabbing their hands with knives? No need to imagine it: it is here. It is the Postmodern.[1]

Fredric Jameson closes 'Postmodernism and Consumer Society' with the following remarks:

> There is some agreement that the older modernism functioned against its society in ways which are variously described as critical, negative, contestatory, subversive, oppositional and the like. Can anything of the sort be affirmed about postmodernism and its social moment?[2]

I want to respond to Jameson by pointing to a narrow margin where contemporary practice attempts to be 'critical, negative, contestatory, subversive, oppositional' and so on. These cultural products which for the moment I will place under the general banner of postmodernism reveal a number of similar responses to consumer capitalism: most importantly their makers treat history as a creation rather than a given; they critique representation as an epistemological problem, thereby questioning what realms of power and meaning are underpinned by existent visual codes. Furthermore, these artists call into question the identity of the subject as primary producer of meaning; they acknowledge that fragmentation and discontinuous 'speech' more closely approximate constructed reality than the modernist notions of unity, purity and closure. I would call artists who address the above problems, the post-structuralist postmoderns, and for the sake of clarity (and acknowledging the risk of formulating bipolar oppositions) would place them against the neo-expressionist postmoderns.

Whatever else postmodernism is, it is the cultural dominant of late capitalism, and its emergence is closely tied to the kind of society that began to develop after the Second World War, with its persistent demand to make the new ever newer. This period marks the moment when, as Baudrillard puts it, the human subject becomes a 'switching center for all the networks of influence' – when the invasion of television, advertising and the media obliterates interiority and intimacy. At the same time culture itself becomes a commodity, as is apparent, for example, in the ever increasing popularity of 'blockbuster' art exhibitions and the enthusiasm shown by multinational corporations which fund and underwrite such exhibitions and pay heavily for the privilege of attaching to them their product and company names. Art can be bought, packaged (e.g., in the form of souvenir T-shirts, posters and silk scarves imprinted with famous paintings by even more famous artists) and sold with greater ease and public enthusiasm than ever before. The more the public consumes, the more the initial context of the work has been ignored. Having lost its ability to shock, the oppositional tone of the avant-garde since the early 1960s has been progressively neutralized by its institutionalization. Where the 'canon' of revolutionary painting and sculpture might have once been regarded by students as a model for political art and action, artists such as Tatlin and Rodchencko are now considered in the same light as the creators of any other modernist work, i.e., as formal innovators who 'advanced' the history of art. With the end of modernism has come what Jameson identifies as 'the waning of affect' – the loss of anxiety which modernism produced, the connections it made with others, in general an 'emotional ground tone' on which modernist works were based.

As a means of determining what postmodernism is and does in the visual arts, it is of use to review the category of modernism. Clement Greenberg's writing is generally seen as the critical core of American modernism in the fifties. (There were, of course, previous 'modernisms' – the utopian proto-political modernism of the Bauhaus and constructivism, and the transgressive modernism of Dada and Surrealism.) Greenberg's modernism, served up in his critical essays, came to dominate American art and criticism until the late sixties; his definition of modernism was founded exclusively on the practice of painting, based on a programme which was self-critical, which constantly renewed itself to 'keep culture moving'.[3] Modern art had two enemies: the academy and kitsch. The purity of its enterprise could be maintained by keeping a constant comparative eye on the high quality of the art of the past, by stemming the tide of art as entertainment (thereby maintaining its high moral and serious purpose), and by ensuring that the aesthetic was a value in its own right. Art, as Peter Wollen has pointed out, was seen primarily in terms of its reflexivity and ontological exploration.[4] 'Visual art', Greenberg wrote in 'Modernist Painting' in 1961, 'should confine itself to what is visual experience and make no reference to any other orders of experience'.[5] By the mid-1960s, Greenberg's call for self-criticism had become rhetorical pronouncement.[6] It was in opposition to modernism's official autonomy and self-referentiality that postmodernism located itself. Yet postmodernism, as Hal Foster has pointed out, is closely related to modernism 'in its discursive orientation: for what self-criticism is to modernist practice, deconstruction is to postmodernist practice.'[7]

Let me begin an examination of the differences between modernism and postmodernism, as Jameson does, with Van Gogh's *Peasant Shoes*, and with his claim that it is one of the canonical works of high modernism. He reads it in two ways. One is as a response and transformation of the whole object world of agricultural misery. He remarks that this drab peasant object world which is transformed into the intense materialization of brilliant colour of the surrounding apple trees, is a utopian gesture, a compensation which makes sight the supreme sense. Elsewhere Jameson holds that art comes into existence through a process of alienation from the social body of primitive communism. As the world becomes objectively and externally fragmented, the faculties of the internal world break up so that each faculty – the emotional, empirical and descriptive – is separated from the others. Sight is now constituted as the supreme sense, part of some new division of labour in the body of capital.

By contrast, and as a means of turning away from this hermeneutical reading, Jameson chooses an image of Andy Warhol's *Diamond Dust Shoes*, a discarded pile of dead objects, shorn of their content. The shoes are fetishes in the Freudian sense, a displacement of the libido, and in the Marxian sense, a fetishization of the commodity. Warhol's work, his Coca-Cola bottles and Campbell's soupcans, may in general be said to exemplify the limited possibilities of art in the period of late capitalism.

Here then are the significant differences for Jameson between the high modernist and the postmodernist movements. There is in Warhol a flatness, a depthlessness, a new superficiality, the death of the world of appearances thematized elsewhere in his work, e.g., in silk-screens of traffic accidents and the *Electric Chair* series. The content drained from the object, we are left with a set of texts or simulacra, silk-screened copies of newspaper photographs. The feeling, creating subject has disappeared altogether.

Jameson's examples are curious, chosen for their affinities of subject matter (new shoes, old shoes) for the opportunity the shoes give him to annotate other interpretations, and for the immediate associations the spectator makes with fetishes. Thus the selection of *Peasant Shoes* enables him to cite Heidegger's analysis of the same work – that Van Gogh's painting discloses the *truth* of the peasant shoes by way of the mediation of the work of art which emerges within the gap between the Earth and the World – and parenthetically to note that Derrida invests them with heterosexuality, an observation which Jameson appears to enjoy because he takes it up later.

But Van Gogh is not part of the high modernist canon. There is too much spatial depth, too much pathos. Greenberg, as the high priest of modernist canons, relegates Van Gogh and others, including the German Expressionists, to a margin where they will not interfere with the mainstream narrative of 'purity brought into being by flatness'. Greenberg's key definition of modernism was published in 'Modernist Painting' (1961), and in his *Art and Culture* the modernist canon was established. In it he argues for self-criticism within each art 'through the procedures themselves of that which is being criticized. Thus flatness, two dimensionality, was the only condition being shared with no other art, and so modernist painting oriented to flatness'. This idea was elaborated by Michael Fried as a concentration on 'problems intrinsic to painting itself'. This definition of the high modernist canon of which Jameson speaks does not seem to apply to Van Gogh at all. Mike Davis has made a similar complaint about Jameson's postmodernism, noting that his system tends to 'homogenize the details of a contemporary landscape, to subsume under a master concept too many contradictory phenomena'.[8]

A more appropriate choice of a modernist work would have been Mondrian in his high utopian phase. Through the instrument of painting, Jameson's object, as Perry Meisel has observed, is to intercept aesthetic form at its historical limit, indicating closures and/or breaks rather than narrating a development. That is why the Warhol example works, as the historical limit to modernism.

If we turn now to what is produced under the banner of postmodernism, it becomes clear that it is not an identifiable style which follows on the collapse of modernism – it is too diverse to be designated as such. As Lyotard has argued, postmodernism is a cultural condition resulting from the erosion of those period ideals we see in Mondrian, and in a shift from an Enlightenment-derived core of assumptions that constituted a humanist code in which the individual mastered the universe. Postmodernism has noted the power of social forces to regulate individual activity, thereby decentering the creating subject. For Lyotard a key factor in this process has been the appearance of post-war techno-scientific culture. In a recent exhibition conceived by Lyotard and called *Les Immateriaux*, he asks how the technological revolution has altered man's identity as a maker, and what the implications are for the very notion of creation. Can these profound, philosophical shifts be represented at all? Can the immaterial be materialized into artefacts? Lyotard asks these questions throughout the course of the exhibition.[9] Lyotard's individual exhibits emphasized the way in which new technologies have forced us to reconsider the idea of creative activity, with the conclusion that postmodernity is characterized by the decline of palpable objects, their traditional manufacture and the producer. An example: a piece of prosthetic skin is shown in a photograph. Skin, the boundary which demarcates inside/outside, is now scientifically produced. Lyotard seems to indicate that in the postmodernist moment it is now appropriate to historicize objectification.

Lyotard's entire exhibition, consisting of similar objects, also called into question the very nature of assimilating material within the confines of a gallery space. That space in itself already creates a unified setting and the unity of an experience which constitutes the subject. Behind Lyotard's enquiry is the notion of the decline of the author and the idea that the end point of the humanist code has been reached. His exhibition came close to Jameson's call for a critical, contestatory and oppositional art practice.

Perhaps we can get closer to this border of the subversive and oppositional if I map the postmodernist terrain by drawing a line down the middle of a page, with neo-everything (e.g., neo-eclectic, neo-new and neo-expressionism) on one side and what I can only at this point call post-structuralist production on the other. Strictly speaking, the space for the second should only be a tiny margin because most of what is being made today falls within the first group, even when it is trying hard to be in the second. This is especially true in Australia, but I'll come to that later, and to the Blu-Tack and Temples of my title.

If we look to postmodernist configurations in the United States, we discover that every return – and there are many – beats a path back to a humanist tradition, even when it parodies modernist thematics. While there have been a few attempts to scrutinize and de-centre the self, and hence to subvert the humanist tradition – for example, in Warhol's work – American artists have throughout the '60s and '70s found this problematic. In the seventies the 'self' was re-asserted with a vengeance. Once again the 'self' became the primary subject of art, in a glut of autobiography and diaristic art. Robert Morris's *I-Box* shows the full extent of this desire to produce ever more innovative styles of self: in a sculpture of 1962, the artist stands nude within a box whose door is a life-sized wooden cut-out of the letter 'I'; the effect of self-satisfaction is topped off by the goony smile of the artist.

The postmodernist style of the self is, of course, neo-expressionism, and its spokesman Hilton Kramer, editor of *New Criterion*. It has been argued that Kramer's conversion from modernism to postmodern neo-expressionism dates from his departure in 1981 from *The New York Times* and the foundation of his own magazine – financed by major conservative foundations. Within two years of its appearance, *New Criterion* was generally acknowledged as the intellectual mouthpiece for Reagan's policy to dismantle government support for the arts and replace it by funds from the private sector. Kramer continues to see the shift from a modernist to a postmodernist aesthetic as a matter of style and a change in taste. In his introduction to the *Zeitgeist* catalogue in 1981, one of the first exhibitions to display and define international neo-expressionism, Kramer explained that what had been lost from the art of the '60s and '70s (presumably pop, photography, video, installations) was poetry and fantasy, the drama of self, the visionary and the irrational. In their place appeared pure, cerebral abstraction. That Kramer's was a highly selective and inaccurate view of the '60s and '70s is demonstrated by his purposeful omission of the political critiques of institutional power by artists such as Hans Haacke and Daniel Buren. But what is important here is what Kramer has welcomed back, that is, a return to history, a return to a historicist tradition where the past is pillaged, collaged, where pieces are gathered together and used 'for their stylistic interest. History is not critiqued, it is pastiched, and pastiche deprives past styles of their historic content and meaning.

Jameson identifies pastiche as one of the two significant features which express the newly emergent social order: the other is schizophrenia. Pastiche, says Jameson, is different from parody. The use of parody implies a linguistic norm, a model against which parody can be voiced:

> Pastiche is, like parody, the imitation of a peculiar or unique style, the wearing of a stylistic mask, speech in a dead language . . . without parody's ulterior motive, without the satirical impulse, without laughter, without that still latent feeling that there exists something *normal*. . . . [10]

Pastiche is thus blank parody, an 'imitation of dead styles, speech through all the masks and voices stored up in the imaginary museum of a now global culture'.[11] When pastiche works under the guise of a return to history it erodes history instead. Pastiche is the *lingua franca* of postmodernism: apolitical, ahistorical, promiscuous. Let me give two examples of pastiche from architecture, before turning to the other challenge to originality, that of the simulacrum.

Michael Graves turns to a tradition of classical architecture, pastiching both historical and pop references, but never questioning these quotations as cliches or interrogating them for their ideological meaning. For example, the keystone is a central motif in Graves's work, although it is unclear from its insertion as to what meaning it takes on. Certainly it is quoted from the dominant architecture of the eighteenth century, such as that of Boullée and Ledoux, architects of megalomaniacal proportions. Graves is eclectic in his choices and, like other pasticheurs, privileges style. Nostalgic and historicist, he makes the past into the present.

Robert Venturi takes another tack, pastiching from main street, from the visual chaos of Las Vegas. He takes a delight in the cityscape of capital, embracing the city of junk buildings and decorated sheds of the Las Vegas strip. It is easy enough to tack on an historical reference (take your pick) to a shed and call it a monument. The result of this architectural pastiche? Not a return to history, but once again its undermining; not the retrieval of history, but its fragmentation.

Let me add an example from painting: David Salle's *Goodbye D* with its layers of signs culled from the past – the primitivizing mask, the nostalgic fashions of the sixties, the model posed like Twiggy, the crouching nude like something from Matisse, the false gesture across the letters at the top. Salle's piracy creates a fusion between the expressive styles of early modernism and the cool detachment of pop. Pastiche here marks the death of the author, for he is everywhere and nowhere, he is no longer the originator of meaning; instead of the unified whole characteristic of modernism, pastiche ends in fragmentation and a shattering of meaning.

What is the alternative? Work which addresses the way in which history is *created* rather than given; work which critiques representation; work which questions how meaning is constructed in visual representation; and work which sets out to subvert those modes of representation, with their assumed references to a given world of reality. Predictably, painting is not a main contender. Rather, photography and performance are. Those who practise the critical opposition are few; among them women in particular have challenged the structures of authority of the modern period and the notion of mastery. Women have long been prohibited from Western representation – not as objects, but as subjects. Images *of* women, by and for men, abound. But in being represented by men, women have remained absent within the dominant culture. Michèle Montrelay has pointed out that women are to be identified with the 'ruin of representation'.[12] In order to speak, women have habitually masqueraded as men. Little wonder that an essentialist view of women is often associated with duplicity, simulation, seduction and false representation. Postmodernist feminists have sought to expose Western representation and its claims to authority.

For example, Barbara Kruger locates her practice between language and text, and through the collision of these questions the truth of visual representations. Her focus has continuously been on the way in which masculine readings of visual texts separate women as objects of the male gaze. Patriarchal order and essences are called into question. 'We won't play nature to your culture' she writes in bold black and white lettering across a surface-painted canvas. 'We are obliged to steal language'. Castration as a theme is played out in a text which locates the threat of lack which women suggest: 'I am your almost nothing'. She uses the same images which commonly set up the structures of male looking and of women looked at, and then manipulates them, sometimes by splitting the image.

Kruger's work is close to that of Laura Mulvey, a British filmmaker whose influential essay 'Visual Pleasure and Narrative Cinema' identifies the process of scopophiliac drives of the male viewer. Both foreground the fetish, voyeurism, the pleasure of the gaze and the pleasure of the spectacle as texts to be re-examined:

'You are seduced by the sex appeal of the inorganic'.
'You molest from afar'.
'I will not become what I mean to you'.

Kruger brings into her textual collages a range of discourses: the place of art, sexual politics, political and cultural power, of gender, difference and the way in which language underlines current structures of power.

Jenny Holzer is also concerned with the power at work in social representations. Holzer's texts, her 'truisms', suggest how language subjects us and how we might disarm it. Those done for the Sydney Bienalle of 1984 mock the certainty of personal credos and are a compendium of received ideas. She uses these texts as a weapon against common assumptions, in order to rob them of their power to compel and subjugate.

Cindy Sherman's photographs are self-portraits taken in various guises, and constitute her as a roving subject. Sherman's photographs show that to express a self is to reproduce an already given type, so that the notions of original copy are now applied to the human subject. Rather than revealing her self, she unmasks the types of selves available to the female subject through film, advertisements, women's magazines. Her photographs are a critique of the way in which women are constituted as subjects and they are also, I think, a resistance against the idea of a privileged interior world. Sherman's photographs show that the world of culture is a construct, that the expressive self is a myth, to which those on the other side of the postmodernist line subscribe. Julian Schnable, Baselitz, Penck and others adopt a rhetoric of the expressive gesture which makes its claims for subjectivity and authenticity. Writing on the allegorical impulse in postmodernist art, Craig Owens remarks that Cindy Sherman's images 'disguise functions as parody. . . [and] expose the identification of the self with an image as its dispossession, in a way that appears to proceed directly from Jacques Lacan's fundamental tenet that the self is an Imaginary construct.'[13]

Finally, I want to look briefly at postmodernism and its alliances in Australia, where the condition of making art has historically been one of relying heavily on visual reproductions, that is, on copies of originals, for information. In the past this has had interesting consequences, an unconcious type of misreading. One thinks of Perceval's response to a series of over-yellowed reproductions of

Tintoretto in *Life* magazine, and of what followed – yellowish images expressively rendered. The copy that Perceval saw was held to be true. This misreading has been one of the most 'original' and interesting aspects of Australian art. But in the eighties copies and the like are not so innocent. Imants Tillers, whose paintings have been critically regarded as exemplars of postmodernism, recently compared himself in an interview in the *Age Good Weekend* magazine against precisely the international neo-expressionists. Tillers has tried to locate his practice as an opposition to the Zeitgeist which he once signalled as being myopic, blind to history. But in the grand statement which hung on the wall at the Australian Centre for Contemporary Art, in a show entitled *How Much Beauty Can I Stand?* Tillers played his hand: *Mt.Analogue*, as he calls it, is a simulacrum based on Eugène von Guérard's *Mt.Kosciusko* of 1864.[14] It is not a neo-expressionist work, but neither is it oppositional, critical, negative or subversive.

We must, says Gilles Deleuze, distinguish essence from appearance, the intelligible from the sensible, the original from the copy, the model from the simulacrum. But we have seen that these expressions are not equivalent; copies are secondhand precursors, well-grounded claimants, authorized by resemblance. Simulacra are false claimants, built on a dissimilitude implying a perversion, an essential turning away.

Tillers's works were placed in that exhibition amongst those of others who have also turned away from notions of originality towards simulacra. In his *Tower Hill* Geoff Lowe departs from the Von Guérard painting of the same subject, and surrounds the large canvas with small paintings of fragments snapped from the the art historical past of Western civilization. Juxtaposing these shattered pieces, now cannibalized and reworked in the eighties in a postmodern spirit, the painter seeks the fragmentary and eschews the unity of time and place set by Von Guérard in 1855. This is global art, outside of time, without place, an art stripped of its historical roots. Von Guérard, who studied in Düsseldorf, home to the romantic painter Friedrich, the Von Guérard, who became the first great landscapist of the Australian terrain, the Von Guérard whose singular aim was to allude to something that could not be demonstrated – the unspeakable sublime – thus becomes the model for Australian artists working towards a postmodernist end.

Fragmentation, repetition and an endless rearrangement of parts characterize the Australian adaption to postmodernism as it has come to be known through the sieve of reproductions and catalogues. Tellingly, its material representation may best be represented by the Blu-Tack used to stick these fragmentary bits onto walls, and by the classical temples which so persistently appear in the paintings of artists such as Tony Clarke and Richard Dunn to signify the crumbling of Western civilization, the 'museum in ruins', and the disappearance of that tradition of Enlightenment which produced a universal civilization. Postmodernism has dissolved temporality and locates us, like it or not, in an ever present present.

NOTES

1. Dan Latimer, 'Jameson and Post-Modernism', *New Left Review*, 148 (1984), p.119.
2. Fredric Jameson, 'Postmodernism and Consumer Society', in Hal Foster (ed.), *The Anti-Aesthetic: Essays on Postmodern Culture* (Port Townsend: Bay Press, 1983), p.125.
3. See Clement Greenberg, 'Avantgarde and Kitsch', in his *Art and Culture* (Boston: Beacon Press, 1961).
4. Cited in Mary Kelly, 'Re-viewing Modernist Criticism', *Screen*, 22:3 (1981), p.42.
5. Clement Greenberg, 'Modernist Painting', *Art Year Book*, 4 (1961), in Gregory Battcock (ed.), *The New Art* (New York: Bantam, 1973), p.74.
6. For a critical discussion of Greenberg and modernist criticism, see Kelly, op. cit., pp.41–62.
7. Hal Foster, '(Post)Modern Polemics', in his *Recodings: Art, Spectacle, Cultural Politics* (Port Townsend: Bay Press, 1985), p.130.
8. Mike Davis, 'Urban Renaissance and the Spirit of Postmodernism', *New Left Review*, 151 (1985), p.107.
9. *Les Immaterieaux* was exhibited at the Centre de Création Industrielle de Paris, Centre Georges Pompidou, from March 26 to July 25, 1985.
10. Fredric Jameson, op. cit., p.114.
11. Fredric Jameson, 'Postmodernism, or the Cultural Logic of Late Capitalism', p.65. See 'Select Bibliography'.
12. Michèle Montrelay, 'Inquiry into Femininity', *Semiotext(e)*, 10 (1981), p.232.
13. Craig Owens, 'The Allegorical Impulse: Toward a Theory of Postmodernism: Part 2', *October*, 13 (1980), p.78.
14. *How Much Beauty Can I Stand?*, curated by Sue Cramer, exhibited Australian Centre of Contemporary Art, Melbourne, March 19–April 21 1985.

Notes on Contributors

Andrew Milner, Philip Thomson and Chris Worth teach in the Centre for General and Comparative Literature at Monash University in Melbourne.

Agnes Heller is Professor of Humanities at the New School for Social Research in New York. Her publications include *Renaissance Man* (1978), *Everyday Life* (1984), and *The Power of Shame* (1985). She is co-author with Ferenc Fehér and Gyorgy Markus of *Dictatorship Over Needs* (1983). In 1986 she co-edited *Reconstructing Aesthetics* with Ferenc Fehér.

David Bennett teaches English and literary theory at the University of Melbourne. His research interests include parody, postmodernism and contemporary literary theory.

David Roberts teaches German and comparative literature at Monash University. His publications include *Tendenzwenden. Aspekte des Kulturwandels der Siebziger Jahre* (1984) and, with Philip Thomson and Pavel Petr, *Comic Relations* (1985). He is a member of the editorial committee of *Thesis Eleven*.

Rita Felski, who wrote her doctoral thesis at Monash, is currently a Post-Doctoral Fellow at Cornell University. Her book on feminist literary theory will appear from Harvard University Press in 1990.

Ferenc Fehér teaches humanities at the New School for Social Research in New York. His publications include *Dostoevsky and the Crisis of the Individual* (1972) and, with Agnes Heller and Gyorgy Markus, *Dictatorship Over Needs* (1983). He is co-editor, with Agnes Heller, of *Reconstructing Aesthetics* (1986).

Boris Frankel teaches sociology at Victoria College in Melbourne. His publications include *Marxian Theories of the State* (1978), *Beyond the State?* (1983), and *The Post-Industrial Utopians* (1987).

Simon During teaches English and literary theory at the University of Melbourne. His research interests include deconstructionist theory and New Zealand literature.

Julian Pefanis teaches at the Power Institute of the Fine Arts at Sydney University. His book on post-modern aesthetics will appear with Duke University Press in 1990.

John Rundell teaches sociology at Monash University. He has recently published *The Origins of Modernity* (1987). He is a member of the editorial committee of *Thesis Eleven*.

Memory Holloway teaches visual arts at Monash University. Her publications on modern art include her co-authorship of *George Baldessin: Sculpture and Etchings* (1983), and 'Minimal Art' in Paul Taylor (ed.), *Anything Goes* (1984).

Select Bibliography

Adorno, Theodor and Max Horkheimer (1979), *Dialectic of Enlightenment*, London: Verso. Translated by John Cumming from *Dialektik der Aufklärung* (New York: Social Studies Association, 1944).

Anderson, Perry (1984). 'Modernity and Revolution', *New Left Review*, 144 (1984), pp. 96–113.

Appignanensi, Lisa and Geoff Bennington (eds) (1986), *Postmodernism: ICA Documents 4*, London: Institute of Contemporary Arts.

Arac, Jonathan (ed.) (1986), *Postmodernism and Politics*, Manchester: Manchester University Press; Minneapolis: University of Minnesota Press. Volume 28 in the series 'Theory and History of Literature'.

Bataille, Georges (1985), *Visions of Excess: Selected Writings, 1927–1939*, Manchester, Manchester University Press; Minneanapolis: University of Minnesota Press, Volume 14 in the series 'Theory and History of Literature'.

Bell, Daniel (1973), *The Coming of Post-Industrial Society*, New York: Basic Books.

Bell, Daniel (1978), *The Cultural Contradictions of Capitalism*, New York: Basic Books.

Bennett, David (1985), 'Parody, Postmodernism and the Politics of Reading', in P. Petr, D. Roberts and P. Thomson (eds), *Comic Relations: Studies in the Comic, Satire and Parody* (Frankfurt/Main: Peter Lang); also in *Critical Quarterly*, 27:4 (1985), pp. 27–43.

Berman, Marshall (1982), *All That Is Solid Melts Into Air*, New York: Simon and Schuster; London: Verso.

Bürger, Peter (1983a), 'Das Altern der Moderne', in Ludwig van Friedeberg and Jürgen Habermas (eds), *Adorno–Konferenz 1983* (Frankfurt/Main: Suhrkamp), pp. 177–97.

Bürger, Peter (1983b), *Zur Kritik der idealistischen Ästhetik*, Frankfurt/Main: Suhrkamp.

Bürger, Peter (1984), *Theory of the Avant-Garde*, Manchester: Manchester University Press; Minneapolis: University of Minnesota Press. Foreword by Jochen Schulte-Sasse. Volume 4 in the series 'Theory and History of Literature'. Translated by Michael Shaw from the second edition of *Theorie der Avantgarde* (Frankfurt/Main: Suhrkamp, 1980; originally published 1974), and from two other pieces, 'Theorie der Avantgarde und Theorie der Literatur' and 'Hermeneutik-Ideologiekritik-Funktionsanalyse' in Bürger's *Vermittlung-Rezeption-Funktion*, (Frankfurt/Main:Suhrkamp, 1979).

Cultural Critique (1986/87), Number 5. Special issue on 'Modernity and Modernism, Postmodernity and Postmodernism'.

Davis, Mike (1985), 'Urban Renaissance and the Spirit of Postmodernism', *New Left Review*, 151 (1985), pp. 106–13.

Debord, Guy (1983), *The Society of the Spectacle*, Detroit: Black and Red. Translation from *Le Société du spectacle* (Paris: Buchet/Chastel, 1967).

Eagleton, Terry (1985), 'Capitalism, Modernism and Postmodernism', *New Left Review*, 152 (1985), pp. 60–73.

Foster, Hal (ed.) (1983), *The Anti-Aesthetic: Essays on Postmodern Culture*, Port Townsend: Bay Press. Reprinted as *Postmodern Culture* (London: Pluto Press, 1985).

Foster, Hal (1984), '(Post)Modern Polemics', *New German Critique*, 33 (1984), pp. 67–78. Reprinted in his *Recodings: Art, Spectacle, Cultural Politics* (Port Townsend: Bay Press, 1985).

Frankel, Boris (1987), *The Post-Industrial Utopians*, Cambridge: Polity Press.

Greenberg, Clement (1961), 'Avantgarde and Kitsch', in his *Art and Culture*, Boston: Beacon Press.

Habermas, Jürgen (1970), *Towards a Rational Society*, Boston: Beacon Press. Translation by Jeremy J. Shapiro of selections from *Technik und Wissenschaft als 'Ideologie'* (Frankfurt/Main: Suhrkamp, 1968) and *Protestbewegung und Hochschulreform* (Frankfurt/Main: Suhrkamp, 1969).

Habermas, Jürgen (1981), 'Modernity versus Postmodernity', *New German Critique*, 22 (1981), pp. 3–14.

Habermas, Jürgen (1982), 'The Entwinement of Myth and Modernity: Rereading the *Dialectic of Enlightenment*', *New German Critique*, 26 (1982), pp. 13–30.

Habermas, Jürgen (1984), 'The French Path to Postmodernity: Bataille Between Eroticism and General Economics', *New German Critique*, 33 (1984), pp. 79–102.

Habermas, Jürgen (1987), *The Philosophical Discourse of Modernity: Twelve Lectures*, Cambridge: Polity Press. Translation by Frederick Lawrence of *Der Philosopische Diskurs der Moderne:*

Zwölf Vorlesung (Frankfurt/Main: Suhrkamp, 1985). Includes versions of Habermas 1982 and 1984.

Hassan, Ihab (1985), 'The Culture of Postmodernism', *Theory, Culture and Society*, 2:3 (1985), pp. 119–31.

Holland, Norman N. (1983), 'Postmodern Psychoanalysis', in Ihab Hassan and Sally Hassan (eds), *Innovation/Renovation: New Perspectives on the Humanities* (Madison: University of Wisconsin Press).

Huyssen, Andreas (1981), 'The Search for Tradition: Avantgarde and Postmodernism in the 1970s', *New German Critique*, 22 (1981), pp. 23–40.

Huyssen, Andreas (1984), 'Mapping the Postmodern', *New German Critique*, 33 (1984), pp. 5–52.

Huyssen, Andreas (1988), *After the Great Divide: Modernism, Mass Culture and Postmodernism*, London: Macmillan. Includes Huyssen 1981 and 1984.

Jameson, Fredric (1983), 'Postmodernism and Consumer Society', in Foster (ed.) 1983.

Jameson, Fredric (1984), 'Postmodernism, or the Cultural Logic of Late Capitalism', *New Left Review*, 146 (1984), pp. 53–93.

Jameson, Fredric (1986), 'On Magic Realism in Film', *Critical Inquiry*, 12 (1986), pp. 301–25.

Jay, Mark (1984), 'Habermas and Modernism', *Praxis International*, 4:1 (1984), pp. 1–14.

Kelly, Mary (1981), 'Re-viewing Modernist Criticism', *Screen*, 22:3 (1981), pp. 41–62.

Latimer, Dan (1984), 'Jameson and Post-Modernism', *New Left Review*, 148 (1984), pp. 116–128.

Lawson, Hilary (1985), *Reflexivity: The Post-Modern Predicament*, London: Hutchinson.

Lyotard, Jean-François (1977), *Instructions païennes*, Paris: Galilée.

Lyotard, Jean-François (1983a), *Le Différend*, Paris: Minuit.

Lyotard, Jean-François (1983b), 'Rules and Paradoxes and Svelte Appendix', *Cultural Critique*, 5 (1986–87), pp. 209–19. Translated by Brian Massumi from 'Règles et paradoxes et appendices svelte', *Babylone*, 1 (1983), pp. 67–80.

Lyotard, Jean-François (1984), *The Postmodern Condition: A Report on Knowledge*, Manchester: Manchester University Press; Minneapolis: University of Minnesota Press. Foreword by Fredric Jameson. Volume 10 in the series 'Theory and History of Literature'. Translation by Geoff Bennington and Brian Massumi from *La Condition postmoderne: rapport sur le savoir* (Paris: Minuit, 1979). With an appendix, 'Answering the Question:

What is Postmodernism?', first published in *Innovation/ Renovation*, edited by Ihab Hassan and Sally Hassan (Madison: University of Wisconsin Press, 1983), translated by Régis Durand from the essay 'Réponse à la question: qu'est-ce que le postmoderne?', *Critique*, 419 (1982).

McBurney, Blaine (1985), 'The Post-Modern Transvaluation of Modernist Values', *Thesis Eleven*, 12 (1985), pp. 94–109.

Moi, Toril (1988), 'Feminism, Postmodernism, and Style: Recent Feminist Criticism in the United States', *Cultural Critique*, 9 (1988), pp. 3–22.

Morris, Meaghan (1988), *The Pirate's Fiancée: Feminism, Reading, Postmodernism*, London: Verso.

New German Critique (1984), Volume 33. Special issue on 'Modernity and Postmodernity'.

Owens, Craig (1980), 'The Allegorical Impulse: Toward a Theory of Postmodernism', *October*, 12 (1980), pp. 67–86 and 13 (1980), pp. 59–80.

Owens, Craig (1985), 'The Discourse of Others: Feminists and Postmodernism', in Foster (ed.) 1985.

Rorty, Richard (1984), 'Habermas and Lyotard on Postmodernity', *Praxis International*, 4:1 (1984), pp. 32–44. Reprinted in Richard J. Bernstein (ed.), *Habermas and Modernity* (Oxford: Polity Press).

Schabert, T. (1986). 'Modernity and History I: What is Modernity?', in A. Moulakis (ed.), *The Promise of History, Essays in Political Philosophy* (Berlin: Walter de Gruyter).

Schulte-Sasse, Jochen (1985). 'Modernity and Modernism, Postmodernity and Postmodernism. Framing the Issue', *Cultural Critique*, 5 (1986–87), pp. 5–22.

Theory, Culture and Society (1988), Volume 5, number 2/3. Special issue on 'Postmodernism'.

Wellmer, A. (1985), 'On the Dialectic of Modernism and Postmodernism',*Praxis International*, 4:4 (1985), pp. 337–62.

Index

Adorno, Theodor xii, 39, 40, 44, 45, 58, 66, 68, 79, 80, 85, 90, 93n, 112n, 114–16 122, 126, 130n, 143, 154n
Aeschylus 59n
Alexander, Franz 152n
Althusser, Louis 33, 35n, 77n
Anderson, Benedict 126, 127, 131n
Anderson, Perry 98, 112n
Arendt, Hannah 11, 36n
Aristophanes 43, 45, 46
Aristotle 9, 149, 184n
Arnaud, Alain 152n
Artaud, Antonin 50–56, 59n, 150

Bach, Johann Sebastian 59n
Bahro, Rudolf xi, 95, 96, 98, 99, 111
Balzac, Honoré de 31
Barker, Francis 78n
Baron, Hans 181n
Barrett, Michèle 78n
Barthes, Roland 22–25, 28–31, 36n, 62, 77n, 134–36, 138, 151, 152n
Baselitz, Georg 195
Bataille, Georges xii, xiii, 133–43, 146–48, 150–55n
Battcock, Gregory 197n
Baudelaire, Charles 81
Baudrillard, Jean 33, 134, 135, 143, 147, 148, 151, 154n, 188
Beckett, Samuel 44, 45, 57
Bell, Daniel 103, 104, 112n
Belsey, Catherine 62, 77n
Benjamin, Walter ix, 18, 24, 36n, 85, 104, 143
Bennett, David xii, xiii, 88
Bennett, Tony 22, 25, 27, 31, 36n
Berman, Marshall xii, xvn, 163, 164, 182n
Blanchot, Maurice 138, 140, 153n
Bloch, Ernst xvn
Bocock, R. 112n
Borges, Jorges Luis 69
Boullée, Etienne-Louis 193

Braun, Karlheinz 59n
Brecht, Bertold 44, 45, 50–54, 59n
Brunt, Rosalind 78n
Buñuel, Luis 50
Buren, Daniel 192
Bürger, Peter x, xi, xiii, xvn, 15, 20, 31, 35n, 39–46, 50–52, 55, 58, 64, 66–69, 71, 77n, 82, 93n

Cachoux, Michael 16, 17
Caillois, Roger 142
Calvino, Italo 69
Casanova, José 104, 112n
Castoriadis, Cornelius [Paul Cardin] 3, 165, 172, 174, 176, 179, 182n, 184n–86n
Cervantes Saavedra, Miguel de 42, 43
Christo [Christo Javacheff] 15–19, 34
Clarke, Simon 77n
Clarke, Tony 197
Clastres, Pierre 143, 146, 152n, 154n
Cohen, Ralph 36n
Conrad, Joseph 117–22
Coppola, Eleanor 119, 131n
Coppola, Francis Ford 117–19, 121, 122, 130
Coward, Rosalind 62, 77n
Cramer, Sue 197n
Crosman, Inge 36n
Crosman, Robert 27, 36n

Dahrendorf, Ralf 9
Dali, Salvador 19, 35n
Dante Aligieri 93n
Davis, Mike 99, 112n, 190, 197n
Debord, Guy 17, 32, 35n, 154n
Deleuze, Gilles 196
Derrida, Jacques 28, 30, 51, 59n, 62, 101, 123, 131n, 134, 135, 148, 151, 155n, 190
Dionysius 56
Disraeli, Benjamin 2
Donovan, Josephine 77n

Index

Dostoevsky, Fyodor Mikhail 81
Dreyfus, Hubert L. 186n
Duchamp, Marcel 18, 44
Dunn, Richard 197
During, Simon xi, xiii, xiv
Durkheim, Emile 141, 142, 153n, 155n, 163

Eagleton, Terry 15, 20, 21, 28, 30–36n, 71, 77n
Edwards, John 131n
Elias, Norbert 184n
Eliot, T. S. 23, 98, 121
Engels, Fredrich 154n, 183n
Euripides 43, 59n
Excoffon-Lefarge, Giselle 152n

Fehér, Ferenc xi–xiii, 58n, 59n, 182n
Fekete, John 182n
Felski, Rita xi, xiii–xv
Fernbach, David 184n
Ferree, Myra Marx 75, 78n
Feuerbach, Ludwig 34
Fichte, Johann Gottlieb 127
Fiedler, Conrad 94n
Fielding, Henry 43
Fish, Stanley 22, 23, 25–27, 31, 36n
Foster, Hal 21, 35n, 77n, 189, 197n
Foucault, Michel 117, 134, 135, 138–40, 150, 151, 153n, 155n, 179
Frankel, Boris xi–xv
Frazer, J. G. 121
Freud, Sigmund 30, 51, 52, 56, 137, 144, 148, 150, 151n, 154n, 155n
Fried, Michael 190
Friedeburg, Ludwig van 58n
Friedrich, Caspar David 196
Fuller, Buckminster 99

Gadamer, Hans-Georg 93n, 186n
Gauguin, Paul 2
Giddens, Anthony 112n
Giotto di Bondono 93n
Glass, Philip 90
Goethe, Johann Wolfgang von 89
Goldmann, Lucien 93n
Gorz, André 95, 96, 98, 109, 112n
Goux, Jean-Joseph 155n
Graves, Michael 193
Greenberg, Clement 188–90, 197n
Grimm, Rheinhold 58n, 59n
Guérard, Eugène von 196

Haacke, Hans 192
Habermas, Jürgen xi, xiv, xvn, 20, 27, 36n, 42, 58n, 71, 72, 77n, 100–102, 112n, 134, 151n, 158, 159, 179, 182n–84n, 186n
Hassan, Ihab 21, 35n
Hassan, Sally 35n
Hauser, Arnold 58n, 93n
Hegel, G. W. Friedrich 30, 94n, 139–41, 145, 148–50, 155n, 158, 166, 169, 176, 182n
Heidegger, Martin 17, 181n, 190
Heller, Agnes xi, xiii, 86, 94n, 179, 182n, 184n, 186n
Henri III 16
Henri IV 16
Hess, Beth B. 75, 78n
Hildebrandt, Curt 94n
Hinck, Walter 59n
Hohendahl, Peter Uwe 36n
Hölderlin, Friedrich 127
Holland, Norman 21, 22, 25, 27–29, 31, 35n, 36n
Hollier, Denis 151n, 154n
Holloway, Memory xi, xiii, xiv
Holzer, Jenny 195
Honneth, Axel 112n
hooks, bell 74, 77n
Horace 92
Horkheimer, Max 112n, 143, 154n
Horowitz, David 37n
Humboldt, Alexander von 160
Huyssen, Andreas xii, 64, 69, 70, 77n, 92, 94n 100, 101, 112n
Hyppolite, Jean 140

Iser, Wolfgang 23, 25, 28

James, Henry 2
Jameson, Fredric x, xi, xiii, xv, 17, 20–22, 25, 28, 29, 31–36n, 99, 112n–17, 122, 124, 126, 129, 130n, 187–91, 193, 197n
Jardine, Alice 77n
Jaulin, Robert 152n
Jauss, Hans Robert 22, 25, 27, 28, 36n, 42, 58n
Jones, Ann Rosalind 77n
Jones, Barry 95, 98, 109
Joyce, James 44

Kahn, Herman 100
Kant, Immanuel 34, 40, 58, 93n, 141, 148–50, 157, 158, 166
Kelly, Mary 197n
Kesting, Marianne 59n
Kierkegaard, Søren 59n
Kisteller, P. O. 181n

Index

Klossowski, Pierre 138, 140, 153n
Kluge, Alexander 77n
Knodler-Bunte, E. 112n
Kojève, Alexandre 140, 148, 155n
Kott, Jan 37n
Kramer, Hilton 192
Kristeva, Julia 76, 136
Kruger, Barbara 194, 195

Lacan, Jacques 28, 62, 148, 195
Lasch, Christopher 12, 105, 106, 112n
Lautréamont, [Isadore Ducasse] comte de 18
Le Corbusier [Charles-Eduoard Jeanneret] 99
Leavis, F.R. 98
Ledoux, Claude-Nicolas 193
Leiris, Michel 140, 142
Leonardo da Vinci 19, 93n
Lessing, Gotthold Ephraim 44, 45
Lévi-Strauss, Claude 123, 145, 146, 152n
Livingstone, Ken 15
Lovell, Terry 76, 78n
Lowe, Geoff 196
Luhmann, Niklaus 159, 161, 181n
Lukács, Georg xi, xii, 43–45, 68, 79, 80, 92, 93n, 94n, 131n
Lyotard, Jean-François x, xii–xvn, 98, 112n, 113, 121–26, 129, 131n, 135, 151, 155n, 157–63, 165, 181n, 191

Macherey, Pierre 63, 77n
Macintyre, Alasdair 182n
Man Ray 18
Mandel, Ernest 184n
Marat, Jean-Paul 49, 51
Marcuse, Herbert 45, 98, 115, 122, 130n
Marinetti, Emilio Filippo Tommaso 99
Markus, Gyorgy 169, 182n, 183n, 185n, 186n
Marmande, Francis 133, 151n–53n
Marx, Karl xii, xiv, 23, 30, 34, 51, 52, 83, 139, 141, 143–45, 148–50, 154n, 157, 158, 162, 166–81, 183n–85n
Masson, André 140, 153n
Matisse, Henri 194
Mauss, Marcel 142, 145–47, 154n, 155n
McBurney, Blaine 77n
McCabe, Colin 62, 77n
McLuhan, Marshall 99
Meisel, Perry 191
Merleau-Ponty, Maurice 140, 152n
Michelson, Annette 153n, 154n
Mitchell, Adrian 59n
Mitterand, François 19

Mondrian, Piet 191
Montrelay, Michèle 194, 197n
Morris, Robert 192
Moulakis, A. 181n
Mulvey, Laura 194

Napoleon Bonaparte 53, 56
Negt, Oscar 77n
Ngugi wa Thiong'o 127, 128
Nietzsche, Friedrich 30, 59n, 81, 134, 139, 140, 149, 150, 153n, 161, 181n

Offe, Claus 9
Ortega y Gasset, José 98
Owens, Craig 77n, 195, 197n

Palestrina, Giovanni Pierluigi da 79
Pefanis, Julian xii–xv
Penck, A.R. 195
Perceval, John 195, 196
Petr, Pavel 94n
Picasso, Pablo 44, 58n
Piel, Jean 154n
Plato 149
Pyrrhus 89

Queneau, Raymond 140, 155n

Register, Cheri 77n
Renoir, Jean 5
Richman, Michèle 133, 151n–53n
Ricoeur, Paul 186n
Riffaterre, Michael 28
Roberts, David xi, xii, 94n
Rodchencko, Alexander 188
Rogozinski, Jacob 155n
Rorty, Richard 186n
Rowan, Caroline 78n
Rubens, Peter Paul 19
Rundell, John xii, xiv, 181n
Rushdie, Salman 128–31n
Ryan, Michael 101, 102, 112n

Sade, Donatien-Alphonse-François, marquis de 47, 48, 51, 137, 150
Sadoul, Georges 151n
Sahlins, Marshall 144, 154n
Salle, David 193, 194
Sartre, Jean-Paul 5
Schabert, T. 181n
Schiller, Friedrich 54, 81, 93n
Schnable, Julian 195
Schulte-Sasse, Jochen x, xvn, 65, 77n
Sennett, Richard 105, 106, 112n
Shakespeare, William 30, 43

Shaw, George Bernard 59n
Sherman, Cindy 195
Skelton, Geoffrey 59n
Socrates 56
Sollers, Phillipe 136
Sontag, Susan 86, 153n
Souvarine, Boris 152n
Sterne, Laurence 43
Stoppard, Tom 43
Stravinsky, Igor 44, 58n
Strindberg, August 50, 59n
Suleiman, Susan R. 36n

Tate, Allen 98
Tatlin, Vladimir Evgrafovich 188
Taylor, Charles 165, 182n, 186n
Thatcher, Margaret 15
Thomson, Philip 94n
Tillers, Imants 196
Tintoretto, Jacopo 196
Toffler, Alvin xi, 95–99, 102–104, 107, 109, 111, 112n

Touraine, Alain 9, 179
Trilling, Lionel 114
Trotsky, Leon [Lev Davidovitch Bronstein] 152n
Twiggy [Lesley Hornby] 194

Van Gogh, Vincent 189, 190
Vasari, Giorgio 19
Venturi, Robert 193

Warhol, Andy 189–92
Weber, Max 80, 98, 163, 184n
Weiss, Peter xiii, 41, 42, 44–48, 50, 51, 53, 55–57, 59n
Wellmer, A. 162, 181n
Weston, Jessica 121
Widmann, A. 112n
Wieland, Christoph Martin 43
Wiener, P.P. 181n
Wittgenstein, Ludwig 25, 30, 123, 160, 181n
Wollen, Peter 189